Here is a poet's re-creation of the intense inner life of a great public figure who has already taken on the dimensions of a legendary hero. Here also are the color and drama of his external life as seen through contemporary press comments and interviews, the recollections of his friends and enemies, his relationships with F.D.R., Churchill, Chiang Kai-shek and others.

As Muriel Rukeyser portrays him, Willkie was a man whose major concerns we all share: the grappling with power, the critical examination of values, the quest for identity. This is *light*, a book which conveys the drama and enty-the magnetic qualities of an American nbia. phenomenon. We believe it is an important literary achievement.

Mu
one yea
The six
last was
solidate poration law, the public utilities, and riter.
Her W national politics; she portrays him as he rican
scientis accepts political defeat and with a sudden leap of his imagination has the alled
her "C vision of "One World." "In
Muriel Rukeyser, commented the *Saturday Review*,
"the age is finding one of its major voices." *The New
York Herald Tribune Book Review* described her as
"One of the most undoctrinaire of contemporary literary minds."

ONE LIFE

by Muriel Rukeyser

SIMON AND SCHUSTER
NEW YORK
1957

Everything has a life of its own
. . . we are all one life.
—COLERIDGE

CONTENTS

real to himself. The fight against Roosevelt. His backers
find more and more to complain about. Flashes of the
actual country and himself, his actual possibilities. He
goads his throat, his words, himself. The last rally, at
Madison Square Garden. 1940.

The count of votes. In the sun; Hobe Sound. He re-
covers reality; he makes, in defeat, the step forward.
He is real to himself again. New Year's Day, at the
Sugar Bowl, he says: "To give those things necessary . . ." January, 1941.

He is writing an article about Britain. How do I know
that? he suddenly thinks. And picks up the phone.
Washington; a visit to Roosevelt, to arrange for the
trip to England. The relation. An inaugural speech.
Willkie's flight: the Azores, Europe in wartime, England. London. The war, no longer the fantasy of a
child; the full destruction of the camps; the secrecy; the
father of Paul. London. St. Paul's and other scenes. A
debate, during an air raid, in the House of Commons.
The Martyrs of Tolpuddle. People in the shelters, at
the Savoy; at Hell's Corner, Dover; a game of darts at a
pub. "Tell the German people . . ."

Return, by way of Africa. The wild rose and the years
of water. A moment between loss and blessing. Say it
depends on the interpretation.

The Senate hearings after Willkie's return. Treachery;
the shabby character, the fool. The witness for what
he has seen, woven into the world. His contradictions.
Questions and answers. The buried poetry of America.
"A most undefeated . . . loser." Willkie: "I have
made a lot of mistakes."

Child of the possible. We go ahead now with the
small boy, Paul, climbing through his mistakes. The
course, comparable to that of the grown man. What
has been true? What has not been true? And when the
cruelty and the unreality finally fall away. When the
child wants, in excitement, to make contact with his
contemporaries. "I dreamed about the mat, the doorbell, the whole, whole, whole, Miss Lorence . . . the
world, the world." Willkie and Paul: the likenesses,
the parachute jump.

Willkie in Washington speaks for the world of the
children. 1941.

His year: the Hollywood hearings, the destruction of a
dam. The commitments that Willkie makes. Pearl
Harbor. A day at the White House; exposed to every
trap and irritation of his own, a man without a job to
match the motion of his growth. The growth in which
he is beginning to move. Unless he himself invents the
next step. The old movement of forgetting. He becomes again unreal to himself in his drive toward
power.

Jennie, a girl in America reaching her powers;
haunted by walls and the impossible, she moves to
reach the sense of her body and the sense of the
world. She has forgotten, she is lost, she is found; she

very slowly begins to reach the forms. "Nothing here is unreal. Making, will break and make."

Toward the world, into the world, around the world. The flight: Cairo, the Near East, all the opposites he knows. The sense of power that everyone feels in this flight—although where does it lie, what power does Willkie have, who is he? Turkey, Lebanon, Israel, Russia. *Swan Lake*, the work that, perhaps more than any other, speaks for the split life and the chance of healing the split through faith. He leaps the railing, carrying flowers. He speaks in his clear voice. China, the journey into the opposite. A second declaration, absolutely clear: a high point, which could also be taken as political suicide.

The return to America. The swarm: contradictions, questions. The long antagonistic relation in attraction with Roosevelt. What was the effect of his voyage on Americans? "To give us a sense of reality." 1942.

Now Willkie moves into the final position. Dreaming we were awake. Too many benefits! He will not endorse either party nor form a third party. The total defeat of his candidacy: Zero in Wisconsin. His appetites will not see him through, this time. But his appeal to make an idea of the world, his story and his song, his eyes your eyes. Surer than ever before. He has become a voice that speaks for these.

From inward and outward, from the concealed weakness. He tries to hide his heart attack. He goes to Mary

Sleeth. But at last he cannot conceal weakness, he must go back to New York, to the hospital. Among the bulletins of cheerful improvement, in the full youth of this part of his life, death. 1944. But his life is not in his accomplishment; his life is in his energies. One way the stream goes is through the consideration of the AEC. The Lilienthal hearing. Power, ideas of power, and human gifts, our deep energies. The hero of this movement in our lives being process itself; in his own terms, Willkie becoming a hero of this process.

FOREWORD

WHEN I began to write this book, the people and the images moving through the story had begun to open up the present for me, and my childhood, and a great deal that I knew and imagined about our bonds with the world. I was writing, but I still sometimes thought of other people who might make shape out of all of this in other ways.

With part of the book written, I began to speak of it to friends. "What kind of book would you say it is?" they would ask. That is still a hard question for me to answer. I don't think it is a biography, although the life of a man is surely one of its chief concerns. Nor a poem, although there are poems here. The other categories: Fiction? Non-fiction? It is a book: a story, and a song.

When I said what I hoped, as the book was nearly finished, a question was raised: "Wouldn't it be better to make a fiction of a man? This is a real man who has already become a legend, and his lifetime was so recent that he is part of the lives of many people now living. And, at one time or another, everybody hated him." But these are my reasons for coming to the real Willkie. He is real; he is a myth; we can see our lifetime through him, with just that instant of distance already. Of course it may be said that he is the hero here;

but the hero is, more truly, his way of finding himself and finding the world. At the same time.

Willkie is recognizable to many of us, I think. Brought up in the tradition we know—a double tradition, full of opposites both true and false—body and soul, two political parties, and these are the very least of it—doubled principles of belief and power, all the way along the line. "Money is power," he said at one period. He was a child in a boom town, playing cards with the Sunday-school pictures; a law student, elated by the future whose doorkeeper was Woodrow Wilson; young manhood in one world war, doing a parachute jump on a bet, getting married; going as a lawyer to another, bigger boom town. He was a young executive, fighting a river system with a few unbending definitions and becoming a hero to executives; a candidate, campaigning the country and becoming unreal to himself. He knew the wish for powers he would never reach; defeat, and the recoil; the imaginative leap, and then the gradual forgetting, in a movement which he was to perform many times and which we all recognize. And he knew, on his voyages, or flashing through his weaknesses at home, the other movement—toward the world, around the world, into the world.

There are stories all the way through this book, based on well-recognized sources of fact. Some are already in print; some have never been printed. Some may be attributed and some not. Some of the sources may be named; some not. There are documents here, set apart in the design of the book. They will be apparent as headlines, news items, broadcasts. And there are poems, diving down through the rest at their own moments.

Many public names are here, in their places in history: Roosevelt, Wilson, Churchill, Bryan and the rest. And the Q of all the questions, the reporter. There are people here whom Willkie knew, sometimes named and sometimes not. And the anonymous: people seen from train platforms, in streets, in rooms visited once, leaning against sycamores.

Along with these are two others who travel along at their own pace.

A small boy and a young girl, offering their own parallels and contrasts in illumination of the central story. As far as I know, Willkie never met Paul, whose childhood is here. He was a German refugee at the Vassar Nursery School. Regarded as a "universal child," he moved toward his powers, very articulate, gifted in his extreme ability to share experiences of great depth and range; like Willkie, like us, moving toward an image of the world, with the help of Miss Lorence, the student teacher who was his friend. She sent me the transcripts of his conversations, and I have drawn on these transcripts freely.

The girl here, Jennie, is also real and comes into her powers as a girl does, to reach the sense of her body and the sense of the world. The elements of her drawings and her story are based on Margaret Naumburg's *Art Expression of Children*. This boy, this girl, are pilot images here; in their ways, which may seem smaller than Willkie's, each may give something to the entire scene. Children, they come in without knocking. They know about doors.

It has been a gift to me to write this book. The scenes and poems, beliefs, stories and meanings have come to me from many sources; the quotations are most often from *The New York Times*, the New York *Herald Tribune*, *Time*, and a series of documentary volumes, *America*, published by the Americanization Committee of the Veterans of Foreign Wars. Several books of senatorial committee hearings have been used.

I wish to thank those people, named and unnamed, who helped this book and me in countless ways, particularly Henriette Durham, Joseph Barnes, Mary Langmuir, Helen and Ira Wolfert, Lucretia Williams, Robert Payne, Bill Rukeyser, Jane Grace, Frances G. Wickes; Justin Kaplan, the editor of this book; and Monica McCall, to whom it is dedicated.

MURIEL RUKEYSER

ONE LIFE

PART ONE Young

Waking at night. Past the trees seeing the towers of fire leap up, superb and blue. A slight motion in the intent sky, at the tip of the flame. Lick, lick, giving a little with the winds aloft. Roaring up, gas burning from underground, or pride.

*

Through. Hot clover; through the dream corn, chieftains gathering, closing in, distinct again with all their silver tuft feathers, their gold-white tuft feathers. Past the deep-gold dust of roads; into the forest air, dark and full of scents and swamp flowers, among pawpaw, sassafras, and the archaic Indiana ferns; the cool brown creek, making the child's arm under water white and very long.

*

Out far. On the branch, he looks down at the station, with the army train pulling in, alongside the platform, in the middle

1

of summer. Shoulders below the branch he grips, the khaki caps and the guns like stalks, hardened, full of instant power. Down into the throats of horns and the spike of the flag. The raw company breaking ranks, invading the cars of the train, reappearing at all the windows, with their heads and arms leaving the train for one more look. The length of the red train waves all its hands. Nothing happens. The big soldiers call one more message home. Nothing happens. The crowd at the station waits and waits. Suddenly something like an idea sweeps over them, and they take out their handkerchiefs. Long strokes of rifles on the train platforms; glitter of white confetti and glass; the tears falling slowly and the glittering handkerchiefs. Out far on the branch, he hangs on, looking down at both crowds. The lucky ones have a gun or a branch or a brass trumpet to hold. Will nothing start this train? The band leader lifts a stick of silver. Perhaps music.

*

A boom town, breathing a flame of its own. The excitements: the certainty of wildness, of the next morning with everything expanded a little, the factories coming in to build, the map of the town staked out like a gambling table; these fields might as well be green baize. Schoolteacher turned lawyer, Willkie's father is now a real-estate man, Herman Willkie, called Hellfire; his strong children all six born and changing fast, the town darkening. The brick and stacks, smoking and darkening. The whole thing riding fast, riding high. The crest of the boom. That speed and taste and blood, that makes you want somehow to match it, to live breakneck from then on.

*

South, almost to Toadlope. Driving the cow, a tall strenuous wall, across the traps of the long grass. Fighting on the tracks. The drawn-out slugging, a long yell of heat on the ties and slipping gravel. The hoarse heavy knowledge of what gives way. Bells, hammers, bike bells, ringing of ice and the sliding runners on the hard surface of snow.

Shine of a field of crosses, many times reflected in dream. Purple flowers, a child moving far away from his grandfather's open grave. Tall prairie phlox between the mounds, speaking to him. He bends—and behind him the hands of bone on his shoulder, the gigantic man leaning down, with all his black rags flapping.

From a great distance he sees, in his dream, the boy breaking away. He hears the voice loud in his head, and he hears himself scream. "Father," he screams. "Father, save me!"

*

His parents, whom strangers say look alike, but who no more do than the two sides of his own face. His mother, leaving in the morning to go to the office—she and his father both are lawyers—leaving the house to the children and the hired girl who will keep an eye on them.

There is a moment late in the afternoon when the light strikes through the window border to the floor. The glass is colored mauve, pink, blue-green; slanting in the air very bright. Going like words.

*

Tin mill, glass works, saloons, whorehouses. The towers of fire always from the open wells of gas. Turn out the street lights by day? In Elwood? No one turns them out, says the boy. It's just as cheap to let them burn. All burning; all wide open. Forty saloons and forty bawdy houses. A law? There's a law forbidding flares. But there are people around here—13,000 of them—and they figure a man can do what he likes with his own property.

*

It is a strict town, too, with the force of its contradictions. These children are forbidden to play cards. The house is very silent on Sundays. Quiet up the stairs, quiet on the next floor. Up the attic stairs there is a small sound, then the little stiff slapping noise. Sitting in a circle on the floor, holding the Sunday-school cards overlapping in fans of pale acid color, there they are. All the children, and Wen speaking up: I'll just take that trick with my little Jesus.

*

Early, before school, he goes out on his paper route. Roll the papers, pack them in the basket, come up to the house, all right now. Steady the bike, aim and throw, give it a little wrist. It will sock right along the doorsill, where they wait, evenings. Where you have seen them, beyond all knowledge. Where they kiss, blurred in the leafy summer of the grown, and then go in: unimaginable Egypt and most daily door.

*

Down from Chicago Bryan came,
His voice was marvelous, silver and free,
He visited the Willkie home;
He said T.R. is all our shame.
Your father has a passion for freedom, Wendell.

When we turn in on ourselves our face.
We are American.   We thrive
Our currency needs a double base,
We are for silver, and we are silver,
Said Mr. Bryan.

The struggle, I heard Mr. Carlisle say,
Finds the holders of idle capital
Here, and those who produce and pay
Here—and where will the party fight?

The party must answer, as each man may.
Don't you agree, Herman?

Don't you agree that there are two ideas
Of government : Make rich the well-to-do,
And their prosperity will rain on you.
The Democrats' idea, however, is
Make strong the base, make the masses prosperous,
Their wealth will sprout and flower for all of us.
Oh, let him do it, Herman.   He's only—what?—four?

They tell us the cities want to stick to gold.
The cities rest on our prairies.   If they burn
And we are all that's left, those stones will rise again.
My throat does tickle.   I think I'm catching cold.
If only my throat holds out for the whole campaign!
Could I trouble you for a hot compress, Herman,
Or perhaps a gargle?

Your father is saying It is hard
To keep the people on their guard
Or to make them take the longer view.
All you are saying may be true, but
What about imperialism?

Our thoughts cannot be stopped by seas.
Oh, no, said Bryan.
But these are sins and contraries,
The founders hated such as these.
And the Louisiana Purchase? said your father.

That wasn't imperialism, Bryan said.
Of course not, said your father.
But if McKinley's ugly head
Looks out from Washington, I dread
The future poor, the future dead,

And Teddy Roosevelt,
Said Mr. Bryan.

Rang and rang, rang in the small boy's head.

*

A child can go through the course of all the meanings and knowings.

*

There is a flare that lowers down the sky.

There are still evenings, his mother's paintbrush pointed between her lips. And then a long green line drawn on the unfired bowl.

There is a pioneer. He sets out, in a rowboat, with his brother. Of course you know that Barbee Lake joins Tippecanoe. Look at this chart. Here's Tippecanoe River, running into the Wabash. From there we go down the brown Ohio. Now the center of the earth: the Mississippi. We're floating to the Delta in the morning.

There is a girl, a bobsled in the deep immense snows of winter, a buffalo killed long ago to the sound of small bells and Indian horns to make this fur of night and branches and a buffalo robe.

*

The big dining room at home. The dark sideboard piled wealthy, the air full of anger and arms, quarrel of the mind getting into these cells of muscle and eye, the cells of the future man feeding and being the quarrel and the strength. Poems, all that reading, debating, every night, as if they were in court!

*

The tall boy hanging naked in the night, rocking at the end of a chain of trousers, swinging against the gas tank, with a can of green paint. Using a good broad stroke, so the whole goddamned world will see the class mark in the morning.

*

When the gas burned down, half used, half wasted, all of it gone; when the railroads didn't save them; when the gas works closed; when the workmen left town; when the enamel pot and the overturned broken chair lay out on the back lawn, with the grass closing in over them; when the plate-glass factory voted for Kokomo instead; when the houses stood vacant. The toy lost in an empty lot.

*

⟨ *In that case, said Mrs. Kohlmorgan. But I wouldn't want for you to go with one of those wild Willkie boys.*

*

And a girl singing in the symbol air, crossing of gold, a polished
       staff of music,
Intent as Wales, enormous violet. Then the edge-lit cloud
Balanced the steeple for a moment, while the high ritornel
Sang slender in her throat, Light of light, God of God,
Sang all the lamps of sorrow, sang figurations of the swirling
      Captives, their rare release.
Sorrow has repetition, sang, but joy, but joy
      Has continuity.

The fleeting furnace moon raising his white powers
Will shiver alive tonight before that ritual face;
Love with her graces and ways, open as peonies,
Running with all the animals of heaven
      In grass of green
Eternal orchards, until the soul of the boy says to the singer,
      Gwyneth, you are my song.

Fifteen years to drift to the shore of this ocean,
Finding the wet and patterned sand, pillars and floor of fire.
All in the mercy of earth, the enlarging flower
That conquers death and sin, that sheds on the village
Of brick, fire, glass, tin and invented money
      Incense and hungry bells.
Ringing and hungering where the enormous ransomed boy
      Now rings and hungers
      In starved and golden air.

*

Summer, time of disease for American money, when the bankers go sighing in their palaces of glass, if it can only live through fall! The Wall Street historian said he was confident another panic would never again be witnessed in this country. Four years ago, and six years ago, the predictions of panic failed. Anyway, everyone knows there are twenty years between two great panics in America.

But, in June, 1907, an iron manufacturer. Eight million dollars. In midsummer, two New York City loans. In early autumn, the street railway, into receivers' hands. A few weeks later, Westinghouse. Thirty-four million dollars.

*

❨ *Early in October, writes Alexander D. Noyes, the storm broke with the utmost suddenness and violence on the New York banks.*

*

But, as it happens, it was not a storm. It was about people. There is nothing so sudden about people as the historians say. It is generally when you call them "storms" that you say these things.

*

◖ Late Monday afternoon, October 21st, the National Bank of Commerce suddenly announced that it would no longer accept for collection checks of the Knickerbocker Trust Company.

*

◖ The Knickerbocker closed its doors the next day.

*

◖ On these two institutions there now converged such a run as was probably never witnessed in the history of banking. . . . The crisis, however, had only begun. It followed the lines made familiar by all former crises.

*

Late fall, the leaves on the church lawn, and he mowed the lawn of her church. The church of his conversion. Every other Saturday, at night, he would go up the frosty path to the heavy door. The big door of the church, and deeper in, and down; the heavy, cold iron square of the furnace door, and in; setting the sticks and the coal, lighting the furnace of song and Sunday morning.

*

When the father of the house comes home in a time of panic, depression, and bankruptcy, and announces that the mill will open. All the wildflowers unfold, double eclipses dissolve over four hundred mountains, night clubs on every block begin the floor show, and the long-lost benevolent anonymous is reborn. All the sons smile. The woman weeps tears of release. The boy goes to the mill. Then white-hot, then cherry-red, the sheets emerge, and the boy catches them and swings them back; run through, and folded; run through, and folded; then plated and done. In the searing noise, in caves of furnace.

*

❨ No, of course we don't take Welsh people into our sorority. Surely she has friends of her own.

*

❨ Shortly after Wendell resigned from the Betas—right after the trouble about Gwyneth's exclusion—George DeHority brought him a message from the rest of the fraternity. But he said he would not reconsider. He was against fraternities on principle, he said; they were European, they were an attempt to divide people along class lines.

*

Major chords come slowly out of the Dakotas. The howl of the wolf, prolonged. Long. You can drink your coffee before his howling's done. Chords come again out of the stillness. The bartender picks up his cloth and polishes.

An all-night restaurant in South Dakota. Homesteads, and Barnum & Bailey coming. Big posters up. The beds and the drunks; the bugs; he is running a hotel, up the stairs, through, and down the stairs again; a back-yard tent which stands to the day of the first thunderstorm. Slowly collapsing in all its colors, flooded together in pools of littered folds and dyes. Drowned and torn, the tent lies down. Huge, Apocalyptic, a beast of dismay.

*

Riding the freights, he reaches Wyoming. Gets off where the Shoshone River hurls down fast, very cold, from the mountains through the big cat country of cliffs and shadows. They are digging the ditches and planning Buffalo Bill Dam. The boy is ripe. They play him for a sucker, sell him a sucker machine. All that new building going to go up, here's a building machine, boy, a bargain, a beauty!

Some days later he has learned all about cement. Enough to

know that where there is none, his cement-block machine is worthless. He buys a red blanket with his last money. West from Powell to Yellowstone, driving a six-horse stagecoach at once into a spill. Fired at once.

East now as a hayfield hand, from Cody to Nebraska; then another boxcar to Ottumwa. Shredded a woodpile for a farmer's wife. She persuaded her husband the boy would make a farm hand. Six weeks of her daughter, the mail-order catalogue for reading, the camp-meeting down the road for entertainment. One night by moonlight, Willkie says, she threatened me with a chance to inherit 320 acres with her if I stayed. So I ducked out. If all the alfalfa hay in the Middle West rots, I don't care, it won't be saved by me pitching it.

Alfalfa money takes him back to Elwood. 1909.

*

What will you spend? Of your body and your will, now home again?

The tin workers are on strike, the company has called in strikebreakers, your father is defending the union against an injunction. Office boy, bodyguard, you are, listening to the meetings and saloon, going into the homes of sick children, men on strike, the smell of barley soup. Food burned during anger.

Now that the summer is over; now that the chance of gain is past; what is left in September but these implacable families, but belief? And courage everywhere. At the hearing, as things peter out. Even fighting with you on the railroad tracks again. Not as you did as a boy, against your friends, but against the hired provocation who gang up on your father. Yes, but go on. What do you see, visiting Darrow in Chicago, there staggered by meeting the great man, and staggered by his fee, and knowing what it means to your father to have the trust of this union and go on alone, at $25 a day instead of Darrow's $20,000 retainer and $1,000 a day in court? In all of these.

Surely, the papers say, although the case against the Association has not yet been settled, surely every last union man must see that their strike is lost.

*

⟨ *The Pittsburgh Labor Tribune has watched the battle against the injunction—an injunction against picketing—from the start. In the beginning, the conduct of the strikers was orderly. Even in the later stages, the men seemed quiet. Their women, led by Anna Todd, waited at the gates. They insulted the peaceable workmen, throwing at them filth whose nature shall not be reported here. Singing, all the time, There'll be a funeral in the morning*

*

WILLKIE asks: But who was going to the factory? Everyone in town was out on strike.

HERMAN WILLKIE: You know the game, Wen; the Company was shipping men in from the East. In carloads. Read the rest.

WILLKIE: If I were head of a big company, I'd give my people a square deal.

ED, HIS BROTHER: That's why you'll never be any such thing.

*

⟨ *When the Company applied again for an injunction, the affidavits started to pour in. Even if this hearing should see a recommendation for denial—a contingency which is highly unlikely —our opinion is that the Union has damaged itself beyond possible repair. We can recommend nothing to Mr. Herman Willkie, legal counsel for the Union.*

But to the men, we say:

YOUR STRIKE IS LOST!

GO BACK TO WORK!

*

Was the case won?
The case was won.
Injunction denied.

*

And at the university, the young man goes up the endless stairs of those years.

Poems of windy Octobers, girls who say I've never been anywhere, brick walls; the locusts of summer, their hot whirling sound; snake dance and bonfire. Endless talk, the political maneuvering of his first candidates. Pressures of argument, the sharp, biting pleasure of that overturning. Coasts of these purposes.

And if you want a course in socialism, you'll have to round up the students to take it, Willkie.

Then, suddenly, when he was taking Gwyneth home one night, she said: But I like them, and I want to belong. I love the dances, too, Wen. I want all of it. I'm going to have fun, and belong to Theta.

He stopped in the road: Gwyn! When you know . . .

I know what you believe. I can't help any of that. I don't; and I want . . .

*

He fought through class elections. The energy that carried him plowing through, like his mother who visited in a storm of will and definiteness. Enjoyment of adversaries. As his father enjoyed. As did the law, for which he now was training. Following, in that way, both his parents. Among the friends: Scifers, Harmon, Hickam, and the rest, and Paul McNutt, gleaming, the peacock. Venus McNutt.

*

College radicals, a term meaning, in the United States, the young who have not surrendered.

Many surrender early everywhere, forgetting their birth.

Forgetting the origin in bravery and full relationship. The surrender is made easy. There is a foam of rewards; you may float along stag lines, festivals and ball games, like the songs. Before they know it, they are surrendered—the spectacular boys, the long adventurous girls, talented, shining. All are surrendered, and then pretending coldness, or pretending they are used to the world. Walling themselves in, from their first adolescence. Beginning at puberty to forget. They begin when they are troubled by what they suppose they should be feeling. The wound is there; the consciousness, which is variety, which is the need for growth and form as well as their perception, the consciousness has begun its own corruption. The rites of change become a memory of jungle, and these—the next people, the most beautiful—have forgotten animal and plant and mud, and nebula; they know only the floors of their own forgetting.

The icicles and the assassins have begun.

How do they conspire to keep from growing? How can you keep the great tree down, force the great thick trunk to open at the top to a dwarf crown? These energies are then driven in.

A faint drumming, in the walls of the room. For the rest of their lives.

*

❨*I am sorry, McCombs, said Governor Wilson, but my statement must stand. There must be no conditions whatever attached to the nomination.*

The nomination was for the Presidency.

*

Murmurs from the earth of this land, from the caves and craters,
from the bowl of darkness.   Down watercourses of our
dragon childhood, where we ran barefoot.
We stand as growing women and men.   Murmurs come down
where water has not run for sixty years.
Murmurs from the tulip tree and the catalpa, from the ax of
the stars, from the house on fire, ringing of glass; from
the abandoned iron-black mill.
Stars with voices crying like mountain lions over forgotten
colors.
Blue directions and a horizon, milky around the cities where the
murmurs are deep enough to penetrate deep rock,
Trapping the lightning-bird, trapping the red central roots.
You know the murmurs.   They come from your own throat.
You are the bridges to the city and the blazing food-plant green;
The sun of plants speaks in your voice, and the infinite shells of
accretion
A beach of dream before the smoking mirror.
You are close to that surf, and the leaves heated by noon, and
the star-ax, the miner's glitter walls.   The crests of the sea
Are the same strength you wake with, the darkness is the eyes
of children forming for a blaze of sight and soon, soon,
Everywhere your own silence, who drink from the crater, the
nebula, one another, the changes of the soul.

*

(When the Governor said to McCombs, on Saturday morning,
So you think it is hopeless? great tears stood in the eyes of Mrs.
Wilson.
    The Governor put down the phone. She walked over to him
and in the most tender way put her arms around his neck, saying,
My dear Woodrow, I am sorry, indeed, that you have failed.
Looking at her, with a smile that carried no disappointment, he
said . . .

At the Convention, the progressive element of the Democratic party—with Wilson as standard bearer—had started as a raw, "new" minority.

Saturday night came Bryan's resolutions, opposing any candidate with the support of the "privilege-hunting" class. Pandemonium reigned in the Convention Hall. Bryan's role was superbly played. When he finally threw his tremendous influence to Wilson, Indiana jumped over, then Illinois, and the fight was won.

*

The student who argued the law. The Kansas history teacher, in Willkie's year at Coffeyville. The lost boy under the golden storm, one of the last days with Gwyneth Harry. The control chemist sweating in Fajardo; in helplessness saying of all the shacks and the sugar, I suppose there are just too many people in Puerto Rico—although he may have suspected that that is only the answer of helplessness. He saw a man hacked to the shoulder for being in the road. Back: the return of the son to the prodigal home. Boomtime in Indiana, wartime yelling around them, cannon and money in every cloud. Excitement and drink to the boom-thirsty boys; a joy like speed, of making and spending.

The distant lover losing his first love, in the groves of attenuation. They drift apart in the twilight distances, young, eternal never. She's married, she's far, in California.

And all around him, rustling, preparing in lace and birdsong. Profiles of laughter, and the weddings of his friends. The stiff clothes and the amazing laughter; in all the muscles, the little inflection and the blush.

He goes south in the state, he is big and glowing in the ease of Rush County.

His long fine cheek. Clarity and decision of the mouth. Unsurrendered blue of eye. Conflict of motives, and the voice that must not acknowledge a thing but certainty.

This in one man. Young.

*

Ribbon of green, unfolding, unfolding, losing green, stubble of death, renewed, the fields of warmth.

Wealth of their well-being. Hot soft rolls, chicken in batter, a cumulus of mashed potatoes, jelly sorghum, will you have some more gravy? And pickles, and jam, and relish, and the best cherry pie. Another cup of coffee? Local beer, and Scotch, squared-off brick houses, and the great horns of choice.

Only now, the heat and closeness of all the easy people in their houses, urging all people to be warm and easy. Be happy and conform, like Indiana where everybody seems to. And perhaps nobody does. Riley stumbling home; Salome and John, a girl handing a boy standing in a flat landscape something recognizable, handing him indeed the ace of spades; Uncle Emerald listening to the women telling fortunes by the shapes of clouds, until one day he got into the piano and shot himself; Dreiser who knows it well, and Anderson unwinding the great secrets. But many women, and many men, leaning a little closer with a sharp-eyed look, saying, Surrender, grow up, go to it, stay with us, get going, conform.

You with your tall stories and your outsize laughter. You'll whittle down.

*

He sits next to the girl, at a wedding dinner. Billie Wilk. Charming, yes, he thinks. Does every heart with its knot of veins go twisting, because for the first time in all the months, he forgets to ask himself when he looks at a girl: Are you free of those days of feeding the furnace and losing yourself in storm? If your heart twists when you forget to ask, he tells himself then, you are free. After all the months when the letters came shorter and more seldom. Now that the old unfailing closeness, their old quarrel, has faded. And the wound. Only the pull of the scar now. Weeks at a time when one does not look at a picture.

He is saying something now about Fajardo. They all laugh, surprising and loud laughter, and it is a pleasure to him to see the ease on their faces. He can crack a joke, talk about the Caribbean, joke again. At last he is not debating at a party. Everyone seems to be looking at him.

He suddenly knows how they see him.

He looks at himself, too, and at the girl beside him. Seeing her, he knows something very simple about himself.

Swarm of brown curls she has, and a pointed look, very pleased. A careful and delighted look, as though she were taking a snapshot of a view she has just seen for the first time. In a moment she will put away the camera, and look through her own eyes.

Now he wants her to begin to look.

*

JUNE AT LAW SCHOOL

The dean, speaking of brilliance and prizes, announces to the audience: The best . . . the best . . . the best . . . Wendell Willkie will now deliver the class oration. His subject will be The New Freedom.

As he goes into his first speech, he tries not to look at the row of Justices of the Supreme Court of Indiana, sitting beneath him. Even the title will be poison. For days he has planned the words, against advice. This is the chance that Indiana now faces. If the state rewrites its constitution, all the promises which Wilson and La Follette stand for will be open to us. We cannot think, can we, of our state constitution as the sure safe past? But the Law School, and the justices, yes, they do.

*

But in these years, what is free, what is strong?
People, strength.   He had heard this always,
The mud of our towns turning into stone cities,
The fire of our wealth, space of our own time
Flowing beyond our eyes.   Now he can see the older
Faces rising : authors of our belief, image-faces of active
Sources like lines his father called in the morning,
The music of difference, all alive.
The founders of law and this people, who set in diversity
The base of our living.
Actual diversity of days and sources, smiling in disagreement,
        strengthened by one another,
Until the idea of diversity becomes our strength, sacred to us.
The range broadening, the potential becoming a way and a song.
Many have fought this reality.   We know the wounds,
On the body of work and of heroes, and in all of us.   Wounds
        of our green belief;
Many have seen in the growing of their lives that dwarfing
        wound, the starving out of their chances by the rigid, who
        have no hope but the static, the dead fact and size,
Not the strength that we laugh in beginning, the pleasure mov-
        ing toward unknown making; but hard control, clanging
        of doors closing like burial, the signals of wreck—
Deforming the children in the galleries of coal, deforming the
        woman in her pride of home, deforming us in our dream
        and in bed and as we look in one another's faces,
Seeing the terrible still poem.
Into this time
Vision sails.   In the midland, thinking of ocean,
Among constraint, brooding on our long hope,
That hope in distinctness rides, full of our powers.
Riding in light
Into the movement of our bodies, into our words,
In all we love.
                    *

Willkie, speaking, finds a way to think of these hostile faces. They will answer me when I am done. He thinks of the quarreling at home, of the debates he takes his pleasure in—looking at the shut lips of these Justices.

He repeats the ways in which the liberty of democracy must be guarded and prepared. Ways have already been found; and he praises the acts which make power again general. The Federal Reserve Act, the Federal Trade Commission, the Farm Loan, all the reforms which open chance. Here is the trusted scholar who has known our people and who makes the "new spirit" felt, particularly on our farms, particularly, among our towns, particularly. In our minds.

*

⟨ *I call your attention, says Senator Robert Owen of Oklahoma, to the fact that the Civil War in the United States was due to a defect in this country.*

We had a Constitution which was amendable; we had a Supreme Court which was not recallable; and the Dred Scott Decision was passed, nationalizing slavery.

We could not change the decision. We fought it out at the cannon's mouth, the Senator is saying, as the only available political remedy.

*

⟨ *"It is no time to tinker with the constitutional dam which holds back the flood of radicalism."*

*

His voice sounds in the bones of his head. Is it going to be unreal to him? No, it is not, it is there as he needs it. Hard as the faces he looks into. Now he tries only to remember his beliefs; he swings into talk as if he were fighting on the tracks again; he tries to remind himself of the roots of things.

The year of the leaf.

*

When the young man reaches his full height, sharpened on
      the arguments of his strong house, mixed in the opposites
      of all he knows, tall in the heat, and waiting to speak.
Has moved finally to the front of the stage, has felt for the first
      time all the eyes.
They are waiting for him to declare his entire form.   Faces com-
      posed in a habit of boredom.
They come from these fields, split by these towns run central
      through them as they sleep; they walked these streets of
      smoke, they drove these heavy horses to the barn, slept
      with the same women, were lost too in these swamps of
      black and ancient green.
Deep in these graveyard nights found girls throwing defies of
      their bodies to death on the grave-grass and on the
      porches and behind the brickyards and under the knotted
      trees.
Judges of all hope work out the same whisky, the same river-
      banks and barrooms, bury in themselves the same bodies
      and the same images, are burned in the memory of the
      color of fire
When they hear the doors strike shut behind them, the gongs of
      time like closed-down metal mills,
And they know now they are called to breathe in air of the same
      belief, the warm deep native earth and air, already sur-
      rendered and done to death,
To cut their time with an edge of new-cut finding.
The young man takes his wavering breath.   He is naming himself
      in the tribe ceremony.

Prepared for speech among many wakings in the lights of his
    lifetime, he speaks to these faces.

Under and before him, faces of judges,
Discovering provocation.

His legs feel very long to him and the ideas feel holy.
It comes to him now that the courts are sworn to these old ideas,
    green stalks of being, that the courts are all of choice.
The choice of growth is of the closing and opening of doors.
Doors of our rock, yes, clanging of mountains,
Through which our grandfathers drove their seed. Mountains,
    and seas of exile and of choice,
By whose unforeseen stars we made landfall, our coast being
    always choice
In another freedom. Though we may land here there is no other
    landing, to choose our meaning we must make it new.

He knows the animals of boyhood and the west.
Freedom to him is a constant and a bond.
Close to our wildness, be fierce and be safe,
Be fast and be feeding,
Be strong according to our own kind.

*

⟨ *We should not let that recur. We have no mechanism, the
Senator is saying, that is adequate to meet our differences if they
arise upon Constitution questions.*

*

Now let us in Indiana, says Willkie, change our constitution
and regain our power. We have built the litter across the way
we must take. But we are lucky, and responsible. Let us clear the
road [this is a class oration]; let us make the road to come. We
know our belief, and we are strong. We believe in our own
liberty.

Whoever threatens this sacred principle, he says loudly in his found voice, whatever stands in its way, shall either yield or break.

He feels a hand on his arm. Seeing only the passion and reality of what he has said, he follows where the arm leads. He is led to the back of the stage.

*

(A MESSAGE TO BANKERS. *The rule of the few in this country is the only element of serious danger to our stability, the Senator is saying. Like Europe, where they made a mistake somewhere— we do not know just where, and it's not for us to say—*

but it is evident that the human brain fell down, in government in Europe. Those people are at each other's throat. They're destroying life on a scale so gigantic as to make the world tremble with anxiety and fear.

Every State government here has in it, as fundamental principle, the principle that sovereignty is in the people; and they have a right to alter, amend, or change that government whenever it fails to meet the requirements: of giving protection to life, liberty and the pursuit of happiness.

And yet we have hardly built the mechanism by which that sovereignty shall be exercised. We still have in this country a minority system, directly at variance with the fundamental principles upon which every one of our State governments was founded. . . .

Now, the Federal Reserve Act will stabilize finance and commerce and industry; means that the public will become buyers in
    gradually increasing degrees;
means that the spirit of confidence
    established in this country will be useful to you in your field.
    It will enlarge your clientage; it will enable you to place your securities in a constantly widening circle.

And the Rural Credits System
> will bring forward the need of those who are cultivating the
> soil of America with those who have idle money to invest; will
> stimulate agriculture and let people buy;
> will mean purchasing power and a larger field for you.

I therefore commend your friendly interest, when these bonds
> are issued.

I think you should take a friendly hand and place those bonds
> with the view to build up this country as a patriotic service;

and above all the service of building up America to make it what
> it should be;

and incidentally you will serve your own interests thereby.

*

The young man is led to the back of the stage, past the
bleached averted faces. They had warned him not to use this
speech. He looks at the justices. One is quite white, with a dry
fury in his cheek; this one white too, wiping and wiping along
his lips the folded handkerchief; that dark inflated man very
red now, leaning to the dean, who moves his head back and
forth, No, no.

But somebody ought to get up and speak for the other side.

In the paper silence everyone seems old, the parents and
officials seem to be aging before a candid look.

Gwyneth used to tell him she must have fun, she must belong,
and he would have to join a fraternity, too. He knew then that
at the last minute he would join. The sick storm in which he
looks at the justices links this scene to her, and Anna Todd, with
her stormy face, telling him about the morning she led the
women to the mill. He thinks of Iglesias, the flame of his revolt
leaping the Puerto Rican canefields, wide flame across space like
leaps of glass. Pride. The towers of uncapped gas, flaming up, in
his first memories.

Names being called now. The list of names of the men around

him, the well-spaced walk forward among a spattered clapping.
The scraping sounds of deference as they accept their diplomas.

A tight formal scene. His name not called.

Tired; he feels tired and unreal. He supposes there must be
some other way to live, if that was folly. But nothing can cancel
it now, that's one good thing.

What do they want me to do? he asks the comptroller. Consider myself expelled?

The man looks at him, cement looking at excrement. Just go
to your room and wait, he answers.

*

They rule out of our justice and our despair
The strength of our strength.   The meanings turn, resolve
Into the play of our night, our flowering.
Not that the day of truth is given the lie,
But cut down long before.   And with ourselves cut down.

Domination of smoke.   The portraits are official,
Say Lie, say Complexity is weakness.
We want our many-rooted heart.   Flesh of our penetration
Allowing the empire of noon and midnight.
The rich, black-fielded life of the center, forests
Of corn and desires.   These fields go deep
While madness and silence stifle the grass.

A woman is running down the moonlight highway
Of buried Indiana, underground.
Whatever slave : factory or teaching woman
She joins our buried life, the floods of secrecy
Told at the riverbank Don't flow, don't flow.

They are passing a law against the life of the river,
The bodies of our truth are in bed tonight.
Horizon of rumor in the Tenderloin, under red light,
Parade of clouds as far as the Barbary Coast,

In the back rooms, in pilot-houses, past thick reeds whistling,
Through swamps silvered with marvelous adolescents,
The girl of Eden admitting all her life.
Singing on the moonridden cry of loons.

Will they stifle the grass and the young lying together,
The Lincoln stories, the twisting and lilacs of New England?
The swarming lives from the Carolinas calling
Truth and the mockingbird, the big river or the sea?
The eyes of the child and the children's zodiac?
Lack, rape, and silence. A summer evening, will you,
Of burning crosses, of instruments of torture
Who pretend not to recognize each other?
Sitting on the corner of Main and Jackson, the half-lit
Limping fortuneteller of all our fortunes.
In this one the generative secrets burn,
And he is all of us, bound in our same false secrets,
Lies concerning the communion of man and man,
Deep lies of brokenness between woman and man,
All torn apart by the mask of men.

*

After the proper interval, they sent for him. Most radical
speech I ever heard, said the President, and then, swinging
around to him, Young man, you have enough other talents,
without trying to be funny. That will be all. They gave him his
diploma and the set of books he had won. Then he went home.

*

That white-faced exaltation. If they had seen revealed what
he meant to bring, he wondered, feet up on his desk in his
father's law office, what would that have done? There was all
that summer to think it over, among the practical hardheaded
problems of his first cases. A barn-burning, which he sometimes

said was his first case. The Justices of the Peace court. The Mayor's opinions; very long they were.

And the haunting of the sea, always at full strength in the buried Indiana. The stinging, rearing seas of distance, the wave toppled in a roar of longing as summer here goes dusty. The deafened fantasy of the guns in Europe. Now a Belgium of horror slowly makes a mirage against the stalks, where a man runs now on the ground now upside-down now on the ground running through a big shelled-out field called Murder, running with his blood flowing like cornsilk, holding in his dry cracking stalks his entrails, beating and wet, throwing his live unwanted brains away.

Naked men with stars and emblem eagles nailed into their shoulders. All being brave.

And all this far away. Often in good weather you can throw it off.

He is healthy and large, and he knows how to forget. Like forgetting that bad hour on the graduation stage. It'd be a weak kind of doing, to go on thinking and all like that.

Better take what comes: the life run through and folded, run through and folded, folded again, that they all want for you. Their calculating looks. Pretty well tamed, they are figuring. Just to get him out of the turtle-neck red sweater. Just to chop off the cowlick, slick down the rumpled hair. Just to see him keeping to the books.

A kind of forgetting sets in.

*

His girl Billie, working in the Elwood library, after being assistant to Mary Sleeth, librarian at Rushville. And then running away, past all his plotting, home again.

The streetcars of that year. The plans, all leading to marriage. Billie, he thinks. Long, rocking streetcar rides into Indianapolis, and the transfer; catching the final rocking car.

Then a rush of time, so that the promise of marriage opens the sound of doors through which words echo, Wilson's words: peace, power, and the sea.

✻

([Only one peace for the peoples of America.

There must be a community of power.

The open path of the sea, alike in law and in effect, free.

The statesmen of the world must plan for peace as they have planned for war.

✻

Ten weeks from those words to the declared war. There is a trick of opposites in America, learned with our language and our history, in which, among many other lying contraries, we set these two. Learned before language. For they are planted with us: a circus teeter-totter, the red clown, War, balancing the black seesaw clown of Peace, the false opposite. The opposite of war is lack of war. Peace has not yet been breathed.

They have taught us that war balances peace as if it were true. So that we are all infected. The marvel people; the little children asking, War, what is war? Then the grownups know the dreadful time, when they must tell the little children. Now watch them as they speak of peace.

And in their congresses: watch them; you can see the flash in their foreheads as the word *peace* reminds them at once of war.

And soon the young men are in their hard clothes.

Because the grownups have failed to respond. What? What did you say?

No, look at the young men, each with all his arms and legs, his eyes, his sex. He has been taught the skills of violence, he has been shown the science of risk. But late risk only, after a long history of the failure to risk.

✻

Begun again, I praise
The fall for being sure,
May I fall whole and perceiving
On the arisen shore.

*

If you look at your succession of desires,
A running flame, a parade of leaders
Chosen for representing true your need,
Or your parade of dreams, the lifetime theater
Telling you everything sacred is remembered,
The lie and the counter-lie are lost in truth;
If you see your life as a procession of images
You will know you have not forgotten a single meaning.
We have known all of this all along.

To find a way to proceed from the revelation.

They have threatened us with the penalties of division—
What became of the war, the sea of immense soldiery
Sent over in endless liquid fields of sunset?
Did it melt to a handful of lies?
No.   The war did not melt away.
Where did your childhood go, and the sword of the garden?
You will see them today.

Questionnaire.   Write on two sides of the paper only.
Do you believe in your body?   Answer yes or no.
Do you acknowledge your soul?   You know they are separate:
How long have you known?

When you say Peace, do you think War?   Two seconds.
When they say Female, do you think Male? Two seconds.
When they say Good, do you think Evil?   Two seconds
We have given you, always the opposites.   Submit.

You have felt stillness, guilt, and the death-wish,
Haven't you? When? How often? How recently?
You know what is meant by these, don't you know, don't you
Know how they were reached and how they were chosen?
The smile is vicious, since the verdict is.

Time and the rose of form have rung your name.
Under the laws of growth, the immortal law,
You may choose in your own voice, and every day.
You need not ever accept their ideas of guilt,
You need not accept their ideas of innocence.

One voice will say in the sounds of penalties
War and No-War, Good and No-Good, Male and No-Male,
And what are growth and form and the human wish?
I will tell you a story.

These are the people who will not stay discovered.
Sunrise over horizons of new eyes, the twilight arch
Allowing spurs of cloud-informed evening, prows of
Cumulus heading west
To the cloudmakers, fathers of clouds and rivers.

This is a man discovering revelation.
America revealed that will not stay discovered.
Continually found.   Related to all finding.
Look at the man, he can be recognized.
Look at yourself.   We are his record.

*

Then he found that it was past. Being scared won't help, he
thought, swinging. He thinks of his mother's fierceness, her
gusts of tenderness. Would Ed allow that first moment of fright?
Would Julia go through this?
    And the ground comes up. It startles him, looking like . . .
At home, the table, with all of them around it, and the small

boy staring down at a plate, a bowl of food set before him. The small boy Wen seeing the streams and creases of the foodscape. Juices in veins converge, and the good strong solid stuff in hills and islands. Waiting under him, there to be eaten.

Swinging down. Among those winds, under that straight pull, now where's your freedom? But it is there.

Now the ground. A shock hammering at all the sockets, and he tries to roll with it as he has seen them do.

All right! they say, and give him his twenty-five. He grins, and pushes his hand back through his hair, that long lip smiling.

He dropped his practice the day war was declared. Herman Willkie started after all the German descendants like himself. Protest of ancestry, another split. The German, Prussian dreams of organized cramping barking authority. Wendell enlisted.

In the blizzard that February, he phoned from officers' training camp. I'm leaving now, he said, and I've got the flowers, and the war (he said wah) can wait. The wedding was announced for Saturday night in Rushville.

Springtime sharpens the difference between the region around Elwood—the marks of factories and making, the smoke and scars and black intensity, industrial signatures—and the Rush ville farming country. The northern people look south, hankering for openness; then they say, I guess they are slaves to the land, and turn back to their machines. And everyone knows what the southerners say. Rushville's in the rolling land. Anyone north of there thinks, More laughter, warmer talk, and pink and white flowery country, women beyond belief. Men as they might be.

And the lupine, the roadside violets all blue in the spring when form emerges changed, when color is form. Red-budding Judas trees and the bellflower and heart-leaf of catalpa.

Deep in snow, this country is buried and waiting.

There is only the wrenched sound of footfalls.

The bride is waiting.

This blizzard twisted over the plains, emptying snows. People here say, Machines want, Crops want. The blizzard wants all to be black, white and level. Every few hours the phone would ring, all day long, and this was Saturday. When Billie answered, the faint shouting of Willkie's rage would come through to the guests. Stranded and hours away, he promises to get there.

He won't let it stop him! says the bride, and her look begs them to confirm the voice they had just heard, taken down to a small rattle of anger. They look away. Darkness is closing down, and no sign the snow will ever stop.

Late in the evening, he called again from the small town where he was at last marooned. Outrage shakes the faraway voice. He has found a man who hires out as a driver. Offered him every cent he has! The driver has turned him down and gone home. He'll keep on trying.

Sunday she weeps. The walls thrown up around woman grow higher and higher as the girl grows. The enclosure she lives in is snowed under by delay. Now she travels through a maze of waiting, under a blizzard of recall; the concealing smile of the wedding guest means knowledge and pity; and every few hours, the phone rings.

On Monday morning, all that is left in the world is the absence of the bridegroom. After the solid walls of storm, the air is thrown open again. And now he bursts through the door, big, shaggy, and handsome-eyed. She sees him from an enormous distance, and then suddenly in close-up. In his hand she sees what will save her. It is the one object that rescues her from the maze—ragged, eaten away, and frozen, the bride-bouquet.

You're not going to . . .

Someone begins to stop her, but the words trail to their silence. She takes the flowers from him, like her deliverance.

*

As soon as they were married, he was sent to France.

If he had mud on him when he went to college, when he came back to Indiana he took a stand on mud. He had gone on tears; stationed at Bordeaux he was lost, looked for days on end in Paris, looking for a town, he reported, and had later looked for it again in Nice. He had always taken big drinks—of drink, of everything. Now he has his army overcoat, he knows Billie doesn't want him to settle in Elwood.

That is only part of what she does not want.

He knows who he is. He wants to move along now. He is perfectly willing to devote years to getting ahead.

And not in any of the ways he knows. Not in Elwood. "In a small town, you have to watch constantly that your shirt isn't stolen off your back."

"Frank!" he says, throwing his hand back from the wrist as the idea opens up. Frank Dailey will know.

"All right, Wen," Frank says to him. "You've trained in the right place. Indiana's a rich legal training ground. We're a litigious people in the Middle West. There are whole towns that, a few years back, dressed in their best every day and went down to sue the railroad. But, Wen," he says, "there's a next move for you. I'll tell you what it is."

Willkie got the job, as attorney for Firestone, and moved to Akron.

He knows what power is. Money is power. Money is pa'ar, he says, to the Legion in Akron, to the newsmen he loves to talk to. They get on well with him. He knows the city at once, and when they want inside dope they go to him.

The Firestone job suits him for a while. But there's more here than a single company can offer. The smell is the *smell* of Elwood when he was three and four. The signs are in the figures: rising production, wages, population. But the impact of shoes on the sidewalk, the sound of riveting, flags of smoke streaming ceaseless over the city. Boom town, where the mutilated soldier stares. The labor spy stares from across the street. Akron seething with spies, wild, full of pride and expanding as it thrashed out. Expanding and shouting, turning it out, living high in a high wind.

*

(*The Akron (Ohio) Employers' Association employed the Corporation's Auxiliary Company to act for all of its members, including the Goodyear Tire & Rubber Co., the B. F. Goodrich Rubber Co., the Firestone Tire & Rubber Co. and a number of smaller plants and companies. The detective agency was utilized continuously for over 33 years.*

The Ohio Edison Co. used the National Corporation Service, Inc. Most of the public utilities used Pinkerton's, or Industrial Utilities, or Railway Audit or Corp. Auxil., along with the Akron crowd.

*

SENATOR LA FOLLETTE: Well, have the activities of labor organizers for outside unions had anything to do with the ebb and flow of your employment of Corporations Auxiliary?

MR. PARSONS: Yes.

SENATOR LA FOLLETTE: They have risen at times when organizing was in progress?

MR. PARSONS: Yes.

SENATOR LA FOLLETTE: And fallen when they were not?

MR. PARSONS: That is about right.

*

The power of these spies is increased by their official positions in unions. Their capacity for wrecking is practically limitless. They reveal secrets, they steal union records and company plans, they blacklist their own fellows. They incite to untimely strikes,

they precipitate violence. Their allegiance is to the detective
agencies.

*

A time of finks and nobles,
With a field office as bond between client and operatives,
The correspondents and crooked men at work in the plants,
And a force of professional spies sent from place to place.
The back-room boys are always on hand, for shadowing, guard
      work or the simpler forms : eavesdropping, dictaphone
      work, hanging around.
When the strikes come the offensive arm, the nobles,
Can round up a slugging gang from the street-corners
And, most efficiently, bring in strikebreakers.
The national officers handle the big accounts : General Motors
      or Bethlehem Steel.

*

⟮ *This work is very profitable, says Sherman Burns in a letter to
all branches—no overhead.*

*

⟮ *The agency makes it clear to the spy that his own job depends
on keeping the employer apprehensive.*
    *Why, you go out and get hold of these ops and tell them;
come right out and tell them flat turkey, "It is your job, too, so
maybe you better use your imagination a little and write something in here that is of interest to the client."*
—from the testimony of Red Kuhl
*

⟮ *This is an amazing and terrifying picture, sirs, of management
caught in a hopeless maze of corruption and distrust. The end,
however, was not reached. A weird framework of spies among
spies was created.*

*

Willkie has his style. Candid, big, quick, a cagey defensive thinker. He is in the firm of Mather & Nesbitt, and among his clients are the Ohio State Bank, the Erie Railroad, and what is now Ohio Edison.

At lunch with A. C. Blinn, Willkie leans back. His suit looks as though he slept in it, Blinn tells himself, and his views are too liberal.

You're a Democrat, aren't you? he asks. What kind of a Democrat?

Willkie laughs. A liberal one, he says. A college socialist, saved my soul there. A Jefferson democrat, is that what you want to hear? An emancipated, 1848 German democrat.

This business needs you, says Blinn, looking at Willkie as though he were going to paint his portrait. We're oversupplied with Tories now. If we're going to expand, we have to reach out in ways—I don't know what ways. But I know what they say about us: if you want to find the best engineering, the stablest and fanciest financing, and the worst public relations, look at the public utilities.

Doesn't have to be like that.

Of course not! We have to get through—not only to our customers, but—how old is that boy of yours?

Willkie says, He's five.

That's a bit young, says Blinn.

Maybe it is, says Willkie.

You're coming up fast, Blinn goes on. You've done a lot already for us. Know what they're saying? Yesterday, in the locker room, a fellow said to me, "You're getting a name for Ohio Edison, as a reformed utility." That's your doing! You handled those well, those franchise renewals. Just let me ask you one thing. It's a kind of touchstone of mine, this: What do you consider you are in business for?

Personally, Willkie says, I am in business to make a living.

*

He is a tall, thin, rangy man, in training. Sitting around on the porch of the country club, he cracks at his friends coming in from the course. He belongs to the club, not to play golf, but in the same way he belonged to Beta Theta Pi. Leader of the unwashed! Paul McNutt said to him then, and dug him in the ribs. What do you want me with? Willkie came back. You and the pompadours and the plutocrats? But he joined, and here at Portage he looks at the same faces, every Sunday. He doesn't shoot golf with them, he doesn't drive a car.

His pleasure is in being one of Newton D. Baker's young men. Pleasure of the horizon.

His pleasure is in fighting the Klan in Ohio. Spy! the note says, in crayon, print-stained, unsigned. The cross burns, furry flame around it ruining the cross-form, the flames blowing and giving it the motion of a martyr on fire. Goblins! says Willkie to the school council, and frees them.

The Klan sends him a wire. He reads on the yellow sheet: WHEN DID YOU JOIN THE PAYROLL OF THE POPE? That's probably D. C. Stephenson at work. Even when he is caught for the sex murder in Indianapolis, his crusade goes on in Akron. And when Willkie, as a delegate to the National Democratic Convention, votes for the resolution to denounce the Klan, he sees the resolution defeated. The flogging, the rides through the peanut fields and the sweet potato fields and the corn go on. A sheeted man, covered and convinced he is sane, polishing up his shotgun. The machine belt nailed to the pick handle. The man and the woman, beaten from the warm sheets, flogged and finally made to pray.

Now Ohio Edison relies on him.

He begins to turn an enormous curiosity on the utilities business.

The power business.

His father-in-law was a building contractor, and there are some locks on the Cumberland River whose details he knows.

Most vivid to him of all, though, is the image of a day when he bought a red blanket in Wyoming. That blanket was the end of his money. But there the Shoshone ran, fast over its stones, the round hard freckled stones of the riverbed real under pure energy, spending itself, glinting and sunny. The stupidity of his cement machine standing foolish and gray.

What did they say in Bloomington? Wendell was always a fellow who smelled like he had prospects. Always had something on the ball.

He might knock a friend down if his friend stood in his way. He'd regret it. But, regretting it, he'd still do it.

And these friends knocked down, and his opponents—they must hate him, don't they? You're his friend. Don't they?

Well, yes, they do. He's always been pretty thoroughly hated by his opponents. He's always felt that the end justifies the means; that makes a strong fighter, you know. Not a man to give or take quarter—but you can get that in any powerful personality, don't you agree? And at the same time, he'll say, Show me a bust of Napoleon on a man's desk, I'll show you a man to keep away from.

The justifying? Oh, means and ends again, is it? I know him well, says Paul, I grew up with him. If the means he uses must be a little shady—if the maneuvering turns into conniving—well, the world is made that way, isn't it?

He's a man of abandon. Of recklessness. Whole family's like that. Should have seen his old man drive a car! He'd take that Model T—you know, the Ford with the generator—around a hairpin curve, on two wheels, or one, Mrs. W. hanging on to her hat, saying, Thank God the kids are all raised. Lucky Wen don't drive. He shouldn't—no sense of direction *or* of time. He's too engrossed in what he's doing to know what state he's in. And besides, you're talking about a man whose only interest is his environment insofar as it can be of use to him.

And his wife fans that fire. She's wrapped up in him. They

don't have much social life either—but she doesn't have anything outside of pouring her life out for Wen. The baiting goes on—Phil gets it at the dinner table the way Wen did at home.

*

⟨ *From a letter by B. C. Cobb, later President of Commonwealth & Southern, about Willkie in 1926: Do not let this young man get away from us. . . . He is a comer and we should keep an eye on him.*

*

GRAND CENTRAL STATION

All the way to the city a crying in the air.
He walks the ramp into this shell of sound,
Acres of goodbye and the noise of the ocean
Of the waste of power.
                          Smell of the rock and metal;
Steel-pale and blue, the names of the calling
Fly up to the ceiling, the names of cities and stars
To justify distance.   And the cries of parting.
Just listen to that, says the outsider in triumph.
Listen to all that noise!
Wheels and galleries of the control of tears.
Goodbye, honey, goodbye.   Goodbye.
Tunnels and wheels of language, an inordinate mouth
Shouting into a skin of echo.   Poison, intoxication
Of immense foregrounds, the deeper bells of the past
Losing themselves in boasts and breakers, each man carrying
Sound like a name, like clothing, a proof assumed.
A man saying Hello walks up the ramp.   His wife.   His son.
Hell, mother, says Willkie.   We'll take this town!

*

⟮ *Nov. 4, 1929.*

T. W. LAMONT SEES MARKET AS NORMAL

BYRD IN ANTARCTICA; NEW GIANT PEAKS SIGHTED

HOOVER CALLS LEADERS OF NATION TO CONFER ON
WAYS TO SPUR BUSINESS

*

The bell-throated past, ringing pain and magnificent
In tunnels diffused to us, wasted among these trumpets
Among wheels riding these arches over sound.
A ground-tremor of cars :   crude yellow, yellow lake, Indian
    yellow.

My God, Herbert, he said in the taxi, looking out; there isn't a
    soul here I know!

PART TWO

Tree of Rivers

ALL the way through the forest, a sound of birdsong,
The lightning-bird singing through the wilderness.
I see him flying before the invented speed. Body of shadow,
    wings of light,
In the leaf forest and the needle forest.   Clusters of song flying
Past the thickets unbroken, and glimpses of river
And the dual-noted thrush, two or three times.

Just after the steaming rains, when each leaf stands up clear,
Individual on the branch, when the tree has made its relation
With the slope of hillside and the strike of starlight, bearing
    each storm of its lifetime in its body, and standing
In the relation to the rest of the forest—just after the form-giv-
    ing storms and the rains of growth
A car full of men drives into this country.   One man gets out,
    slams the car door,

Saying, "I want to walk. Wait for me up the road."
His smile suddenly brutal, "I want to see it before it sees me."

After the road, the woods are axless and pathless; the great mists
Hang over the sycamores, darkening and thickening in the still-
    ness
Above the black-green, into the green. The man's walking
Bends the small pliant branches. One note of the car horn
Gives him direction : he keeps his shoulder to it, and goes with
    his arm braced
Pushing through the forest. Deep grass and moss bed
Cover the rock, cover the ledge, cover the fallen tree.
Far ahead, the distant green of spring shining on dogwood where
    the light falls through,
The ribs, the braces of trees. Along these arches
He sees the bear turning away from him, browner than branches.
Everything glitters. The full drop hangs
On the hard bud.
Underfoot, moss springs down, leaving water.
The drop trembles.
He goes invading.
Bright the drop falls.
His face hardens with his inward glare.
Goes plunging through the forest.
Spruce, firs. The oxalis ground, the fern of the woods,
In delicate tolerance, the patience balancing,
Bending and recording.
                         Now the sawbriars
Catch him, and his breath hisses caught.
Before his foot. The snakehead prodding the air,
Erect and advanced from the thick coil,
Silent, not calling on his rattles. Touching and touching
The space between them.
He stares at the snake. It glitters and glistens before him.
The guardian; and a darkness winds his face.

The forest stands as free behind as it stands before him; but
      a limit
Has been marked, a threshold indicated in the coil.
He waits.   He knows that if at the end of the long waiting,
Unendurable waiting, if then he can go ahead, he will come into
      a further country.
A leaf comes down, a hand in the air
Rocking down, and the snake withdraws his head,
In an arch over a coil assumes his next shape,
Looks once at the man, a flat unlit stare
Before he pours himself away.
A little moving water is left where he was,
Moving silver like the model of a river
Before it exhales upward into the branches.
The man walks over the earth where it was.
He pushes further into wilderness
With a stirring in himself of sadness,
Of past fear and of recognition.
A word has been spoken in a language
For which he has been homesick.
This is a language which he cannot remember,
All he knows is that he knows the word.
The word of the snake.

Deep grass and moss bed
A murmur of wells.
Before him, a cleft of rock
Holding water moving and curving.
Strung from rock to rock across his path
He sees his way crossed by a spider web.
Spiderspan wider than spears met to guard
The gates of the forest.
It shivers in the light, a faint breeze
Sways it like fantasies of bridges in India.

The man knows this is the final obstacle.
The bull of dream lowers his head now, he shuts his bull-blue
    eyes,
Now he is running and he jumps the water,
Tearing the web.
It is torn, it sticks to his fingers and his hair;
He has cleared in one jump the forest; he is standing
On a shoulder of rock above a hidden farm.

The man is dropping down, dropping down
To a green yard and growing grass
And a woman with a water-pail
Standing in the doorway.
This is a young woman, big-breasted, slender-waisted,
Sets her pail on the floor, smoothes her straw-bright hair,
Waits for his nearing.

    Morning, he greets her. Morning, she answers. You came
down from the overhang. That's a knotty way. There's the path
just beside you. She looks at his thorn-caught legs. He smiles;
for anyone else he would feel a fool. He has only a city answer:
It's been years since I walked through anything but streets or
parks. I wanted to see them building from this side.

—Streets and parks are far from home
Can you hear the river from here?
The sound of building in the air?
—All I hear is rushing of water, very near.

—Down in the gully, come and see,
April water doing ruin.
We've had some ruin here.
You've got honey in your hair, Mister.

He puts his hand up to his head and touches
The sticky places.   The web adheres.
I came through a spider-web, he says and laughs—

They look through each other's eyes.
—I'll take you across, she says.   Just let me look,
I'll make sure the baby's asleep.

She takes the bucket in.   When she comes out,
She narrows her eyes against daylight.
The sky gray, developing purple.   That's storm, she says.
Yes, he's asleep.   I can go down there now.
You a government man?

—Not on your life.   I'm with the company.
You know the wires strung along the valley?
That company.   Do you have light in the house?
—They haven't brought light in, she said.   We're going to,
        though.   We're going where it is.   The dam's moving
        us out.
He tries to say he is sorry.   They are walking past the yard,
        through the stand of hickories, then along the road.
There's no loss, she says.   It's hard for the old ones.   They
        think of the doors and the steps, they think of the graves
As if they were children.   I'm ready to go today.
My child's a baby; he's one; I'm alone with him.
His dad went to West Virginia to build a tunnel
When everything here had been bad for a long time.
Built the tunnel.   It gave him crystal in his breathing,
His chest turned to crystal, they say, before he died.
I'd like to move to the outskirts of town.
They'll move me, they say, and the boy, near a school.
They tell me I can learn.   A trade, something like that.

I'm sorry about your husband, he says.   And you don't hate to
        leave?
I should think having them tell you what to do—
How can I say it to you?   She turns on him.   Her eyes going
        dark.
The boy was born just after they broke the news.

I didn't know how I'd get through.   The birth
Was so much leaving and putting away myself and starting again
Another birthing seems easy and right.
When the man talks about The Valley, he tells me
What I have thought and kept secret, telling it open and plain.

They have come to the rushing of the creek, foaming tawny
        and white.
Endless and potent along the road, violent and turning
The rocks downhill, dragging the whips along.
—It looks higher than the road over there, said the woman.
—You had a bad time of it last year, he said.
—Twisted the door off, spilled mud ankle deep in.
But down in the cove they had real trouble, where the houses
        float by.
And their cattle drown.   The chickens are swept away
Afterward.   There was fever, too.   The creek's just as high now
And they do say the rains are still to come.—
The sky dark, the clouds very fast.
—Next year! she says.   The wind blows it away.
Next year it'll be built.   There! she says, pointing down.

Down past the treefall slopes, the bend of the river.
Past the darkened branches, below the darkened sky,
The treefall slope, thick forest down to a wild river
Choked purple, raging upon the curve, pale in the rapids,
Insane noises driven by storm.
                                        Over them
A stroke of lightning is laid across the river
Stopping the rush, the rapids, the windflowing leaves.
Law blazing across the river.

The moment is stopped.   Then blindness, lifting of blindness.
They see the smoke-forest.   Command of thunder.
Streaking of light, Moses across the river.

Inexorable light.   A wall of law.
—Where the lightning struck.   They mean to build there,
The woman is saying.   They talk about a highway
That will reach the dam, somewhere along here—look,
On this tree.   Over her head, a slash of blue color
Painted on bark.   That's the surveyor's mark.
They think to build where we are now.—

The forest leaves whistle in a forerunner breeze.
Now the rain, says Willkie.
I must get back to the highway.

*

Not leaves, not lightning, not that greatness of rivers.
The woman who sees herself in her lifetime, moving,
The man at work who uses the valleys
And still sustains the valleys.
The water-spiral turns the fire
That breaks upon the miles of air,
Leaps through the furnaces of change
To make and make. From those steel pools
The healing of earth is given a man.
He rides his pastures to the sun,
The great sun pours hot power down
To feed the feeding mouths, to bind
Earth to earth and man to man,
Until earth stores the waters up
To course the water-spiral new,
Whirlpool and embryo.

*

⟨ When Willkie came to New York City as partner in the firm
of Weadock and Willkie, he was serving as general counsel for
Commonwealth and Southern Corporation, of which he became,
at first, a director—as he was of Consumers Power Co., Ohio

Edison Co., Alabama Power Co., and others in the same system —and soon, president.

*

Q: What is Commonwealth and Southern?

A: C. & S. is a big Morgan-Drexel-Bonbright utility holding corporation. In the Tennessee Valley, C. & S. and another holding company serve all the customers with power. There are various rates, of course. Wholesale power is cheap; small towns and homes pay up to 18 times the wholesale production cost of 9 mills per kilowatt-hour.

WILLKIE: The private companies have foresight. We are equipped to supply 33% more power than the valley is using.

Q: What is a holding company?

A: A combination organized for the express purpose of controlling one or more other corporations by virtue of its ownership of their securities. A pure holding company has nothing in its assets but the securities of its subsidiaries; a parent holding company engages in productive operations as well. Most commonly found among public utilities.

*

Back in Akron he had eliminated the graft wasted in getting Ohio Edison franchises. There was no need for that sort of thing. His friends said of him, He's a complete realist, he has no scruples, and, back and forth, over a drink, "Would you say he's a type who would fundamentally operate by bribery?"

"What do you mean, fundamentally?"

Laughter.

"No, all right; not fundamentally. But when there's real need for bribery, Willkie makes use of it."

He studied. He spent his nights in preparation. Sat on his appetites. This was Akron, booming. When the depression hit, he knew. This was his chance. The utilities were in a jam, and he could be their spokesman. The power lobby was discredited. Willkie was with the founders of the Edison Institute. "A shiny translation of the old lobby, wouldn't you say?"

"I don't know. He gave it color and class. Sort of an educational front. Took the curse off. He's a good man for that. And he's sensitive to corruption—gets the full flavor of the corruption at Washington. Not that he's above using the same dirty tricks, when they're of help to his side."

"In court, he plays it up the middle. There was a conviction he got in a will case—described St. Peter and the throne, and St. Peter's disgust with the plaintiff."

"And the time he got the girl for being coached! On the word 'profile.' Said that wasn't a word she knew. Tripped up her lawyer with it."

"He's a great courtroom lawyer: looks solid, has that intense, serious, driving way. Great publicity sense, too. In Akron, he used to give all the newspaper men free legal advice."

"Straight as a string, too."

"In city politics?"

"Oh, *city* politics! He's a fixer, that boy. A fixer, and coroner, too."

"I wish he'd never gone. He came to me, and I told him not to go. Too ambitious to stay. I suppose he'll fill out in New York—all those banquets."

"Who does he see there? Morgan? And what is he smoking? Cigars?"

"He sees the Attwoods. His apartment is in one of the big Fifth Avenue buildings, but it looks like Indiana. He still likes fried chicken and rat cheese, and cherry pie! He smokes Camels."

"Well, I guess the worst you can say about Wendell is he's a Democrat."

*

❲ *This is what Willkie is saying: I have no desire to become one of those business men who thinks he can solve all the problems of the world.*

*

B. C. Cobb told him to figure up his income for the past three years. I'll double it, he told him. Pretty soon Willkie was president. He has not been a reform president. But what he did when he looked at his Board was this: he invited the operators in. This is unheard of in a holding company. But Willkie got the functioning men in: I am a strong believer that those who direct the destinies of the operating companies should be in close and constant contact with the problems in the field. He couldn't ask Morgan out, or Bonbright; but when he looked around the Board and saw not a single banker, he was ready to go ahead.

What he wants, he says, are big sales and low prices. He has gone up and down the Tennessee Valley, plugging electrical gadgets. The stunts—The Power Girls, the streamers across the streets, the reduced rates—have built up a volume of sales up in the top brackets.

*

❲ *Get out the juice, says Willkie, and we'll bring the industry out of the woods.*

*

He's planning, he says, to sell the pants off the power question. "Meanwhile, I'll stave off the wolves."

Q: Who are the wolves?

A: Lilienthal, Norris, La Follette, Roosevelt.

And in his appearance before the House Military Affairs Committee—this was before the act creating the Tennessee Valley Authority—Willkie spoke of the possible act as unsound and uneconomical. It threatened grave injury, he said, to the security holders.

*

⟨ *May 18, 1933. Over the signature of Franklin D. Roosevelt: It is clear that the Muscle Shoals development is but a small part of the potential usefulness of the entire Tennessee River. Such use, if envisioned in its entirety, transcends mere power development. . . .*

*

A tree of rivers flowing through our lives;
These lives moving through their starvation and greatness,
Masked away from each other, masked in lack.
Each woman seen as a river through whom lifetime
Gives, and feeds.   Each man seen giving and feeding.
Under all the images, under all growth and form.   The energy
   of each, which is relation,
A flare of linked fire which is the need to grow,
The human wish for meaning.
                       Roots of diversity
Each being witness to itself, entering to relate,
Bearing the flood, the food, the becoming of power,
Which is our eyes and our lives
Related, in bonds of flow.

*

⟨ *For fifteen years they tried to sell Muscle Shoals as if it were a shovel or a slave. A remnant of war. They regarded it simply as a power plant.*

*

⟨ *Roosevelt writing, The use transcends.*

*

The power of war leads to a plan of lives
Involving rivers.   The many-stated million
Human concerns.   This touches, this gives life
To all its forms.   Now clothe our force,
Make it as flexible as a man venturing
To fend for himself in his own enterprise.

Now in the unity of all vision, unity of the land, the forests
    and water,
See nature, the nation, as a web of lives
On the earth together, full of their potencies.
The total unity, reached past images,
Reaching past the naming of religions.
We reach to create.   That is our central meaning,
Suggestion of art and altar in all our passwords,
For the meaning of "mirror of nature," the meaning of "image
    of God"
Is a simple fiery meaning : man is to create.
Making, singing, bring the potential to day.

*

(*This, of course, is not what the creation of TVA means to most people reading their papers. Even today, it is thought of as a "power" project, in public ownership.*

The threat and the yield of the river cannot be split. If our lives are split and fragmented, the river's is not: it is not separately a flood and a source of development, wealth and pollution; the washing away of farms and the stream where the fisherman stands with his thread. Here is a seamless whole. This whole being a region part; in the flow of many—ores, growing of soil-born, the wilderness our memory, the farms and cities—all these with the river in relation to the lives of the valley's people, streaming through years, and the lives they touch, which are endless and which with them are whole.

*

⟨ What happens on the river is based on what happens on the land. On other rivers, there are power dams, Lilienthal is writing; they were not built with the thought of the river as it is in nature, a unit.

These power dams are not thought of or used against flood. They do not provide a channel to take us down.

The lands have been washed away in a cycle of ruin. In the long Chinese reaches, earth is laid bare. The rains run down. India, Brazil, Missouri have such rivers, running the world away. The fields need, the wastes need, the children need. The hero they need is themselves, living in full relation to one another.

*

Nothing can be walled out. Another kind of thinking must come into use.

We have been trained to think of all things as separable. All day today we worked separately, many alone. The feeling of the unreal day.

In the flashes of sight, we pierce the mask: behind the eyeholes and the mouth-holes that every day we deal with, the living light; inseparable, ourselves.

*

⟨ The U.S. government, says Willkie, is in the power business.

We can absorb all the power that TVA can generate. We can sell it over our own lines. We can change our rates; if there are savings made, we can keep those.

*

SLOW DIALOGUE BETWEEN PAIN AND ROOSEVELT

Warm in the pool the wasted man
Among his mutilations swam.
Lay in the sun of his despair
While time ran around the year.
    Legs of his wounded days
Refused, refused.   He turned to pain,
The arrogant and dwindled man
Saying, Do not surrender me.
Though frightful time outrun my praise.

PAIN: I remember the player's thighs,
The skill and locking of the knees,
The ruthless muscles of the wise.
Time running frightful in sunrise
Outrunning you, outrunning light,
Races through the dream of night.
Torment lays forfeit all your dream.

THE SELF: The core of my arrogance
Has been transmuted, but your fires
I cannot yet meet with praise.
When the boy's muscles are my dream
And the man's withered legs my day
All I am and all I seem
Will find the way, will find the way.

PAIN: I am the thread, I am the bait,
I am the pride of your despair.

THE SELF: There are legs I shall outrun.
Speed of this resurrection

Will find me in the spectral dance
Before the real, before the real.
Somewhere my next life waits and sees
Time and the heart of man at race.
The wish can heal, the wish can heal.
There is such freedom in this place.
Warmth of the many-minded free,
Outblazing personal liberty.

The cause racing, and the root
To be found.   A young man wrote
All of this long ago.
We believe ourselves by slow
Turnings of the living heart.
Pain of that growth will give us start.
To stand so braced will be my pride.
I have been born and I have died;
Pain sends me on my wandering,
Warns me of enemies about:
We Refuse is their war shout.
Pain sets my hand a growing root upon,
The weapon of the wounded king.

In the warm pool the wasted man
Swam laughing in the sun.

*

❲ *In 1926, Roosevelt, preparing to build, writes to the President of the Alabama Power Co., complaining of the "usual high cost and inefficient service of small local power plants" around Warm Springs.*

*

Willkie: It is this precisely that justifies us. This region has always needed big inter-connected power systems. We've poured $126,000,000 into these operating units.

I've given the House Committee a plan. I've proposed amendments.

If the government were to be placed on an equal competitive basis with privately owned companies, I swear to you *(thumping the desk)* government power would disappear in three years. Disappear!

*

(*People are the most important fact in resource development. Not only is the welfare and happiness of individuals its one purpose, but their genius, their energies and spirit are the instruments by which that development is accomplished.*

*

Willkie looks around at the Japanese furniture, the overstuffed chairs, the fringed lampshade, and thinks of his farms, the hogs and the Herefords.

"Billie," he says.

His wife answers. "You have a good time when you go back to Rushville for a week. But how long could you talk farming over a fence?"

"I don't belong in New York. I ought to be in Indiana, Billie, sitting on a crackerbox, talking about politics."

"You wouldn't be satisfied. There's more power flying around your crackerbox on Pine Street."

He laughs, and she tells him it's time to go downtown. He's a man who never carries a watch. He likes to be told the time.

He kisses her good-by and hears his unlocked door close as the elevator goes down, in an oiled silence. Across the still lobby on soundless carpet. And out into the bright wind. A shouting of two boys going to school, and a near car horn echoed at once, a block down Fifth. A flight of pigeons lifts into the sharp blue sky over the Museum, wheels, now dark, now bright, and settles on the cornices.

Willkie feels as though it had been weeks since he saw sunlight. Half the time, he does not know if it's raining. I'm fighting something, he thinks. Just drive me down to Pine Street, let's get on with the thing.

In his office, he stares at a telegram and calls Miss Grahn back in. He slaps the yellow paper down. "I'm sorry I acted irritable a minute ago. This upset me for a moment. Excuse me," he says, and smiles his instant smile.

"Oh, that's all right, Mr. Willkie," she says.

"No, look at this." He gives her the telegram. "That's a follow-up from the Forum." On the air, he had said that it was no worse for a utility holding company to own two companies in different states than for the President to have landed estates in New York and Georgia. The utility companies are called every name in the book. What about the railroads? You know, don't you, that they made their money by creating a landless tenantry? Isn't that worse than any utility?

Just then a question is asked: You attack the President, Mr. Willkie. Didn't you support his campaign?

"What did you tell them?" Miss Grahn asks.

"I gave it to them," he says. "They asked me for five thousand —remember? I gave them a hundred and fifty. And I said last night I didn't mind telling them I wish I had my money back.

"And three of my best friends in Akron send me this! Murray, George, Frank!"

*

❲ WESTERN UNION: *Before you became a plutocrat, you were a good Democrat. We now are astounded to know you contributed only $150. Not being owners of any holding company stock, we still like the New Deal.*

If you are quoted correctly, attach evidence of such contribution to a draft on us and we will reimburse you.

*

"But you don't own any stock!" Miss Grahn says.

Willkie throws his hand out and back, laughing. He roars at her. "That's beautiful!" he says. "What do you want me to tell them? That my money's in farms? My estates?" He stops laughing. "No. Send them this answer. Wire them my acceptance. Tell them I advise all disgruntled Democrats to do likewise. And give the story to the press."

Early in the fight between TVA and the power companies, the full scale of the plan could be seen in its beginnings. The twenty-one dams of the TVA were to be the model. After the Tennessee, there would be fifteen other TVAs, said Willkie, and he added, The utilities will turn to Congress. We will bring pressure to bear. If the government is going to fool around with the power business, he drawled, they have to charge enough to get a fair return. They have to buy or condemn the lines that exist—everything that now exists.

He was very touchy about being called a Morgan man. I wouldn't know a member of the house if he walked into this room. Unannounced, he said. Unless I'd seen his picture, he said.

But he kept saying Money is power, too, and he loved what he was doing. As I go from smaller business to larger business, he told the president of his university, I find more and more integrity.

You were always open-minded. You could be influenced.

If I think a man's sincere, yes, says Willkie.

If you think he's sincere, of course. It impressed me very much to see you feel the ideals of another man, with all your own strength of will, going into action. I'll never forget your conversion. I'll never forget the influence that banker—what was his name, from Kansas, that banker?—had on you. It was he who led you to the Presbyterians, I do remember every step of that.

What was your family? Episcopalian?

Willkie is silent. He swallows; the meat rasps in his throat. He reaches for the water glass.

Damn fool, he says to himself, at the high window, at the end of the day. Why should a few harmless remarks have raked you over?

He suddenly sees, clear and small, the cement machine out in Wyoming, with the Shoshone River rushing behind, pure, cold and fierce. Then, following upon that, with spyglass clarity, the lines of faces of the old justices. He puts his head down, and feels the giant spider web, sticky as honey on his black hair. He shakes his lion head, and goes back to his desk.

Not that he is tired. He is never tired. It is only that a curious sense of unreality has overtaken him. From the first moment, today had driven something deeper into him. He feels like a man tortured, not by something he cannot see, but by something he cannot remember? What do they do in Germany? Knock at your body with—no, that was Spain.

When the questions were asked, at lunch, he had felt as if a great ax had split him open. Now he tries to hold the shaft; he tries to think his way through the boiling confusion now exposed. What did that reporter ask him? "What is the greatest joy in life?" To keep one's thoughts uncontrolled by formulas. To be a free spirit.

He is the man who said he would punch Morgan in the nose if he found that he was being bossed. The boy who said he would not join, and joined. It was easier at home, in the kitchen, when everything could be laid on the table, argued out. You could change from night to night. Change your views and your subject. In this world, it was a matter of constant defense of a vast property—a property as big as a country. Defense, slugging.

I always wanted to be a college president.

Who can connect a circuit-breaker? Not I. Read a vector diagram? Not I. Compute the dielectric strength of stators? No.

But in the labyrinth—among the traps of the legal, financial, purchasing, promotion, engineering, governmental and public relations jungle—I know my way.

It is only that, today, I am unreal to myself.

That woman who lives on the flooded farm near the new dam—I don't suppose she ever found herself directly at opposites.

He realizes that his thinking is of the same nature as the opposites he is trying to think through.

Supposing the opposites are false? he says aloud, and swivels around to face the window. Evening darkens the deep blue; lights seed the towers. New York, that's my city, he says. There's no contradiction in me that I can't match down there.

But that was true in Indiana, too.

Two Scotches aren't enough tonight, he thinks. I wish I could talk this out. There's not a man in this town to do that for me. I'll fight the Washington crowd, the White House—they are consistent, I'll say that for them. Rich and undermining, or flighty and crackpot, they cohere. But I'll beat them down.

He shakes his head like a boxer, and rubs his nose. One day of weakness in seven years! That's a day too much, he thinks.

*

([*Stripped of unrelated items, the power question is finally revealed, says Willkie, as a drive for government ownership. And this bureaucracy, climbing to the driving seat, has disguised the package it is delivering. They talk about flood control—that's popular; or reforestation, or the soil, or shipping. But what are they marketing? Political power. And at the same time, they are cutting prices, underselling the utility companies, and letting you—the taxpayer—make up the loss.*

*

Willkie looks back over the twenties. He doesn't see the wings sprouting on anyone. Then: No group has a monopoly on that—not on virtue, he says. But the spurs to progress—we need them, and the profit motive, he believes, is one of the principal spurs.

Really, says Willkie, we can handle all the power you can turn out. And sell it, too. And not lose on it, either.

All right, yes. We sent out salesmen. We sent out Home Lighting girls. What do those farmers say? The Power Trust is a Money Trust? Well, money is power. All right. The holding companies will—tell you what we'll do: we'll restate our values.

*

Q: Yes, that's not a bad idea. But first, Mr. Willkie, may I say that you are, to many of us today, the sign of the next kind of industrialist. The next kind of executive, who sees his place in a structure.

WILLKIE: I am just holding off the dogs of war, so the fellows on the selling end can do the real job. By the time people buy all the electricity we've got for them they won't be able to help feeling good toward us.

Q: Feeling good toward you—that's it, isn't it?

WILLKIE: It sure is. And I don't mean agreeing. I like a fight. But I want the other man to like it, too.

Q: To like you.

WILLKIE: They don't hate us. I don't believe it for a minute. They haven't much kick. Look at the rates—the phone company's the one to get after. But that's a tough proposition. So they attack the utilities.

What do they want? What can the government do?

Q: (*Smiles*) I'm here to ask the questions.

WILLKIE: Well, ask them, then. What would you ask?

Q: What can you do? What about new construction?

WILLKIE: I tell you. Business needs money, like anyone. And the money—the capital market—is soft now, reluctant, shy. Girlish. It makes business reluctant to borrow. It's the uncertainty.

Q: What have we got? A startled princess and the god pursuing through the forest? The running of the virgin?

WILLKIE: I wouldn't say that. I'd like them to be young and fair. They are to me. But it isn't that pretty a picture. Put it this way—I can raise money on a one-legged man, but not on a two-legged man on the amputating table.

Q: And TVA is the surgeon?

WILLKIE: The butcher! Look. I want them to buy us or leave us alone. The way things are, they're running an illegal business.

Q: How about competition?

WILLKIE: (*Exploding*) Competition, yes! It's our lifeblood! But this is destruction of property! They won't split up the area; they won't let our lines be the only lines—they're subsidized. Subsidized competition! They know power is a natural monopoly. Every college boy knows that; and before I'm through, every high-school kid will know it, too. Power—this force, coming down from the mountains. You can't haggle over that. Anyway, we want everything the government wants—plenty of power, low rates, and protection for our stockholders.

And what does the TVA do? Tries to impress Congress. Its magnificent accomplishment! Its accomplishment is magnificent, all right: a flow of public funds, without let-up, flowing into the hands of the directors to spend without any check worth the name.

Is TVA a power project, or are these electricity plants incidental? Is this really a program for flood control and waterway? I question the worth of a navigation plan in this country of hard roads and railroad tracks.

We're giving that part of the country plenty of juice for its money. They've been lapping it up, down there. Sure, the TVA wants to increase the use of electricity. So do we.

The question is: Do we run the power business inside or outside the profit system. Can two conflicting systems of doing business exist side by side? That's something for the citizens to decide. After all, they'd have to pay—they and their children.

Q: About profits—how do the rates stand now?

WILLKIE: That's a hard thing to compute. Just as the value of our companies is hard to fix. Our average rate is about 3¢ now.

Q: What is the "objective rate" you've devised, Mr. Willkie?

WILLKIE: That's my pet invention. It's a method, really—a method to keep lowering the price without jeopardizing the revenue.

Q: And what are the companies in the TVA area worth?

WILLKIE: $600,000,000. (*After a moment*) That's their book value. I told you we'd restate values, didn't I? That figure may be higher than their actual value, and I hope some day to write it down. But I can't see that competition is the kosher way to force this.

There's been a lot of talk about big write-ups in industry. The public thinks they're colossal. They're only 10% or 12%. I'm not making any excuse for write-ups, but there's not a serious problem. The public thinks there is. It's just a lot of leftist talk. Let it blow off in Congress. Then we'll see where we are.

Big figures always impress people. $5 million sounds like $5 million; that's not so much of a write-up, on $200 million.

Scripps-Howard's talking about 100% write-ups.

Let them get after the truth. You won't get it in hearings without a defense—defense. The big deals and the Insull collapse made the public see us as big-time robbers.

And who is there to defend the utilities? Some of the old

guard are afraid. The politicians or the journalists are scared of being called "bought."

As for me, look at my brokerage account, my bank book, anything.

Q: Why do you suppose people are suspicious?

WILLKIE: Because a utility is a monopoly. It's the closest thing to government, in some ways.

Ever meet anyone who wasn't suspicious of the government?

We have certain powers like the state's. The power to condemn. . . .

Q: Then what is the argument against government in the power industry?

WILLKIE: That's Red talk. But I'll tell you. Power under government would become another post office; a center of intrigue. Look at the New York waterworks. They're a key to Tammany's hold on the city. That island! When an island has a water problem, you've got real trouble.

What's the value of water to New York?

This question of value: it's tricky. Take a canal that was built by slaves. How do you figure its cost? What is it worth?

Q: How would you judge value?

WILLKIE: I would like to have a fair value determined as of a certain date, and go on from there. On some sound theory that we can get together on.

Q: The prudent investment theory?

WILLKIE: I don't think it's sensible.

Q: But you think a theory can be agreed on?

WILLKIE: Maybe. It's hard, of course, with government men.

Q: What would bring the kind of men you like into government?

WILLKIE: Not that I blame them. I couldn't do it myself. You can't keep the best men in public service as long as there is any private industry. Talent goes for its reward.

What do men talk about?
What are they interested in?
Getting on.
It's that extra money,
    that extra lost hour of sleep,
    that extra toss in the bed,
    that idea at four in the morning.
Missing the dinner party. That extra five or ten per cent
    of effort. That's what does it.

Q: Suppose the men want to go in public service?

WILLKIE: If they do, their wives won't let them.

Q: What about Lilienthal?

WILLKIE: He's a master. A master of short-range finesse. Now that you ask me. Lilienthal! He's no radical. A radical has fire in his throat.

Lilienthal's riding his horse, that's all.

And what could you expect? Coming up from Wisconsin with no sense of anything! No responsibility—you get that in a man who's advanced in business, slowly. All this sudden power! It makes him unsure of himself, unsure and cocky. Now, a business man: he doesn't take a criticism of his business personally. But a guy like Lilienthal does. Supersensitive! Maybe all that flimsy legal underpinning—know what they've claimed on navigation? Maybe that shaky foundation makes him extra cocky.

Q: He gave me a message for you.

WILLKIE: Dave Lilienthal did? Well, he knows what he can do with it—No, let's have it.

Q: He said, See if there is a chance of agreement—an area of agreement, he said—that will permit governments to undertake projects like this and help, not hurt, business. I think there is, he said.

WILLKIE: I'll give you a statement. Ready? "There is no real conflict between private enterprise and public service. What is needed is more of a social consciousness in the men who head industry.

"We need business statesmen."

Q: Thank you, Mr. Willkie. (*Prepares to go*)

WILLKIE: (*Watches for a moment, then, softly*) You know, this fight against the holding companies—I see it as the crux of the whole thing. It's not against size—Con Edison is outside it. It's not really against rates: C. & S. and North American— we're with the lowest, there. If this was a fight against lobbies, you think they'd concentrate on the lobbies.

No. It's sheer Norris-Wheeler emotionalism.

And this Lilienthal—one of the best things that's happened to me, personally, in this fight, was the release of Wehle's statement in my support. When it came out, Ben Cohen asked Wehle: Why did you do that? And Wehle said, Ben, I'll tell you, but I warn you, you won't understand. It's because I'm a gentleman.

(*He laughs in approval, the color of vanity. Pleasure shows in all the changes and tilts of his face.*) I like that remark.

I expect a lot of lies. I've got one job in all of this: to get the juice out as fast as I can. Till the whole utility picture can be seen, in its full strength and beauty. Endless power, cheap power for all the customers! They'll see the picture, just as soon as the cloud of emotionalism has blown away.

That's what it is—emotionalism!

Q: That's a very fine and clear statement. Just as it is. Was it hard to get money for gas plants, ever? I suppose not.

WILLKIE: (*Startled*) Gas? What's gas got to do with it? This is water power, a giant of giants. The conversion of all our energy resources into electricity.

Q: A great network of wires across the land—

WILLKIE: Exactly. And more than that. Our resources pooled— How does gas come in?

Q: This is to be an article about you, Mr. Willkie, as a leader

in evolving organization—the type of dynamic leadership that
can cope with the present.

WILLKIE: You say that very well.

Q: We know your interest in the origin and nature of authority.

WILLKIE: That sounds very fancy. Of course it's true. But what
has that got to do with the gas business?

Q: Nothing really, except that I've just come back from a week
in Elwood. The gas boom was still going strong when you
were born, wasn't it?

WILLKIE: Sure. Hell, I remember the sky at night. That was
something to see!

*

⟨ What river flows through 7 states and drains 48?

*

Gullies as deep as halls held these surveyors,
Their bobs and blueprints. But men have drowned in the eaten
Land, the river ate them too.   You know the river
Cannot be looked at unless you see the forest,
The forest will not speak until you call the people.
Look at these people's lives and you will see it clear.

After explosions filling these valleys, clear
Outlander voices ring across the sky, and people
Prepare to move the dead from the graves, the river
Is coming over the bottomland and forest,
A little fightin creek would have eaten
The porch, the chickencoop, all but the surveyors.

The spools of cable, the pylons like surveyors
Walk, signal to the lives of all these people.
Their lives are real and face the tree of the forest,
And face the tree of time and the tree of the river

Singing a secret of growing and not being eaten
Until they are given as food.   And the valley stands clear.

*

([But what is a river for, Mr. Davidson is saying, if not for navigation?

*

They say that Willkie could never understand Lilienthal.

I cannot understand her, a man will say of a woman, or, I cannot understand it, of a poem. He will sit back, as if he has spoken about the woman or the poem. It is only about himself that he has said anything. And not enough.

During the lawing, Lilienthal and Willkie spent a certain amount of time together, or thinking about each other. The clue to this spare, direct, and dedicated man—Willkie cannot conceive of any clue.

I don't get it, he will say, he could be making twenty times that. It isn't that he can't plan—or count. Or choose. But he seems to see only one choice ahead of us. What is it? I don't know, something about science. Something about using science for good or evil.

*

Now that the river has changed, my dear,
And summer has changed and the winter weather,
I cannot foretell three days together,
I cannot foretell two days, my dear.
In the hills or in the town
The landmarks are all gone and down,
The signs are new and strange, my dear,
The signs are new and strange
And how shall I foretell, my dear?
What one thing do you need to hear?
What shall I say will come?   —Change.

*

The land has flowed into the river. The great crops of the land
have been shipped away. The raw crops eating the earth. Babies
in the yard, blackberry juice painted on them. Wilbur, you take
your squirrel gun. In town, they get that lovely Saturday-night
honking; and lots of fire alarms.

*

The tarpaper shack and the red rose bush.
Smoking crystal of the hill.
The brush of the shorelines, fever in its sting.
Don't tell me the water's still risin!
Go down to the rail gate, see where the rundown is.

There is a cloud on this house and the smoking crystal
Holds waters that will drench the oil lamp out.
One flashflood left me only my coffeepot.
That's nature's way, my walnut Granther said.

The dragons of burning ran along the mountain
A scar lighting the overflow; the forest
Pulls back from the highway, in mortal insult.
Spring bringing floodwaters.   Now the Negroes come
Over the runoff sloping, ankle-deep, with their blues
And watermelon smiles.   They know the suffering flood,
They are dark and they sing.   They know potential joy,
Flames, lightning, and the gully-buried man;
All the sky-stars and all the leaves on the tree.

Joy white and absolute, potential joy.
Ice and snow melting in the spring.   Amen.

Who shall bar with his arms the heavy rains?
Had me a man, the man pleased me.   Amen.

From kinsee to caintsee it's been rainin here,
I never longed west of the Mississippi.   Amen.

Downpours standin up to the bankgrass,
I've been a good wife.   I want the snowfed Trinity.   Amen.

Water spread over a lake to the windowsill
The tin cans silver, my kitchen window plants.   Amen.

My brooms, my yard goods, the honeysuckle vines,
And three left shoes go washing past the bank.   Amen.

Drowning of a deal table and eighteen head of cattle.
The whole section's under water and me singin Amen.
          I do sing Amen.

But next life, next life, or maybe next year, Lord,
Lay lightning across your river and your poor woman's Amen.
          Amen, Amen.
          I do sing Amen.

                              *

([*Willkie in action is beautiful to see, says the* New Republic. *Think of Toscanini, think of Eleanor Holm. He should have been Welsh.*

                              *

They dug up the grave, while a banjo and two guitars
Were quiet.   Hush your music, Sourwood Mountain,
We'll dance the Bird Cage again tonight.

Move the peacock quilt, pack up your favorite kettle,
There's extra homespun and the kerosene stove.
You will never forget the time the floor moved.

Frail pillars of reason held you with a creek gone crazy,
At five-thirty we heard the millrace and running stone.
The stars are nearly out and the legless shadows

Are men who have come to help hurt that my river done.

A LEGAL STORY

In the fall, Roosevelt calls a power pool conference at the White House. He likes the English grid system, against partitioning of electric systems. He wants a power pool in the Tennessee Valley.

Lilienthal and Willkie meet. Engineers are appointed, but only to gather physical data. Nobody asks them to find out what they can about the sources of power. In the meantime, the courts have a certain number of claims against TVA.

Willkie: The operating companies will put up a relentless fight. However, the problem could be solved amicably. Private property does not have to be destroyed by subsidized Federal competition.

The government, he says, is hurling abuses at us. At the utility industry. But, this time, it's put its great foot right through a beehive.

*

The words they use are rigid in definition. Going into this country, you cross a frontier that is not guarded well, as guards go. There is only a small, shriveled man on a high stool, saying: There is a human tendency to give a "reality" to concepts. Reality does not exist here. These terms must never be confused with concrete phenomena: they are things.

Value—signifies the worth of a commodity or service. Value in exchange is not the same as value in use, which is a subjective term implying worth *to a person*.

Utility—a subjective ability of a good to satisfy human wants. It is assumed that the utility of a commodity to a person does not change with time.

All the cost, value, investment, profit, words, the ideas like intrinsic value, the materiality of wealth, loans that can be sweet-

ened, the yardstick itself, are based on the *status quo*. They deal
with things as they were *the moment before*.

*

Everyone knows, says Willkie, that after the scandal at Muscle
Shoals, the equipment of the dam was rigged to fool Roosevelt.

*

❨ From the Chicago Tribune: *There is no longer room to doubt
that at Norris the communism of Lenin and Stalin has taken
root in the U.S. . . . Can anyone doubt that in the inaccessi-
ble mountains of Tennessee is being grown the germ culture that
is intended to infect America?*

*

The utilities men came down, snapshot the privies, and
laughed. These farmers buy power?

Ask, rather, whether it allows these lives to grow. Whether it
summons us. What can it show about development? Or democratic institutions? Or peace?

Perhaps there is a step here. Has an opportunity been defended, or has an opportunity been won?

Is there Jim Crow at the drinking fountains at Norris Dam?

Has the generation of power been used as the means of . . .

Can 19 companies stop TVA? No.

And the power pool?

*

❨ For the first time, we are to see our resources whole, in their
potential life and ours. The valley is a unity. So is my life.

*

Willkie drives past the monuments. Through Washington,
raging, away from the White House. From the hotel he sends

a telegram to his wife, who would be longing to hear about his meeting with Roosevelt: CHARM EXAGGERATED STOP I DID NOT TELL HIM WHAT YOU THINK OF HIM.

Q: But what really happened, Mr. Willkie?

WILLKIE: Nothing much. I was ushered in, there was some general talk.

Q: He draw you out? Famous for that, of course.

WILLKIE: I guess he did. It was all very pleasant. Then, without any opening for it, I wanted to ask my question, and I said, This is all very pleasant, Mr. President. But why did you call me here?

Q: What did Roosevelt say?

WILLKIE: He answered, Well, I want to know why you're against me.

Q: (*Slowly, with skepticism*) Is that a fact, Mr. Willkie?

*

If you think of it as a power fight between monopoly and government, you can go on with the statistics, proving whatever you choose about returns, taxes, whether a power dam is useful for flood control.

However, there is another way to see the fight. It involves an entire way of seeing, in which you acknowledge fully that you are dealing with the lives of people in relation to a valley. Not one river, but many rivers streaming together; not the tree of rivers, but the land itself and the future time.

This, in its structure, is a translation of the facts between private and public enterprise. It has its lawsuits, its quarrels; it also exists without the worship of the state.

Is the purpose of the Valley project to make a system of relation between people and a valley—their environment—beyond any idea of the state? Unless the state is allowed to be a growing system of relation. Unless we think in this way.

Elwood, they say, is a gas town; gas determines its history.

Rushville is a farming center. In Akron, rubber is the pivot. New York is power and reach.

Gas does not; people determine Elwood; they are using gas as an extension of themselves. Rubber does not turn Akron, or any other place. These are people. You will have heard it said: War does this, technology does that. We in America are very imaginative, we have hurried toward a mysticism of matter. Nevertheless. People.

*

Willkie was never one to stop short of the rabbit punch.

Take out full-page ads in these papers, all through the territory! Tell them the government's wasting tax money and needed materials. This is no time, tell them, to waste either money or material on socialistic experiments. The government stepping in and taking over the electric business! Or any business! That's red revolution! Are you going to stand for it?

ROOSEVELT: You will join the power pool study, then?

WILLKIE: Sure, if TVA extends the C. & S. contract.

ROOSEVELT, looks at Lilienthal: Let C. & S. drop its suit against us, first.

WILLKIE: The moment TVA promises to suspend line construction.

LILIENTHAL: No . . . we can't do that.

Then WILLKIE: Let's have no more of these misunderstandings, Mr. President. If anything here is based on the chance that we'll change our ground—don't do it.

Willkie thinks, watching Norris: Power and sin, power and sin! Old boy, muttering now? You'll be all right, and needed, too. The Court fight's coming.

A few months later, when the question of power is put aside, Willkie talks to the press:

*

❨ I cannot believe that the President has turned thumbs down on further power pool conferences. . . .

For me to believe this would be to believe the charges made when the President called the original conference: viz., that his object was political strategy.

I cannot believe this.

*

In the crested country, among the copper fumes, among "niggertowns" where our resources flood away, among the steep cities where streets cave in, limestone leached out by the underground water. The nice houses are near the shacks.

Willkie walking through Knoxville thinking, Of course we'll string our lines. The spite lines go up, miles of copper, and Mrs. Tate with a rifle in her hand shouts up into her big hickory tree, Come on, you. Come down out of that tree. Slowly, the lineman climbs back into the yard.

These are fine people, says Willkie. They know which end is up—some of them, anyway. A doctor from Georgia was walking these mountains, knocked on a cabin door, as night was falling in Tennessee.

Might I spend the night here?

Farmer says no. His wife's expecting a baby.

Fine, I'm a doctor. I can help.

The farmer at last lets him stay, and they go to sleep. Next thing the doctor feels his shoulder shaken. Time for the child, Doctor! shouts the farmer.

It is a long, hard night. The child is born at last.

In the morning—a minute later, it seems to him—the doctor wakes again, yawns, and for laughs, asks the farmer how much he owes him.

Twenty-five, says the farmer.

Twenty-five what? says the doctor, amazed.

Dollars, says the farmer, spitting.

But, says the doctor, my services are worth far more than that. If this is a matter of money. As it seems to be.

OK, says the farmer, let's go to the judge.

They walk to town and find him. When the judge has heard both stories, he looks at the men. Everything hangs for a moment; then the judge rules for the farmer.

They go outside and the doctor takes the twenty-five dollars from his billfold.

Oh keep it, says the farmer. I just wanted to show you what a goddamn fool we elected for a judge here.

*

WILLKIE, to Roosevelt: But there is no confidence. You can't get junior money in, these days.

ROOSEVELT: Can't you?

WILLKIE: There's too much uncertainty. I blame a lot of it on all the talk about "yardstick rates"—

ROOSEVELT: That was a bad image, at best.

WILLKIE: It's something that you admit—

ROOSEVELT: You people wanted to talk about rates. Now a yardstick seems to most people to be stable; reliable; conservative. When I measure a field at Hyde Park, I may use one. But you and I know, Mr. Willkie, that—Dutchess County or Rush County—we must have a yardstick of the standard temperature, we must be sure the stick is not warped, we must be sure it is a stick, and not subject to—if you will forgive me—electrical forces. And we must specify, the physicists say, the way in which our yardstick is moved from one position to another. . . .

(*Willkie, when Roosevelt said,* I measure a field, *is struck for the first time with the reality of the withered legs.* Wounded! *he thinks,* wounded!)

. . . And this yardstick is to measure nothing so simple. What are we trying to gauge? Human wish, human need; as they are today. And we are trying to meet them, we are engaged in a perpetual experiment. (*I'll play right into your hands, if you don't mind, he says, smiling and glittering.*) We'll meet and feed that wish. We'll try for central lives instead of marginal lives. As far as electricity goes, we'll produce electricity for their use. And then we'll see what they wish for!

All we know now is that they will be changed.

Their lives will be changed.

They will need a new yardstick, or some new measurement.

Their wishes will be changed.

*

To the press, Willkie: President Roosevelt represents the forces of discontent against business.

He did not create these forces. He has done, at most, no more than lead them. And then—I'll go along with the prudent investment theory of valuation; although the method the Supreme Court upholds is more satisfactory to you, the consumer, in my opinion.

You know, when I see him, I can't get a word in. At Tupelo? He was a liar. And Lilienthal? Lilienthal was a traitor.

*

To the press, Roosevelt: I tried to find out why these companies have had difficulty in raising money. All he would answer was "The general feeling." I know that the general feeling is more important in selling than most details. But it seems to me that our business men are getting too emotional. No good in being hysterical about private ownership. And he laughs the easy, relaxing, famous laugh.

*

All of these rigid arguments are about the flow of water.
Willkie, his voice rising: This means that all flowing water
would come under the Federal bureaucracy. Any farmer with a
creek would have to go to a political officeholder if he wanted
a bridge or an irrigation ditch.

*

PORTRAIT OF A MAN, WITH A BACKGROUND OF.HOLDINGS

Standing against the gorge, he sees the slides of light.
Where lightning lay, they are building.   The surfaces are lit.
The dam that is almost finished stands in seamless night
Declaring its form with a clear speaking.
The man leans on his railing.   He thinks : I will listen.
Bulbs of violent light swing on their own wires,
Lines of the downstream face flow down the slope of dream.
Spillway of loyalties shining, the gate of fire.

He forgets the police on a hot summer night long past
Later finding the wound between his shoulder blades;
He thinks of the women opened before him, flowers of summer,
The first cry of his son at which all waterfalls
Waited like streams of wine bitter in Spain.
Riches of breathing, fantastic poverty.
The running of stones in this riverbed.

Corngreen and fields of thirst, he thinks.   I know a woman
The river of whose mouth, whose sea of flowers
I saw in the hot fields of the past, at night.
Over all images a lightning stroke of law
Has been laid across, white structure on the river
To stop my profit's streams, to make a tree
Celebrating the years of growth and form.

The pacemaker image.   A pulse and pattern of light.
The mirror image of my waste, in the ferocious cities

Whose roaring and giant fibres find my exultation
Outward in the shout, while what I stare at is
The dam I tried to murder for years; or sail
In a boat the color of violins among
A school of condoms floating in the Sound.
Beyond naming, waste!   The legs of the withered man.
My summons from the great web and the woman
In glimpses accepted, for long forgot.   I think
I am wheat dormant in the seedman's hand.

*

Roosevelt, at his press conference, looking at Willkie's memo to him and talking: It is the same old story about trying to lump all business together. We have got away from it now, but this memo was based on the old-fashioned idea. . . .

Among Mr. Willkie's proposals is one that asks that the power valuation established by the courts apply to a set date, and for the future the prudent investment method be adopted. Of course that is impossible.

If the thing is wrong now, I cannot see where you have any right morally to compound a felony by law with the Government saying that the crimes of the past will be entirely forgotten and forgiven.

He wants us to leave the water or the wind in the existing capital. Two wrongs do not make a right—that's perfectly obvious.

He asks for a modification of the "death sentence." I showed the other day that four per cent of securities controls ninety-six per cent. That's a ninety-six-inch dog being wagged by a four-inch tail. And we're right at the heart of it. He wants the four-inch tail to be legalized for all time to come. We cannot agree on that, ever.

*

❨ Q: *Sir, are you leading up to eliminating holding companies entirely?*

ROOSEVELT: *Yes.*

Q: *Is that a fair question?*

ROOSEVELT: *Yes.*

Q: *Mr. President, is this what you call docking the dog's tail?*

ROOSEVELT: *I'd say, "cutting the muscle."*

Q: *It might be a case of cutting the tail off right back of the ears, Mr. President.*

ROOSEVELT: *I would hate to destroy his looks. You know, he could have a perfectly good tail if you cut the muscle in it.*

*

([Gunther hearing Willkie say, That fellow in the White House is just too smart to live.

Such use, if envisioned in its entirety, touches and gives life to all forms of human concerns.—Roosevelt

*

In a song, in a clear look, the heat and blood of history may come, through a child, to us all. The enormous dams, the dome of the Capitol, are now no larger than the dream of a child: in the hot clover, through the dream-corn of a boom town, running, in Indiana summer; or, later, another boy, a four-year-old, with the bells of the great dreams going through his blood also.

Rang and rang, rang in a small boy's head.

A child goes through the same course: the meanings and knowings.

*

A man riding on the meaning of rivers
Sang to me from the cloud of the world:
Are you born?   Are you born?
My name is gone into the burning heart
That knows the change deep in the form of things.
—I saw from the treeline all our cities shine.

A woman riding on the moon of ocean
Sang to me through the cloud of the world:
Are you born?   Are you born?
The form of growing in leaf and crystal flows,
And in the eyes and rivers of the land.
—From the rock of our sky, I came to recognize.

A voice riding on the morning of air
Sang to me from the cloud of the world:
Are you born?   Are you born?
Bring all the singing home;
There is a word of lightning in the grass.
—I stood alive in the young cloud.

*

A STORY

There is a child. He comes from far. By boats and trains, cities that move, houses that sail away. He comes from the country of war to a field at peace. Day lilies, yellow daisies, Queen Anne's lace. A barrel, a box of sand. He is four years old; he looks up into Miss Lorence's eyes. Many children, playing.

CHILD: Look, look!
MISS LORENCE: Yes. I'm looking.
CHILD: I'm way up in the sky!
2ND CHILD: Moo, moo. I don't like you.
CHILD: I do magic.
2ND CHILD: What magic?
CHILD: Want to see?
                 I do magic very well.
                 Step there. Put one foot there.
                 Now I need the latter.
                 Hold it! (To the young woman)
                 What's your name?

MISS LORENCE: Miss Lorence. What's yours?
CHILD: Paul.
MISS LORENCE: Paul is slight, Paul is small,
Paul wants to feel, he wants to smell,
He wants to taste, to see, hear.   Everything.
He is slight, his eyes blaze blue,
White-skinned, cocky, knobby, as
Fragile as a closed-down spring.
PAUL: Where is father?
MISS LORENCE: Far.   Your mother does not know.
It is the war.   It is the war.
PAUL: Who is Hitler?
What is sound?
How does it feel to die?
What does a worm think?   Miss Lorence?
How long does it take to grow up?
Miss Lorence—I will talk to you.
The little house I like, the kitten I like.
It went to a little wood, to a little Paul,
When it came to Paul it cried.
In a basket, like Paul the baby, in far land,
To Paul's father.   The father of Paul
Kissed the kitty and cried.
Unhappy was he.   Why is he?
Because I have no kitty, because the father
Of Paul is in a far country.
Not in this town is he,
Not in this house,
Not in the room or the bedroom.
Far away, far away.   When will he come to us,
When will we be happy, seeing him company?
Not for long, for long, for long.
Cry we, for it is a long time, and far away.

ANOTHER DAY

MISS LORENCE: The child among his powers gathering
His words, his rich articulate joys and fears.
They are our fears, our joys, the questions of all.
His creations are real.   His agonies
Are curiously related to the trouble of the people
of the world.
PAUL: There was a boy once, lived in a little house.
A big man came, started eating and eating.
He got to the boy, boy said, Dog, dog save me.
Dog jumped the ocean and saved the little boy.
Then they lived together.
The giant was discouraged.
After a while he saw his mother.   Yawn I.
A man came and ate up the little pig.
How discouraging!   How sad!
Discouraged little pig.
I am tired.   Rest I will.

ANOTHER DAY

PAUL: And then the cow did write.
His mother said sleep, sleep,
The other cows are outside,
You have been bad,
More than the black cow,
More than the white;
Go to sleep.
You are a baby cow.
Your father is in the creek.
I had no home and I cried
Master, master!
I want some water or I will be sad.

ANOTHER DAY

PAUL: I will now sing a song for you, Miss Lorence.
Will you write it down?

MISS LORENCE: Yes. I'd like to.

PAUL: No. I cannot sing today. My songs are tired.
They are unhappy.

MISS LORENCE: I can write down your unhappy song.

PAUL: No. You sing me a song.

MISS LORENCE: Shall I sing Sacramento? Buckeye Jim?

PAUL: No, no. You must not sing those songs.
Sing your new song. About me.
Sing about that grownup downstairs
Who lives in a tree.

MISS LORENCE: Who lives in a tree?

PAUL: The man with the grass in his lovely hair.
The wild, happy man, with the bears,
and the large scamper.

*

MISS LORENCE: The words are masks, the words are a stream;
they mask his open fears. The apprehen-
sions stand there.

*

PAUL: I don't want to rest. Once upon a time there
was a Miss Lorence, who was going away,
away, away, away. Don't go away to
leave me. Sit on my bed not to leave
me. A skylark am I, wildly I walk, walk,
walk, walk.
Mittens here in my bed.
There. I hit you, but I love you.
When you die you stop. Don't really worry,
dear you.

I do not really die.   Do not believe anything I
      tell you,
Or unless you really see.
Sometimes I joke.
This is school.   Not sky, not home, but school,
      school, school.
What is my shadow?   It is me,
But not a mirror.

ANOTHER DAY

PAUL: You sit there because I like to look at you.
                I would like to live with you.
                Why don't you come live with me?
                This little fish went in the water,
                But there came a boat and smack,
                Killed at once.
                That is the end of my story.
                Which is a love story, Miss Lorence.
                What do you know about love, Miss Lorence?
                Once upon a time there was a big, big, big man.
                A zero man.
                I dreamed about the school and people.
                Miss Lorence was a snowman.
                I dreamed about me, sleeping in a box
                Because I had no house.
                And we cried.
                I dreamed about a hundred miles on a boat.
                And the boat went on swimming in my head.
                Wicked witch. Pony. Zero. Clay.
                All my head is gone.
                Shot off by a gun.
                Your head will be gone too
                If the men, the men, the *men* shoot you.

It will be too bad when your head is shot off.
You are a dear little baby.
Once there was a man called Jew
And he was chased and he was shot
And he ran but he was shot
Wee Willie Winkie.
—Antonia, you are a zero.
Have you ever "rapping at a window, tapping at
    a lock," Miss Lorence?
I am a quiet little boy because I must be quiet.
Come sit beside me, Miss Lorence.

*

They talk to each other, and he holds her hand. The small, knotty boy, with a young woman bending over him, curved and evocative, giving him his rest and his stories as November deepens.

*

PAUL: Miss Lorence, you are a tree with leaves on,
            A strong stone, a brook. Look,
            Water running in brooks, in brooks, in brooks,
            Which are purple and white streams,
            Screens, screams and cries and loud noises.
            Oh, what a singer am I.
            Little songs and cries.

            I want to want to want to get up.

            But I will sing a loo a loo a loo.
            The old man named Loo
            And he went to an eye
            And he lived in the eye.
            What a lot he could see.
            Once upon a time

There was an end of my story.
I do not like the black sky.

*

His gay words, words of delight. But the real fears, the questions, the real real emerging. Father, Hitler, war, shooting, Jews, death, safety.

*

PAUL: What do you write?
Write me a song.
What about? The fish I do not know.
—The man had little streams.
And a bright pain.
It was bright when he pushed
With a noise and a bar.
A tooth. With a hole.
There can be holes in the ground,
Can there be holes
In the white sky?
The sky is a tree. It spreads.
Does it hurt the ground to have holes?
Why, the sky was *white*.

*

PAUL: Do you know Hitler? Does he like you?
I know him.
MISS LORENCE: Do you?
PAUL: He doesn't like me. He shoots people.
MISS LORENCE: Why doesn't he?
PAUL: Because—I don't know.
I lived away over the river.
MISS LORENCE: In Germany?
PAUL: I lived in a million houses.

My father is in Krieger land.
Not this land, not this America,
But a Krieger land.
That is a land of guns.
That is a shooting land.
I remember the dogs in the park.
Far away.   I remember.
That park we saw the dogs.
When we went home again
We stepped the leaves apart.
I want to get up.

*

ANOTHER DAY

PAUL: Miss Lorence, we are new to each other,
Because I have not been to you for long, for
     long, for long.
You are a dear little tree.
Sit by me close.
I am a little horse who is going to sing.
Such a lot of songs I have to sing,
For I have not been to you for so long.
Did you ever have a red pain
In your throat?   Mine was, it was mine.
Now I am here I can sing to you
A little song all for you.
You make me happy.
Shall I say it in German, in French?
No.   I will not.
I will just say it to you in talk.
It is a little song about me.
I am happy with you, happy like happy
At birthday candles

And little gold shoes
That Jesus wears.
Little gold shoes.

*

Yes, a nice child. Isn't he a nice child?

*

ANOTHER DAY

PAUL: You can't come with us.
                We have business to do.
                We have to go over to Germany
                But we'll be back in a minute.
                We have to go to Hitler's land
                To shoot him.
                But you are a lady so you can stay home.
                Men take care of ladies.
MISS LORENCE: Who are you going to shoot?
PAUL: Hitler of course, the bad wolf.
                If you are in trouble with Hitler you'd better not
                    come on the ferryboat.
                If you are don't come here with us,
                You'll make more trouble than we have.
                Are you a Jew?
                It's being Jews that makes the trouble.
                It makes people worry.
                Are you Jew?
MISS LORENCE: No.
PAUL: That is why you are not worried. That is why
                    you are happy.

*

His father is lost and away. Paul never asks for help or sympathy. He is detached and proud. Now, around New Year's Day, he stops being Paul. The brittle four-year-old turns into something else: the farthest he can imagine, the oldest he can travel. He announces to everyone that he is Timmy Torin, he is nine and can do anything. He is his own hero. And his father is lost.

*

PAUL: My name is Timmy Torin.
I can do more things when I'm bigger.
You like me big don't you?
If somebody was lost I could find them
Any time my mommy tells me or you tell me.
I'm a very big boy.
I'm not afraid.
You know about Jesus, little Lorence?
Some day I will tell you all about Jesus.
My father is dead, he is an angel.
When you are blind you cannot see but black.
When you are blind, it is like you are nothing
And are dead.   How is that?
Somebody says, When you are dead you are
       stopped.
And other people say
You go to the sky and watch and sing.

Miss Lorence, I am tired.
You can have one of my blocks.

*

The sea has opened, the limit of his dream
Has split; now lights announce him to the day.
He is born; and asleep, awake, and soon the warm
Taste of the second world calls him to understand

Power drawn on the tides of sweetness in.
His strength allowing change, letting him choose and grow
Again, and the curve of the world is breast, the breathing land
With his own breathing tells of peace and form.

Not now, but much later, does the world fall away.
This is myself, says the child.   My self, we all did say.
There is my mother, whose pleasure, whose deep need
It was to feed me singing, or recoil.
And then the fable, the terrible forgetting.
A cold distortion twisting past the leaves.
Was there a Garden?   Was there a Tree of Sin?
What was my exile but from memory?
Refusal, flowering, was the only tree.
It grew until the truth was almost lost.
Cast, the obliterate spirit sang its loss.
Dream and the sea open.
All things find their change.
        The child remembers : the child is the tree;
The tides, the leaves, the city, the true relation.
The world was the mother, the world; it was always the world
Pure, fierce, all moving and all reconciled.

*

A structure is rising.   It takes on shape, it takes on meaning
Where there was formless waste.   Go down the valley,
Eye of creation, sings the voice of the girl
Through cloverfield.   Green water is the spring of the year,
Jade green in summer; autumn bright blue, for winter water-
        black.
The wall's detail, discrimination of blue
Standing above the wall, where developing water
Coils, sheathes, transforms itself turning, into light.
Fusing of images and further change.

Fire and music, interchangeable.
Fusing of flow, dividing and further blue.

There is control here, for all things in relation
Find their offerings and give.   A tendency toward life.
The man at peace with his life and its flashing,
A climax forest at peace with its fields.
When the storms come, there is something in us
That has always been ready to greet the storm.
An impulse running through a valley of process
Quickens the blossoming, whose orange on evening
The fiery action of men and women emerges.
And daughter-stars, daughter-forests of our range
Dance with the central prince the dance of reign.
We know the light incarnate, we have seen
At last that the flashing is our old light, and flesh.

Under stones, under leaves, under links of purpose,
Appetite up so tall, the power is given
Along the hillsides of risk, the spiral dances
Within its own symmetry.   But women, but men, but women
And men in the dances and risks of birth
In which love and the spirit are reborn.
This also from lightning given and growing power.
Lightning which is the word.   The gift and power.   Love.

                                        *

(*From a letter: You know what this is. The yellow-bellied
scoundrels from north of the Line have hacked away at our land.
From another letter: They have flooded it, ruined it, and mutilated it into a colonization scheme for Yankee Republicans, trying to make our children talk like that.*

   *From Westbrook Pegler: What's this place? Norris Village?
We'll call it Camp Fauntleroy.*

Lilienthal: I am against basket weaving and all that that implies.

*

In the last hour of night, a zebra racing dawn,
Black-and-white hour that feeds the night and the light,
Feeding the strong infants; when the well is open;
When all the birds of day begin to sing.
He turning in sleep finds through a journey of dream
One woman in whom all the rivers of his storm
Cluster and fill, as words, as woman.   Finds
The running of stones in a riverbed
Troubling hillsides with their leaves
Over black branches.   Swinging-to of mountains
No heavier than sails riding to rendezvous.
Dense in our blood, abstract as the idea of God.
As smoky misereres, as the birthcry.
The big few clusters, the body of a man.
The clusters of her body.   Sleep of gardens,
Sleep of rain, always distant and present
As your own deprived childhood.   No.   Not deprived.
Yes.   For it never saw it was deprived.
But there was the unknown, the great dream of the poor
And of all men; your childhood found that friend.
Was it the faceless, the man in the purple graveyard?
No.   Hidden.   And kind.   In endless offering.
And now in early sleep, a ripple uncovering
The roots of the diverse, the city of love.

A note in music.   His sleep going long and along.

*

Fields where we slept
Lie underwater now

Clay meadows of nightmare
Beneath the shallow wave.

A tremor of speech
On all lips and all mirrors;
Pink sweater and tornado
Act out the spiral dawn.

South lies evocative
On one fine Negro mouth.
Play of silver in streams
Half lake under.

High on the unplowed red
And waterweeds respond,
Where Sheriff Fever
Ordered me to trial.

Where once hatred and fear
Touched me the branch of death,
I may float waves of making
Hung above my lost field.

Remember they say and Incarnatus Est,
The fire-tailed waves, never forget the eyes
Of the distorted jailers or their kindness
Even while they were torturing Mr. Crystal.

Psalms awake and asleep, remember the manmade
Lake where those barren treecrowns rode.
Where air of curses hung, keel of my calm
Rides our created tide.

*

He turns through the lucid stars of a lit city
In sleep.   He is walking past the snake and the spiderthread.
"And they do say the rain's to come."

The flood-woman ankle-deep, staring upon his eyes
In a dream of rivers, water whirls here like the sound
Of voices, of swans. The faring. Below him turns
A house swimming, a broken-legged table and three chairs.
Past him in all that filth, a message in a bottle,
Too far to reach, and four stiff-legged chickens.

Ocean of our refusal, pouring its waste
Over the mind of man.
A choice between evils.
These evils are of us, that we did not respond:
Poverty, hunger, war.

The flood and the woman staring upon his eyes.
This flowing away is the lives of all I love.
Are you saying this is not water but lives?
Of course it is water. Fool! Of course it is lives.

*

⟨ *The agreements which preserve freedom, says the Dean of
St. John's, rather than destroy it. The most extraordinary thing,
he says, at present: that dam on the Dnieper, because of its possibilities. But it does seem that the Tennessee Valley has come
closer to revealing such possibilities than anything else.*

*

HIS DREAM OF FLOOD : AND EDEN

He breaks as the river knots about their knees:
I thought I could bring life to such a pitch
That you and I and all things might be seen
With our own fire burning. Something like Eden.
She is water to the thighs. Relinquishing daylight, cries,
Where four rivers meet!
I like Eden our parents alive and corruptless,

Our parents thirteen years old, each one his own,
Slenderer than time, meeting in their first powers
And making us again.
Now her voice twirls past domes and nebulas,
The tilted courtroom sailing by as columns.
All stars, all cities variable.
And sondes and angels, swimming
Flood at his throat.
He knows something is safe.   The whirlpool,
He says, the embryo.
Before him floating and grave
The face of a child within the water-spiral.
A thin boy carrying a growing shoot.
Image of the continual self he shines
The edgewise spiral of all the hourlines.
Because you do require, the child is saying.
These are the bonds among things; they are the spirit
When you do recognize.
Even when all the voices are denied.

*

He starts awake in the city.   Orion believing
And erect stretches the sky of night.
That's all very well, thinks, seeing the clock; but I
Am practical : I can forget.   And sleep.

*

〖 *Flood control! No flood this year, says Roosevelt. Willkie
grins at the newspapermen. Have you looked at the almanac?
It hardly rained.*

*

〖 *After five years of fighting, Corcoran says, Well, Wendell, at
last I think we've got you cornered. You've been the only effective general against us.*

Wait and see, says Willkie.

After six years, they call in the photographers. Yes, says Willkie. Tennessee Electric. Sold. To TVA.

He accepts, from Lilienthal, the check for $44,728,300.

Willkie: This is sure a lot of money for a couple of Indiana farmers to be kicking around.

*

In a new domain, we will be secure only if we expect new facts.

*

Dewey inviting him by phone to be his Secretary of State. Dewey foretelling his own future, and liking the taste.

Willkie speaking into the phone: No. I tell you, Tom, I don't believe in your foreign policy. . . . You don't say? You don't, either? . . . Well, I guess I just wasn't brought up on your side of the street. Good-by, Tom.

He hangs up.

*

⟨ *Willkie saying: The heart of the American system is the control of power—the prevention of the accumulation of power in any hands at all.*

*

On Washington's birthday, a few men talking in the evening about the Presidency. Among these, Arthur Krock, of the *Times*. After the debates, the poles of hostility and the old longings with their masks, Willkie's name comes up.

I like him.—William Allen White

I doubt that Mr. Roosevelt has done as well with the government as Willkie with C. & S.—Kansas City *Independent*

The strength of Wendell L. Willkie is the strength of the
good Indiana earth.—John Watson

He has the longest upper lip in the U.S.—Damon Runyon

*

An evening on "Information, Please."

A petition to politicians in *Fortune*, called "We, the People."

The memory of the Herald Tribune Forum debate with Ar-
nold and Douglas; of the Town Hall debate with Jackson; the
Press Club debate with Ickes.

The face of a candidate.

*

⟨ *Willkie, ruffling himself for the cameras: In my business it
pays to look like an Indiana farmer.*

*

The White House. May, very late at night. A light on the
switchboard; a bedside phone ringing. Scents in the warm, still
night. The phone ringing. The sound cut off for a moment;
then Missy Le Hand telling the operator to pass the call on.

The phone beside the President's bed.

Now the voice coming through, relayed thin and high. The
ambassador to France, speaking from Paris: They are only sixty
miles away, now, he says in a frantic well-bred wildness of war
and distance.

*

Willkie wants to aid democracy "without jeopardizing peace
for our own land." Ten years ago, or with the League. But you
cannot postpone jeopardy, or a meaning, or a talent, or a woman,
or a man; these gifts live in time. He looks at his friend, with
her dark, witty face, and he thinks, yes, she may know. She may
very well be right.

*

Under the banners of "reform," writes Willkie, there came to Washington—and to power—men whose hatred for business and businessmen surpassed the bounds of reason.

For indeed it is *business* that has made the American people so great. . . .

The first characteristic of a people's platform—a platform built for all the people, for national prosperity—must be a *businesslike* approach to the major economic problems of the day. This is just plain common sense.

*

([For 11 years he has lived in New York, yet at heart he has never left Indiana. His office is only a block away from Wall Street, but Wall Street has never felt that he really belonged.
—Bruce Barton

*

In a restaurant. He stops to talk to Faulkner about *Sanctuary*. His friends all know that writers and the society of writers mean to him a particular prize. The evenings of Irita Van Doren. At Dorothy Thompson's. The men who write his speeches.

He seems to want people to be quick, emotionally alive, he says in the jargon of the time. He respects, he says, mental experience. Locked in a fantasy of the *status quo*, he draws to him those who are so locked.

*

The tree of rivers seen and forgotten,
With all its lightnings laid over it, the white law.
Strokes of the spirit on the flowing spirit
Seen, forgotten, and seen, until the source.
But the source, simple and various
As possibility, the nest of light,
Is open; what do you forget who have forgotten?
At home or hunting, forgetting takes your throat.

This dream of rivers responding, as many lives respond:
The cant of a dam and the running of fresh waters
Allow discovery deep in the city of your days
Starting up, before your faces born,
Born and reborn of your perceive,
Of your smile that you recognize
The meanings as they move.

PART THREE Convention

(Out over the country a sort of murmur, they write, is going up for Willkie. He sits in Pine Street with his feet on the desk, says Markey, or debates his head off, saying, The heart of the American system is the control of power.

It was as a supersalesman that he got to know America.

*

(This is a different world from Roosevelt's, they write. Here's the air of the plains, the small frame houses, the stories of successful migrations and business successes. Willkie, says Anne McCormick, means the big, anxious, fluctuating world of the middle class.

*

Q: Why should anyone seek to assume the burden of the Presidency?

WILLKIE: I am 48 years old. I've done a lot of thinking on our problems. I have certain ideas about our government. I want to do something about it.

Q: Why should anyone seek to assume the burden of the Presidency?

ROOSEVELT: Somebody has to face it.

Q: Which do you consider the better answer? Give your reasons.

On a separate sheet, you may submit your own answer. Write legibly. In marking these papers, spelling will be taken into consideration, as well as neatness, family background, religious practices, sexual practices, superstitions, penmanship, color of hair, color of eyes, color of skin (area visible when fully clothed), color of skin (area invisible when fully clothed), color of distinctive body markings, color of political beliefs at the following ages: 7, 13, 18, 20½, 24, 29, 35, 41, 50, 80; color of political beliefs one month after start of first remunerative position, color of political beliefs one month after loss (for whatever reason) of fifth remunerative position, color of fifteen typical friends, color of employee (present), color of five typical enemies, color of landlord (present); color of campaign backers: (1) over $5,000, (2) under $5,000; attitude toward England, attitude toward twenty selected corporations, attitude toward U.S.S.R.; attitude toward any four of the following: (1) children, (2) the tariff, (3) baseball, (4) Charles Chaplin, (5) hybrid corn, (6) old age, (7) the movies, (8) theater in Washington, (9) vice in Washington: (9a) financial, (9b) sexual, (9c) supernatural, (10) regular church attendance, (11) your nearest Chamber of Commerce, (12) spirituous liquors, (13) quiet evenings at home, (14) human burial, (15) masturbation, (16) mothers, (17) group games for growing children, (18) the party system in the U.S.

Write an essay of not more than 200 words on any of the following: (a) New England and the South, (b) mining and

farming, (c) oil wells and relief, (d) war and peace, (e) male
and female, (f) brandy and Scotch, (g) good and evil, (h) God.

*

❨ FORMIDABLE BUSINESS MAN CANDIDATE, SAYS GENERAL JOHNSON

*If the Government, says Willkie, continues to take over my
business I may be looking shortly for some kind of a job. General
Johnson's is the best offer I have had so far.*

*

When he debates, he calls up furious applause from his own
backers. Now he is taking them on: Frankfurter at the Harvard
Club, Jackson at Town Hall, where Willkie buys 200 seats.
Jackson has the regular six seats. This open slugging on the announced subject, Can Business and Government Co-operate,
brought the letters in, starting the next day. And brought the
questions. When Willkie says he is a member of big business
who never hired a labor spy in his life, the questions begin.

Did he ever have to meet a payroll?

Was he a businessman or a mouthpiece?

Was he, as fixer, doing deficit financing on his preferred
stockholders' money?

How could C. & S. buy power from the government at 2 mills
and sell 90% of it at 6½ mills?

What are the ethics of the Edison Institute?

How can the French Popular Front be blamed for everything
that has happened?

And the answers, denying the charge of labor spies, being
proud of having nothing to do with "that phase of American
economic life." Now Russell Davenport comes in as campaign
manager. Now Joe Pew, Cyrus Eaton, William White, Dorothy
Thompson, where are you? Where are you, Booth Tarkington,
Claire Luce, John Lewis, Irvin Cobb? Where are you, Irita Van

Doren? Bruce Barton? Oren Root? Henry Mencken? Have you
placed your bets?

*

This is going to be about smoke.
Blindness, shouting of smoke, the dice pitted with mines and
      tunnels.
Black hills, flights of paper over the lines of glaciers,
Railway stations in the zebra hour of morning
When the only ones awake are the mothers of infants
Staring at dawn, sky of the fountains.
                               Smoke
Of hotels, of women wanting to be raped, of the plush sofas
That long only to float into empty houses.
Smoke of concessions, the crystal chandeliers
Whose teardrops ring and say, Choose between evils,
You live in the world, you must learn to choose between evils.
Two gray colors of smoke waiting to be chosen.
Will nobody tell them?   They do not seem to know.
I will.   My brothers of smoke, my brothers,
You do not have to choose between evils.

*

This is what are the hunters of smoke and the paths of the for-
      est. The tracking and the advantage of the steaming
      quarry,
This is what the pillars of fluted thought, the image vibrating
      through all the dances to the unknown where the leap is,
This is what the event and the battle-rags, the women secret in
      their suffering, the long rages of the pioneers, the glory
      standing over a final valley,
This is what they led to in their charts of vision : the sweat of
      bargaining and the smoky gold eagles,
The indirect lighting and the gamblers' despair.

Shifting landscapes of a Convention Hall.
This is a bazaar where there are nothing but drugstores
Each one has a single drug tested only on mandrills.
This is a dry arroyo expecting the avalanche,
Thirty-seven men offering foolproof ways of survival.
They trade their partisans.   That is their method of choice.
When they say survival, they do not mean living under the ava-
    lanche.
They do not recognize the existence of the avalanche.
They mean how to set up shop in the arroyo,
And show a profit after the first six months.

                         *

In a summer forest, when the profuse season
Let fall as burning flowers the burning flowers.
The cities of Europe fall as people chopped down and dying.
The skies see hairy fire.   The children see
Their mothers opening as nobody had told them
People can open.   News sometimes comes of Father.
Then no longer.   What horror the children see
Will not be acted out upon the world
For fifty years, or a hundred, as horror bursting
Or anti-horror working in their children.
A neat correctly dressed man with a picnic smile
Is drawing his feet up under him in a dance
In the summer forest.   He makes a little stamping
Pulling his knees up, a shiny little dance
Called Hitler Jigging.   The Forest of Compiègne.
The beds and chimneys and toys and linen and wood
Of many houses are not interested in this dance
And in China they have been fighting for a long time
Dragging thousands of miles the idea of man.

                         *

❡ *The day after the fall of Paris, the Manhattan Project was organized by Roosevelt.*

        *

❡ *Perhaps it means something that there rises up out of nowhere a discursive Hoosier. . . .*

                         —Anne O'Hare McCormick

        *

Under the lights and the eagles, they are shouting and shifting votes. It is pointed out that all the right hats are here.

Joe Martin: He stampedes everyone but the delegates.

Four days ago, nobody thought of this man as a candidate. Now that he is here, now that the Ballad for Americans has been sung by somebody, not Paul Robeson; now that Joe Pew has looked at him and thought, How can we do it? We all know no simon-pure businessman can be a good President; now that the Elwood house has been made vivid and plain to them: ramshackle, with its shade maples and its two tones of green; now that his youth has been made palatable: full of tippin-over privies and cop-fightin; now that his early politics have been made gay and irresponsible: he liked T.R.'s trust-bustin and Jack London's socialism—now we can get down to the real work of the hotel suite.

        *

❡ *Willkie, to the newspaper men: I don't have any organization but you fellows.*

        *

A very soft woman in a red print dress and a jacket covered with blue print flowers pushes past the jewel-covered ladies near the door. In the second room, she pushes past the delegates. A pale man waves his arms and says, Blood! We'll have their blood! The soft woman can hardly push past these people; they are milling very willfully, and according to a set pattern. She pushes past the next two rooms of people. Bourbon, cheap bourbon is what she has been drinking. Paper cups. There he is: very big, square, terribly tired and rumpled (he's two inches shorter, he's so tired, says a reporter), with the fifth room shut behind him.

I could love him to death, she says to nobody at all, pushing very hard, and stamping her high heel on the white shoe just before her.

Now in front of him, he is talking about playing poker. He's learned that bluffing's fine if nobody calls your bluff. I even liked the girls an awful lot, he says, and a high giggle mixes with the smoke.

Honey, says the soft woman, honey. Her voice wavers, her wavering cheeks with their invented color. She looks at the door behind him. Now there just must be a bed in there—could I have a little time with you alone?

He looks at her. Raddled. Drunk.

Just five minutes with you alone, honey?

No no, he says, moving his arms away from her. Then he remembers the code of all these assumptions. He grins mechanically and says, looking away: Tomorrow.

In front of the hotel, the taxi driver, making his shrewd face: He'll get the nomination. Or the double cross.

Look at the fat little shine, says one of the delegates. He says he's a bishop, the man goes on. What do you know? They like this kind of efficiency, dinges do, the man goes on, and by efficiency I mean the finesse with which they are approached, the man goes on, bought, and delivered.

The Taft delegates get through to the second room. To the third room. But they never get in. Willkie, in his second sleepless day, near collapse, his voice gone, has been put to bed.

Sounded like shucking corn, didn't he? says the man from *Time*. His voice has gone to pieces. Yes.

Now out again and talking, trying again to mollify the professional politicians: Yes, says Willkie, I'm for a two-ocean Navy; yes, says Willkie, outlaw the Communists.

But the professionals cannot see it: this renegade Democrat who talks about Civil Liberties.

Willkie saying: Some of these beauties were selling the regalia while I was defending the lodge.

And what is he, anyway? You hear every kind of thing around here, but . . .

Willkie saying: Why, I heard myself called a Jew at noon, and at two-thirty they say I'm anti-Semitic.

*

⟪ *The New Republic prints his defense of civil liberties. He wants the Communist Browder and the Nazi Kuhn to have their say. The Dies Committee, he says, destroys reputations, by publicity, by inference, and by innuendo.*

*

⟪ *The Saturday Evening Post, in an article rejected by the New Republic, has him say that the common denominator of the liberal lies in a common purpose: to make men free. Not secure, or rich, or powerful. To prevent such limitations as insecurity, poverty, and weakness may impose.*

*

⟪ WILLKIE NOT AGAINST FDR AS A MAN

Statement: The New Deal has gone reactionary in a big way . . . most reactionary government the United States ever had.

*

⟪ *The strength of Wendell L. Willkie is the strength of the good Indiana earth.*

*   —John Watson

Willkie saying: What I am against is power. Power ruins anybody that has it. It's the most corrupting thing in the world.

*

(*After Dorothy Thompson proposed, from Paris at war, that party politics be adjourned, and a Roosevelt-Willkie ticket admitted, Roosevelt wrote to Morris Ernst: I shall be delighted to see Dorothy Thompson when she comes back. She has been here several times as you know. Do try to get this silly business of Wendell Willkie out of her head.*

I like him, writes William Allen White. His propaganda stuff is by all odds the slickest literary goosegrease that I have taken out of the second-class mail for a long time. He is somewhere between Jackson: "To the victor belong the spoils" and Commodore Vanderbilt: "The public be damned!"

SWELL
SALES
TALK

From the Kansas City Independent: The American people are tired of a smoothy in politics, even if he is honest. What about Hague? What about the Memorial Day Massacre? What about Kelly and Nash? What about Jim Curley? Here's a flaunting rebuke to Groton and Harvard, Lawrenceville and Princeton. Don't be fooled by that dimple. Don't let that adolescent smile deceive you.

*

And his backers? And William Rhodes Davis, and Sam Pryor, and Verne Marshall? Is Roy Howard here?

*

❨ FORTUNE POLL SHOWS LABOR IS NOT ANTIBUSINESSMAN!

*

When he hears Hoover still opposes him, he waits until after dinnertime and then takes a taxi to Hoover's hotel. Face to face, he can talk it out. Jim Watson, however, can't see him; he wants a day-in-and-day-out Republican. I am now, says Willkie. But Watson has no use for converts: if a fancy woman truly repented, he says, he'd take her into his church, but damned if he'd ask her to lead the choir. Willkie looks at Watson and almost mentions Mary Magdalen. But he decides against it. For a moment he sees the whole thing clearly.

*

❨ WILLKIE NOMINATED ON SIXTH BALLOT

*

❨ FIRST CONVENTION SHOWN ON TELEVISION

*

He stays up till four in the morning that night. Next morning, at the Warwick, he has breakfast with Mrs. Willkie and Philip, holds his press conference just after noon.

That day, he breaks away from his escort, and is seen around Philadelphia. What he does is to rush to the three papers. Sitting on the desks of the editors: My name is Willkie . . . he begins.

They like him. They all like him. Tired, with a fever blister, they notice. But he shakes it all off, none of that can touch him, they feel. They know the smoke of the meetings, they have been in the suite at the Benjamin Franklin.

Smoke of our time, the obscene harrowing of our lives. To let us curse ourselves? To let us represent ourselves, smoke of our torn lives.

The editors are pleased. He is informal—natural, like Roosevelt, they say. And did you hear him? More than once, he said it: You Republicans . . .

That day the Willkie family leaves for a short cruise on the yacht of Roy Howard, the publisher. Then New York. Colorado. Rushville.

*

([*It's getting so, said Mary Sleeth, on his farms in Indiana, every time a cameraman shows up, the hogs run right over and strike a pose.*

*

What were his dreams during these nights? Unknown.

*

Ice-gate over the land, a shock of closure.
Across the country now, a many-worded crying
That masks a silence.   The rising water and the entrapped air.
These are ice-crises in the history of ice,
And nothing is known of the life of ice in earthquake.
But all of this is about applause,
All of this is the fullness of values,
Commitment and refusal, the demand of the root
And the freezing of shallow streams.
When ice first forms
Snowfall and frozen rain may be its friends,
Deep roots recapture

Sleep of the heavy rain, the water rains,
Much of the gathering is underground.
These forces are not delicate, they are subtle,
They are like quicksand, not a material,
But a condition.
They are not forces, they are men and women.
The crest gates waiting,
The wheeled gates sealed.

*

⟨ DEAR MADAM,

Holding your science in esteem, I venture to ask the aid of your wisdom now. This is a man I think I believe in. The front page carries enough about him every day to trouble me. No, I am not being honest. I have a personal reason for wanting advice, and for remaining anonymous. Enclosed is your fee and his birthdate. Thank you.

UNSIGNED

P.S. *Please print your answer.*
P.P.S. *He wants to be President.*

*

Bertha S T U C K E Y
Ohio's Foremost Astrologer

Skeptics Invited

Scientific Astrology Will Solve
All Problems

July 10, 1940

Aquarius—Feb. 18, 1892, Elwood, Ind.

This is a man of vigorous activity, enterprise, determination and practical ability. He is firm and confident, but abrupt and impulsive, to much so for a place such as the office of President of our country and its affairs as they stand today.

He is courageous, masterful and agressive. To much so to keep

America out of war, it is indicated that at some time in his life he is likely to help in carrying on revolutionary changes. But under the planet of Mars where this is found it would not be by peaceful means, for Mars would rather fight.

Of all he is very keen in his judgment, yet his impulses are likely to overpower it.

His warm hearted yet passionate nature was sure to bring him this popularity and friends.

He is fearless of the opinions of others.

But at best from this time on in his life He will meet with many dual experiences; and if he should be elected President he would not be able to avoid some sort of inclination to tragedy.

For he is a man of much duality, with a very stern, radical and impulsive side to his nature as well as a very philanthropic, hospitable, quiet, unasuming, kind and charitable side . . . at present the suptle Neptune is transisting such progress with quite a strong undercurrent.

Now I would say that he can not work very well along with others. He is to powerful an individuality by himself.

He is a big man, and look perfectly healthy, but his health has not allway been the best.

There are some favorable aspects for advancement to public positions of responsibility and trust . . . . .

He is very impressionable and psychic, and no doubt a good speaker. He has a bright, witty, alert, and humorous side to him, but also another just as satirical. He has many other abilities that favor him much more than being President of our U.S.A. His tendency to the reformers spirit would no doubt lead to radical changes in the new deal that would be disasterous in one way or another. Poetic and musical inclinations are in evidence in his family or the relationship. He is a man whose feeling quickly respond to kindness or sympathy. And his sensitive side will get the full effects if he meets with defeat.

He has strong aspects for change, and a new beginning, but to me it does not seem that this is in the White House. It seems rather to the honor he is getting and to better conditions that it may bring. In the face of defeat if it comes, he will realize some ambitions coming true thru this, that he had for years, that seemed impossible of realization. He is entering into accord with the planets into a period of adventure that imbuse a powerful spirit of activity and enterprise. He will become acquainted with people of a pioneering instinct, or in some way recieve an impulse that will start him upon a new venture in life. . . .

When one finds a chart so dualistic as this is, it is hard for the best of us to reach a definate decision. But I feel safe in predicting by what I find that he will not be elected to the White House.

*

PART FOUR **Campaign**

Sun on the taces.   On the knotted rocks.
Sun on the iron.   Sun on the dust of the roads.
The ravel of cloud, the silver chalkings of track
Lying westward through the dappled pass
South of the city where the mist flowed in.

Distance and the crowd.
The train goes dark-green westward
Over the free, light-gray crystals of rock.
Early morning the moment of thin air
4 A.M. and the cattle lying down
And all the cattle get up from their knees.
Early morning, the chill before the sun
And eleven men standing at a railroad crossing
The arm of the signal swinging Stop red Look red Listen.
Stop.   People standing, looking separate in the morning air.
The little river over speckled stones

117

Passing the section crew. They wave. They wave.
The iceman and the gandy dancers,
And three blasts on the whistle for a penny.

In the smoke cities, sitting on the fences,
They shine in their leather, but they make no sign.
They hear the speaking in a pause of worlds
Roaring, in the haze roaring, in the stench
Of the slaughter of animals he roars. They make no sign.
In their stained aprons they listen, standing; they turn
Back to the cool immense bloodyards.
                                          His voice
Diminishing down the raspit avenues.   Promises
Individual Man, but vaguely, and the vague cities
Promised, and downward through industrial
Illinois, vaguely, and
                              through the blaze of town
Downstate, glowing, the summer leaves, the faces
Lit by September and inlit by the deep
Summer-end need for spiritual change.
                                          The hoarse raven
Croaks in his throat, Rock Island, the swaying
Train carries these panicky friends, advisers of symptoms,
Sending their telegrams.
                                  *

⟨ *A noted throat specialist from Chicago has boarded Willkie's
train.*
                                  *

The man sits in the rocking bedroom, claws
Hooked in his throat : anger and rage, pain
And refusal of pain. All right. Finally, Let him in.
But I don't need him.
                                  *

([*A statement. The famous physician:*
  What the man needs is a nightstick, not a doctor.

*

From the throat he can rally strength.   Remembering
Words to light home of track with the light of concentrated
Meaning and love past stupid pain.
But these are the towns listening : Galesburg, Joliet,
Peoria glowing, the ramshackle uniform and painted
Houses waiting : Missouri. He had puddled steel outside
      Chicago,
Where the huge fires roar, opening night, smoking
Pink smoke, yellow smoke, white, on the ochre
Air over Gary.   Here, in broad dayland,
Had lain on the freights among the metal noises
Hiss of sand, relief of steam, and a bell wagging
Where now the faces ring unanswerable
And the limitless ragged sunset
Serves only a man on the grass
Exhausted, in overalls, not hearing,
Or not caring if he hears.

*

([*Our first line of defense lies within ourselves. We must stop*
thinking in terms of personal power, and start thinking in terms
of national power.
or
  Let us start with the resolution that we are not afraid to stand
for what we believe in.
or
  Then let us recognize the fact that one man's loss is another
man's loss, and one man's gain is another man's gain.

*

We are faced with a crisis.

Let us define that crisis in terms of materials, men, hours, and dollars.

Let us not be afraid to define it.

And let us go forth and meet it.

*

There is a knotless line westward, past terraces
High on the roads, the black form of a car
Traveling under.   Here, the clear glittering throat
The long pull of track that seals the black
Of quick sleep among the counting, among the hammering
Until the machine, blades whirling, dances the dance
Of Steel, and the machine chips and tightens and screams
A man saying, "A good steel rail will last."
A man saying, "He will need more than parades."

*

❨ Dr. Harold Barnard, of Beverly Hills, has arrived by plane. He is not a tall man; not a big man. He has treated certain movie stars. He is quiet-spoken. He says, Lean back and open your mouth.

Willkie: Go to hell and take your tools with you!

Dr. Barnard says: Some twenty million Americans may have an interest in that throat of yours. Lean back.

He does lean back. The muffled, impossible throat. It rests; it responds. He will require . . .

Bulletin: . . . overcome what had been almost a paralysis of the muscles of his throat . . .

*

His throat clenches, and he begins to be haunted by the thought of Roosevelt's legs. He remembers the despair of the

legend: a swim in Glen Severn, tiredness, chill like a predatory
heavy-clawed animal on the legs: paralysis.

                        *

(｜ *But then I saw Father on the stretcher, being carried down to*
the beach head first. His head was lower than his feet, but he
managed to wave to me, and his whole face burst into a tre-
mendous sunny smile. So I decided he couldn't be so sick after
all.—Elliott Roosevelt

                        *

How was he first aware he would never walk again?
How did he ward off his mother's submissive hope?
How did he master his eyes?　Unlock his knees?
Did he know the danger for his back and arms?
Did he suspect he might never have his hands?
And his hope?　And his will?　And his wife?
And the night visitations when the mutilated
Processions filled the world and his room of dream?
Water did this, the pool told him;
He panted, he swam : Water will get me out again!

Voice did this, Willkie heard the memory,
Voice, get me out again!

                        *

Street corner to corner he will talk all day,
Feasting on talk at midnight to the last
Listening man. In Willkie, the child's food
Made breath, the bread made word, where love
Is the word.
            Doctor Barnard hearing
The rasping impossible voice under the beating light,
Rocking among the train : My God, I can't make him stop.
He goes right on night and day.
                  Words traveling

Straight on the land.   A train traveling, white
Plume over her back, over the rusty spurs
Never seen varnish; the network of glitter over
The network of track.
                              Down into Oklahoma,
Stretched beside overgrown dry creosote
Over the track, broomcorn, and again
The crowds at the tail platform,
Willkie talking : You mothers, you fathers . . .
                              *

⟦ *Willkie says FDR will have boys on transports on their way to
a foreign war, within 3 months, if re-elected.*
                              *

The track cuts west.   Slant roof, sun-catcher,
Outhouse, and barbed wire, the scrub growing up hill,
And a man in overalls walking the eleventh furrow.
The hard eyes of bigots.   The hard eyes of the poor.
Full moon at Skelly Stadium, the crowd
Roaring through Tulsa, the screams of wild turkeys,
The underground black sounds of strength, Negroes and oil,
In a growing city.   After the tents and clapboards,
The spinning of chance, the spinning dance of derricks
On the horizon through the pecan grove,
Across the broomcorn, across the tumbleweed,
Past the false-fronted clapboard, the pipeline, and this crowd,
Deep-throated, hard-riding, impoverished as by war,
Eaten away by dust the eroder, water,
Poverty the eroder and the eroder oil.
Waiting for fullness under the open moon.

I saw the footpath beside the telegraph poles
Waver among the knotted weeds,
Straighten.   A child here

In faded clothes among the faded words:
The sheetflood washed me clean.
My hilltop when I ran alone
Is put to pasture, ridge the contour round,
How shall I be, how shall I be found?
Furrows hold ice, furrows hold snow,
Plow the slope that I name home.
Dust my mother overturned,
Sand and dust and wind have come,
To burn my days, until I go
To find the garden of the wind,
The pleasant garden of the world,
Where the sheetflood lost its force
Wrapped all its water in a bud,
Where bud and seed and fledgling bird,
Where the child will tell his word,
Where all the streams are from.

*

⟪ *Only the strong can be free, says Willkie, and only the productive can be strong.*

*

I used to press tools in the Texas oil fields.
We produce 60% of the oil of the world.
        (Let the streetlamps burn all night!)

Amarillo in the morning heat
Away from the boom-town, infancy,
Used to be made of buffalo-hide,
Ain't made of buffalo-hide no more.
Little boys of the Panhandle
Used to pitch pennies at the yellow houses
Used to gather buffalo-bones.

Ship away the buffalo-bones.
Barbed wire was invented here:
Sing me a boardwalk in an old ghost town,
Gun play near the courthouse : Now vote me in,
I'll give a lot each for every vote,
Turn the LX into Amarillo,
Hot in the morning.

Down the Staked Plains the color winds
Rising through mirage.   The still
Elusive colors graze these hills,
Drink at these caves, go hunting in this sky.
The colors feed; or go hunting; or they hear.
Pause of colors before change.
A stranger, from the East, and talking fast,
Looks at a unique man,
The man from Tucumcari
Knows cattle and tourists.   He stares at the candidate.
The great pure Apache watches from his eyes,
Ferocious dawns do climb the Walls of Bronze.
Two from Gallup remember the strike.
A carpenter from Conchas Dam,
A handful of people from Mimbres Valley,
Alamogordo, the Oscura Mountains,
A few curiosities down from Taos
Listen to Willkie.   Spit.   Shake hands.

Out of the throats of volcanoes : rocks : volcanoes forgotten : a
        word craggy and pinnacled:
Shiprock : the shape of a cry issuing : as people, as rock:
Among the rivers in a dry country : invasion of dunes, the white
        sand in the wash : from the cave waters
Given, erect crystals : pinnacles in the flows : a cap of lava over
        the rock:
Cliffs vermilion and undermined : retreating cliffs

For the rainwash, the sheetflood overthrow
Reaches them : they deploy, in summer thunderstorms
In the shale, in softness, until the softness goes;
The ruined villages of rock, and the people.

*

《 *There were floodlights at Albuquerque. They said it was the largest rally in the state's history.*

   You could scarcely hear for the yippin and whoopin.

*

There they slept.   They left the train.
Three planes from the plateau airport.
Through the low overcast into the phoenix sun.
Willkie then looking down, burned in his rage,
Hostile and sweating, saw the eaten country
Pinnacles into waves receding, the treeform famine
Of water vanished; the waves minimized to a ripple of terraces.
And all the people invisible.
Came down
To bleachers piled with local cotton and beef,
Hills of oranges, glass honey-hives.

*

   The professional Republicans hate this nonsense: a state with only 3 votes!

*

The professionals see the signs in the dice, the signs in the cards
       and clouds,
Over their drinks they curse at the candidate, a renegade enemy
       whose sudden cause
Was rammed down their throats; he is wrecking their only
       chance.
The Dream of Business is a failing image.

Among the predictions, statistics, in the crowds,
The explosive seeds of defeat.   Their deadliest fears
Run damp in their bones.   More than torches by night,
More than pennons, candy, and speechmaking,
A campaign is slavery, they say,
The tiring slavery : to plan, to counsel, to control.
Above all : to carry out.
Willkie shows courage.   Willkie will shout.
Forthright, alone, he speaks his mind.
But the party needed another kind—
A man who will accept support.
No benefit here of party or plan.
Joe Martin sacrificed himself, wanting a giant to fight a giant.
—He's not a giant!
He draws his crowds.
Dead whales on flatcars draw their crowds.
Nobody votes for a dead whale.

*

⟨ *He is so interested in ideas he cannot take action.*

*

⟨ *He cannot be induced to plan a campaign.*

*

 This is America. Some are at home, some are in exile, here.
He wants to campaign in every corner of it, says Marquis Childs.

*

Parades.   Rattle of palm trees.   The silver planes.
Statues : Prometheus and General Otis.
Searchlights demanding.

This is the journey into the people, asking for consent, for sanc-
tion, for belief.

Concrete parades, stabbings and fortunetelling,
Gin, roughage, the studios on Christmas Eve, spotlit groceries
     and the prayer marathon.
The rose window copied from Rheims, the Aztec temple de-
     signed by the architect who believes in function.
Great ancient lizards and tar pits, the skeletons of pale fine
     starlets,
Some Rembrandts, a cafeteria (white tile and potassium broth)
Where you pay what you think the meal was worth.
The Strip, the Bowl, the Derby, the Easter Cross,
The Troc, the Wee Kirk; the neon in the graveyard,
Saying on and off, Father.   On and off.   On and off.
The oil well in the sea.

                    *

⟨ *Southern Cal. possessed no natural resources whatsoever—no
lumber, no minerals, no coal.*

   People and sunshine

                    *

⟨ *"I had half a million wiped out—what's worse, five hundred
in cash."*

                    *

They pray.   Security against oldness
And death—for the gilding of all things.
Under the lights.   On the porches, rocking, and at the Iowa
     picnic.
Drugged by wanhope, seduction, or the drugs.
Among the filling stations, between the orange trees,
Burst with illusion, listening for the faint
Tympans of rumor.   Fame.   Disaster.   Or the sudden
Wild nimbus that cheats prediction and the grave.
A tower of linked intestines, cemented, climbing

Over the orange faces, digesting the world.
It cannot; it turns to digest itself.

But the incredible fifteen-year-old
Uncorrupt in her moment, standing at Vine.

*

❴ From the Committee to Aid Migratory Workers:
  We were accused of contributing to radical causes.
  When you are told a person is sick or in need,
  You don't ask him his religion, nationality or politics . . .

*

They will be obsessed by the word "security."

*

❴ When Hollywood gets aroused, it gets aroused.

❴ This is not a campaign. It's a crusade.
—Willkie at Long Beach

*

Up past the burnt hills.   Distance and the crowd,
The track, development, the tracks on their light-gray crystal,
The knotless, nodeless line.   Struck into water-light.
No but knotted, cloved, notched, scarred, traveled brightened by
      tears,
Good steel rails and riding them
Development riding on the tracks of law.
North in a ravel of cloud, into
The dappled pass south of the city.
Mist flowing over toward San Francisco
The power towers walking, Spaniards' ghosts,
The silver-white unborn.

*

❨ *And in the words of Winston Churchill: There is one way above all others in which the United States can aid the European democracies. Let her regain and maintain her normal prosperity.*
—*Willkie at San Francisco*

*

A network that emerges.   At the ocean
Two musics tighten, floating gongs, bells inward
From the network to the eyes of a man
Whose pulse burns in his blue eyes when he sees the bridge.

*

A red bridge fastening this city to the forest,
Telling relationship in a stroke of steel;
Cloud-hung among the mist it speaks the real,
In the morning of need asserts the purest
Of our connections : for the opposites
To call direct, to be the word that goes,
Glowing from fires of thought to thought's dense snows,
Growing among the treason and the threats.

Between the summer strung and the young city,
Linking the stonefall to the treefall slope,
Beyond the old namings of body and mind
A red bridge building a new-made identity:
Communion of love opened to cross and find
Self the enemy, this moment and our hope.

*

It was when he began to make promises that a change began.
It will be . . . an Administration . . . wants to do something
for labor . . . jobs and jobs and jobs. . . .

*

⟨ As for the charge that Miss Hepburn is against me, I can only say that Mary Pickford, Robert Montgomery and Walter O'Keefe are on my side.

*

Now the professionals are feeding him another tactic: he would call Roosevelt a warmonger.

*

Eggs thrown. Eggs, eggs. A rock. His voice slurring now so that sometimes the sense is lost.

*

⟨ Words on a banner: ROOSEVELT FOREVER, WIN WHAT WITH WILLKIE

*

". . . If we do not prevail this fall, this way of life will pass."

*

The campaign train on its journey eastward. Willkie goes deep into America; into himself.

*

Power never dominion.
Some other power.
Some force flaking in light, avalanches of lilies,
Days and the sun renewed in semen, pure
Among the uncorrupted fires, fire's ancestor,
Forgotten; worshipped secretly;
Where the vestigial Lucifer regales
Craters of memory; where leans
Some fleshly girl, the shaped stones of desire
Leaping in color at her human cunt.

They will translate this girl.　She will appear
In textbooks as a sacrificed antelope
Guilt running shiny over the short fur.
Ideas of shame did split that throat.
But none of that is true tonight.
The girl was leaning over the crater, I dreamt it,
The shriveled flowers twisted in her hair,
And jewels budded at her throat.
The girl of choice, remembering the past fires,
Praising the word, the columns in the grove,
Arbor vitae uterinae
Locked by such branches, light in the dense forest,
Praising the world unknown and feeling beat
Among her branches
A human child.
Brambles of sense! and that responding power
Rocking the fullness of time.
Until it shall be, what never was:
River and born and dream.

Canals of music downward serenade
New satin gleams under her haunches;
And, running laterally,
And backwards across ripples,
Passing the lower stairs,
Even above the unforgettable murmur,
The sound of oars.

Body of the splendid, bear me now!
Completed by orbits of unhorsèd comets,
The bronze, paternal stars.

Cave of their messengers,
Thalamic cleft where the divorcèd myth
Begged to be nursed through hysteria that leap year,

Sank at the window—O the famous view!
This side or that side of the balcony
Falling, the graceless sanatorium swan,
Breaking nobody's kneecaps but her own.

Passes the pear orchard near the middle hill
At the wind's moment when all sails are lowered,
A small bird kiares, slope of his flight, the blue
Yielding flutes of his feathers, that small wing
Bounds us above—kiar! Inscribing our horizon.
A high note over our necessity.

*

His speeches begin to be unreal to him.

*

A filament carrying morning through the waves,
A nerve singing branches.
Orbits of pear blossom
Recurring while the wars declared themselves;
On the red rails, the train hurling his words
Down all the arteries of tears.

Endure, grandmother of all music,
Crystal in Asia, indelible pinnacles
Color of going to sleep
Above the breastës gold.
Endure, sing : deep night in Abyssinia
Waits for a messenger, heat
Of that ancient waiting
Rising from tongues of lions.
The jagged time, the jagged time of clues,
All broken inheritances riding home
Past columns and ruins, down the edge-lit clouds
Reaching back to the well at home, a twilight girl

Wherefrom new breasts, new sources, feed the dawn.
Singing develop
The sapphire climbing song
Flaring, a woman's eternal jugular cry.
An Ethiopian Jew praising the world,
The flying psalm inviting creation come.

Osiris in his veins praising the world away.

Wine that is poetry—inclare! inclare!
The conqueror of all attractive dragons
Is in that vice and white and steam.

He waited.   He saw the water.
But the recurrent branch
Flew backward on the track in early day,
Warning him against compliance, breaking
In blossom said, Willkie!
You must defy them or be lost!
The foam spinning on water straight beneath
Will tell another myth, and spin and drown.
Far down under the trestle invisible.
His sense of the real leaves him.   Dizzy and blind.
Will go to Washington.

*

❲ *On the campaign train is a lounge car for the "boll weevils."*
The local politicians. They are criticizing Willkie's inability to
"get political." Willkie is finally getting around to his farm
promises; they are vague. His emphasis on industry—industrial
freedom, economic freedom—leads to the inference that a busi-
nessman is better suited to be President than Roosevelt.
  His only solution for our problems is "business confidence."
  Every now and then we wonder whether he isn't beginning to
talk mechanically. If you listen to many of his speeches . . .
  Willkie: I feel as good as this beautiful morning.

*

THE YOUNG MEN

The surface shine, the inner steel of track
Carry September ringing to a boy
Miles down and decades past, a maroon sweater
Haunting a plexus of rails.
A spur leading nowhere.
And silos, like ill-launched rockets, hurling tall
Such faulty upright weight five miles downtrack
As feeds the colored cattle, as feeds the governor,
As feeds the party wheelhorse as feeds me.

Ascending ties, a hymn of ladders.   Colder.
I urge my wretched urgings clamber out,
Holding the frozen ironwork.
Coldbitten indecent lavender and white,
The naked noses and naked stares recede.
I hear the patching words that ring like coin
Behind the platform, my penny monument.

At a certain moment the railway forfeits metal,
Speed seizes this track, we are going fast.

The calendar's contagions, days, declarations,
Flaunted away on a Hollywood montage.
There must be a darkened third-run movie house
Behind that ice-clad coalyard where they show
Quiet.   A willow.   Some hammock-pampered girl
In a Middle Western college; pipedreams of reassurance
And a low speaking voice.

Waterfalls
Narrow, behind me.

All the American rivers
Controlled into metal systems,
Narrow as rails.

Firing down endless, successful rapids,
The tiny inconspicuous steely rapids
This train, my dragon, a Cherokee canoe
Clipping back birchbark over carbon paper
Pouring the smoke of my statement,
Tobacco that is the barn-hung skins of prophets
Pouring smoke out, that hardens into scars.

Effigy and belief!   The track flattening south,
Splits from before backward, far into silver,
Opening into the small lost villages.
Sidings of young men propped against sycamores,
With eighteen miles between any two of them.
Their hopes are hanging three feet above their eyes;
Their girls away at a dance; all their big powers
Lifted up, and alone.
Lost villages, my frontier; our crest and crown;
My brothers who will never vote for me.
My lost self who will never vote for me.

*

He forgets. 30 states in 7 weeks.

*

Until I stand on the January platform
(Bunting and boards), Connecticut Avenue
That lowcut archway into the histories.
Speaking the inaugurals of these same young men,
Declaring a specific amnesty.
Then, eighteen miles apart, the muscular young
Arrogant fools, the founders of our future
With their ideas of freedom as relation
To human process, will push their shoulderblades
Against their treetrunks
And rear, like a tidal wave upon Peru.

Some fool with space on his left hand and his right
Will stare down-track.
The free, watery, liquid rails
Will seal our fire across the seamless land,
Fusing, fusing.   Fusing
A new age.
The streaming hours of man,
The plant spread to the green sun.

That's what it'll take; not anything like these
Seven long years of Washington afternoons,
Shaking official syllables out of my creases:
Pork-barrel and candy-stick.

*

⟨ *Freedom is not just a set of laws.*
   It is the ability of men to make these infinite combinations between one another, and between the communities in which they live.
   . . . And so we say to you: Bring us together.
                                        —Willkie, May 1940
*

Then I forget.
The star in the nets of heaven
Blazed past my breastbone.
Did I forget that fire?
I forgot.
In my net of growth, my words are unreal to me.

*

⟨ *The campaign train went through all those states, doing 17,300 miles in 7 weeks. People standing, still and lonely-looking in the thin, chill air. The prairies fled by, with people waving; little houses, flat plains. Over rusty freight spurs that had never carried* a passenger train. The dark-green, 12-car special. With bull-thewed Willkie in rocking corridors, talking torrents, his arms making giant swipes in the dark air. He lived and worked in the last car, the Pioneer.

Chorus: Only the productive can be strong.

In the car known as the Squirrel Cage, they roughed out drafts of his speeches: Russell Davenport, Pierce Butler, Bart Crum, R. L. Buell, Elliott V. Bell. Willkie would be using perhaps 20% of the hashed speech.

Chorus: Only the strong can be free and
only the productive can be strong.

*

Help us, he says.
   Help us, help us. Help us.
   Then the gray land, the gray hills of industry, the cities.
      "The rest of Tuesday was spent in West Virginia, the
      only U.S. state which has no upper class."
   Button, reading: ANOTHER PAUPER FOR ROOSEVELT
   Leaflet on newsprint, reviling Elliott Roosevelt
   Button, reading: I WANNA BE A CAPTAIN TOO, PAPA.
   The politicians, complaining: Willkie makes his long
      speeches from the rear platform, sometimes to a hand-
      ful of people—300 people. It's his nearsightedness.
      Remember when the man came through, saying—"I'm
      afraid the court reporters are lost!" Three cars of the
      train were missing, uncoupled somewhere. Those re-
      porters now, they followed us 30 miles, riding in police
      cars, doing 85. There they come, waving, yelling, wav-
      ing us to stop the train. And Willkie? Nearsighted?
      He waved back at them from his rear platform.
Help us, help us, help us.
   JOHN L. LEWIS ENDORSES WILLKIE, says Roosevelt's motivation
and objective is war.

Of Roosevelt; a Cadillac press operator: He's a good man.

Of Willkie; a Timken shop steward: Willkie is Wall Street and everyone knows it.

Of Willkie; a grinder at Allison-Cadillac: He slings too much mud.

A Cadillac janitor: There ain't no other President, no suh. I ain't heard of no other.

Jackson: Willkie preaches sacrifice to the people, but he defends the profits of his big-business friends. He bitterly opposes conscription of wealth or of plants.

Irvin S. Cobb: The New Deal is a rotten egg. It's yellow and it stinks.

H. L. Mencken: I've also bet some money that Roosevelt will be re-elected which I would lose most cheerfully.

Willkie: We're going to win. Write it down. Write it down.

Button: I didn't raise my buck to be a soldier.

More buttons: I WANNA BE A CAPTAIN TOO, PAPA.

*

Willkie to a citizen with a button: You don't belong to the right family.

*

⟨ 16,000,000 *to enroll today in first peacetime draft.*

—Oct. 16, 1940

*

Roosevelt began to stump 13 days before election. He never mentioned Willkie by name, but he accused his opponent 32 times of falsification.

*

Jackson: I have done all I can to stop the increasing concentration in this country of great aggregations of other people's

money in the hands of lawless, irresponsible and ruthless men
like Wendell Willkie.

*

A Boston debutante, working as a volunteer in Willkie campaign headquarters: I hardly know how to tell you what happened to me when I shook hands with him for the first time.

*

❆ *The "official Jews" being full of trepidation* . . .
*The Democratic National Committee calling Willkie a "nig-
ger-hater"* . . .
*Willkie at Schenectady: They deal in the lowest type of poli-
tics and smear; they deal with the most corrupt of political
machines; while their candidate makes lofty speeches about
world leadership and foreign affairs.*

*

Help me.

*

❆ *Roosevelt stirs up class hatred and divides our people* . . . *the
tactics of Lenin, the strategy of Hitler and the preaching of
Trotsky.*

*

MADISON SQUARE GARDEN

The Garden was full of screams and flags. Women throwing
hats, the searchlights pouring heat, the cheers, the circular portrait of Willkie, the banner as tall as a brownstone house, NO
THIRD TERM.
2 bands, 7 mikes,
3 blue spotlights on each side,

1 photo of Barton at one end,
150 reporters and telegraph men,
40 feet of portrait of Thomas Jefferson,
500 lights in a ceiling constellation,
8,000 lunches in paper bags and boxes,
room for 23,000 in Madison Square Garden,
number of tickets passed out: 145,100.

RUMOR: All Roosevelt people are paupers who earn less than $1,200 a year. And aren't worth that.

QUESTION: Did Willkie say Roosevelt's secretary kicked a Negro policeman in the stomach?

JOE MARTIN: Shall we take the first step toward dictatorship?

THE CROWD: No.

JOE MARTIN: Shall we take the first step toward war?

THE CROWD: No.

JOE MARTIN: Is the presidency a personal dictatorship?

DOROTHY THOMPSON: No, don't boo, but listen—

CLARE BOOTHE LUCE: Politics makes some pretty strange bed-bugs . . . Miss Thompson will have plenty of time to scratch herself after the election.

VOICE OF SPEAKER: This is the method of Roosevelt.

THE CROWD: But it is *not* the method of Democracy.

(*At 10:14, a trumpet.*)

(*At 10:16, tremendous ovation. Willkie, wearing a light blue suit, a white shirt, a blue-gray tie, appears. He laughs and waves to the crowd. He seems not to care at all for the passage of radio time.*)

Joan Crawford is autographing.

WILLKIE: A free people now arise to write a single word across the vast American sky: Liberty, Liberty, Liberty.

COMMENT: His voice was simply Willkie's voice.

(*The crowd goes wild.*)

Two-thirds of the way through, in his unreal voice, he starts

to go to town: I want to unite all the people in America; I have
no prejudice against any of them.

(*The crowd goes wild.*)

Who can bring all these elements into unity?

(*The crowd goes wild.*)

You can hardly hear the *Star-Spangled Banner.*

The organ music, the chanting.

The crowd.

A man, pushing through the press: Willkie, by God, you're a
man.

Oren Root, campaign manager, was having . . .

*

❨ *Willkie has come out for Puerto Rican statehood; for Leif
Ericson, for Rosh Hashanah, and for Christopher Columbus.*

*

Oren Root was having a joy fit.

PART FIVE

Election

⟨ *FDR's colossal self-confidence stood him well when the going was tough, said Mike Reilly. Usually, he clearly showed his emotions. And he just wasn't the nervous type.*

I saw FDR's nerves give him a real rough time but once, said Reilly afterward. For some reason beyond my comprehension he got a mild case of the whips Election Night, when Wendell Willkie was his opponent. He was getting the returns in a small room off the big dining room at Hyde Park.

*

All evening long, at the Commodore, Willkie stamps out cigarettes and listens to fortunes and numbers. Voices in the room, carrying numbers in. He looks at the radio. A man he would not have in his house, counting at him face to no-face, reading returns-by-county out of the machine, here in the room where his brother Ed plays with the broadcast pictures, trying to bring

143

them clear. The scenes do sharpen, but in their moment blur, darken and flash.

Only the numbers are steady, pouring in.

Willkie goes down to the ballroom. They have the numbers of two minutes later by the time he reaches them: a constant, increasing flow, carrying all the eyes he has seen along the track, all the active faces running through, casting votes drop by drop and spreading.

I hear some people, says Willkie, shouting to me, "Don't give up." I guess those people don't know me.

Confused sound of counting.

A few people are leaving now. The crowd packs these rooms.

I still can win, he thinks. The elevator takes him up. Philip looks at him, and with a surgeon's look; you can see that he knows. All his worries washed away, by numbers, thinks Willkie. But tonight they are my chance, too. Statistically, he thinks slowly and seriously, I still can win.

Now the voice breaks in. From Fir Cone, Oregon, McNary conceding.

*

❲ *McNary: I am wishing Mr. Roosevelt and Mr. Wallace grace, and their administration prosperity.*

We shall try to furnish them a worthy and vigilant opposition.

*

Willkie is turned to the radio. He hardly moves now. Only his breathing and his eyelids, each with their kind of counting.

His wife says, I wish Wendell would get ready to go home. I wish you would, Wen.

Many cigarette leavings. In the ballroom, litter of cigarettes like firecrackers, white and for the deaf. For counting people, deafened by numbers. They widen, the numbers, flowing in until every state is spoken. Through the thinned crowd, fluted water-green bottles can be seen, piled and fallen, rolling in curves on the floor. Chalked on the board, the immense numbers, wiped away and chalked up new.

Across the hall, the yellow pads of markers and statisticians in their elaborate systems of prediction. He remembers suddenly Uncle Emerald, telling fortunes by the shapes of clouds. I suppose you could do it by the flights of planes. Tickers with their erratic sounds; deadpan sounds of the race reported as if it had no human meaning or human agency.

Willkie changes his shirt for the sixth time.

The last guests are going. Ah, says the man from *Time*, just one eleventh-hour professional gesture! If he would only give up and send in his congratulations. Jump over the net and let's go home.

They do go. The ballroom thins out, and the suite upstairs, until he sits there almost alone. The boy from Columbia, putting his notes away, looks up at Willkie. Numbers still streaming in past his eyes, easily, gently, filling in the almost empty room. Over the old streams, other millions, hardly any without its opposition. Never enough. None without its opposition. The boy from Columbia meets Willkie's eyes, exhausted blue; sits down again and pretends to write.

Suppose I were president of Columbia? Willkie thinks, in the elevator. What is it like for him, up at Hyde Park? Or for Wallace, with LeCron? he thinks, or for McNary, so quick to concede, so early out there to bed?

Now he has spoken his last to his formal guests; spoken his last to the campaign people downstairs; to the newspapermen and their knowing foreheads. All of them walking well. As if on dry land.

2:15 in the morning. Cold 42nd Street outside, unbroken dark. Box of the radio silent, filling without a sound in waves of numbers, little hundreds pouring.

He looks at his underwear hung long-sleeved on the chair. He slowly puts on his green pajamas.

*

❲ VOTES: for Roosevelt, 27,243,466; for Willkie, 22,304,755.
STATES: for Roosevelt, 38; for Willkie, 10.

*

Late Wednesday morning, he sends at last his telegram. He would broadcast on Monday night, to the nation. He would work on his own speech. The squirrel cage could go home. Ed could go back to Libby McNeill, Philip to Princeton.

And he and Billie to Pryor's place in Florida. Gratefully.

*

Now he is strong, and drives through these days. But lying between the sun and this earth of sun, Jupiter Island he sees, as soon as he stops talking and smiling. His hurt throat darkens and relents. His eyes are shut and darkened against his bare arm. He is aware slowly of hard work going on.

What? he thinks. Really hard work! Far under, essays he has never known. He hears the women's voices diminishing near him. They suppose he is asleep. He is not. It is a work of images, like mourning or falling in love. A mask is off and the mirrors will not again show him that stare. The work is difficult and bare. Very slow.

*

He broadcasts on Armistice Day. In New York, from the same hotel, with all the mouthpieces live as ever before him. He begins distinctly, sand and sun in his voice. He is calling for strength in opposition, alert opposite, a delicate equilibrium of his old appetites. He is asking for himself as Loyal Opposition.

*

❲ TIME says, *He awakened Business' conscience and, for a while, restored its belief. His cause was democratic capitalism, which*

the U.S. was arming to protect. Yet he failed to identify himself
with that cause in the public mind.

THE NEW YORK TIMES says, Now he is head of a party. He cannot move wholly as an individual now.

The HERALD TRIBUNE hears from a friend of Willkie's 3-point
program:

1) A realistic attitude toward international affairs.

2) A liberalized view toward economic and social problems.

3) Ridding the party of its old symbols.

TIME says, He could not recognize the emergency. It is political, its very force gives politicians control over business men.

*

In the Grand Ballroom of the Astor, 1,000 bankers, brokers
and executives are watching the *Financial Follies of 1940.*

Before the curtain, the market-writers sing:

> We're recording angels of the deeds of high finance,
> We watch you big good-natured boys go through the
> public's pants—
> We're the saps who think that business has romance.

The curtain opens. Scene: A freight car, from which descends
a posse of tramps. They speak. They are discovered to be railroad bondholders. They sing:

> Oh, I got plenty of nuttin',
> Ah don't git interest when due;
> Ah had some stock,
> Ah had bonds,
> Ah had preferred shares, too . . .

Willkie arrives in time for the finale. The football team of
the Blues has a captain who is himself. He, with Al Smith and
Hoover, McNary, Taft and Dewey, Hugh Johnson and Stassen,
Martin, Barton and Fish, are playing the Reds: FDR, Hopkins,
Wallace, Hague and Flynn, Ickes and Miss Perkins and La
Guardia, Corcoran and Cohen, Steve Early and Kelly and Nash.

The scrimmage has some byplay in it which the audience feels is witty. It concerns Hague. Finally Willkie is thrown. But just now Uncle Sam announces a challenge from the College of Foreign Aggression. Reds and Blues form an "all-star team for defense" and sing, opening their mouths and working their fists:

"Crash through your prejudice and make the whole . . . darned . . . country . . . one . . ."

Willkie is chosen Number One in the Hearts of the Financial Newspaper Men.

*

At the airport to fly south again with Pryor, Gene Tunney, and all their sons, he is asked about his plans.

Willkie: You don't know where I can get a good job, do you?

*

Lying in the sun, his eyes shut and downward, he falls within himself, falling the moment the mask is gone. Something is slipping slowly and far, like a rock sliding over in all its veiny crystal, giving way. Like many other meanings. There is some reason to fall now, he thinks, and he acknowledges all the hours.

There is no fall now. Something like a footpath, a narrow search.

Just before he wakes, in one moment of extreme intense darkness, he lets go, even of the moment that was his rage to hold. Then, without any vision, in dark of sleep, he knows perfectly well that there is something underneath that does not need a mask. That will not refuse anything except masks and defeat. What a simple answer, he remarks to himself brightly in that split light, like a boy. If it is an answer. Yes, he thinks, it is, and mine.

Lighthouse, a woman's voice is saying. Wakes. The two wives

are looking across at the old lighthouse. Billie is saying Indians? And Negroes? There?

Yes. And then they moved them west.

He remembers the ghosts in the Smokies. My grandmother, he says aloud to the women; she moved again, after all her voyages. When she saw them look at the Negroes in the square. She had come from Europe on her ship; and before that, lowered into the little dory, with her best shawl, and a book of Goethe.

The cadences of his mother speaking clearly among all this surf. She has a book opened as white as sand upon her lap: All things in leaf, she reads.

All things in leaf. Four notes he hears for many days, up in New York seeing the few he needs to see, even in Washington, telling them he is "undecided" when they ask about the future. He goes fishing in the stream, and brings in two sailfish. Large ones.

Hearing that sound, and out of the wounds of the unreal, a slow hesitation of response begins.

*

They are trying to work on him again. Davis, who is in some way linked with Hitler, who gave $40,000 or perhaps $55,000 to his campaign; Verne Marshall, and Roy Howard. They come down to Pryor's place, and they begin by reasoning, and move in on him with their enormous pressures, until the rows become too violent for Pryor.

But slowly, there is a change and a quietness. A kind of rejoicing takes possession of this man.

*

In the glare sun, on New Year's Day, he rides to the stadium, and is pushed through to his place by a wedge of policemen.

The slow enormous sounds of the past month and the past locking years fold in upon themselves, fold over and change in a curious music no larger than his voiceless, new-stirring self. He is saying, during a football game, in the Orange Bowl, to the holiday crowd:

To give those things necessary; to aid, so that the free; living; may continue; in other portions of the world.

He has been asked to speak about aid for Britain, and so he is doing. But, very slightly, the words have altered meaning. Value and cost, he is thinking. In the sunlight, the blue flaring sky. After defeat. If we allow the year be born, he is thinking, as all the colors wave at him, and the cheers enclave. For I am born, I believe myself again.

Glitter of microphone, the air of the sea, carrying voices in. Now I speak only the words I can believe, throwing away the rigid corroded terms of hatred. The sly resonant pity.

In this sun, with the young and the game, throw away nightmare. Make friends with the dream. Half daytime over, fire screams through this air.

PART SIX A Coast of Images

WILLKIE at his desk. He looks away from the window, back to the paper where his question is, and he writes:

We cannot be indifferent to what happens in Europe.

We cannot forget the fighting men of Britain.

They are fighting for—

He puts the pen down; leaning his big head on his propped-up hand, he stares at the paper and through it. Then he writes:

"We will not stay out of war because of brave assertions. We will stay out of war—" very slowly—"in my judgment, if the men of Britain are supported at once."

Then Willkie thinks, How do I know that?

*

Knowledge my nakedness,

Where is the accurate, the innocent skillful man,

The accurate shining, behind whose forehead lie what young
    dreams?

I am the present, and I know your face.
Mercy must enter grace,
Wisdom this wilderness.
These are thick forest fears whose hidden rivers
Are the past under leaves feeding each taproot of our lives.
The present touches again, again, again, continual music.
The touching by majestic images of common day.
Have you looked at the Bible since you changed your mind?
Certain Mozart applies, recurrences of Beethoven;
All are true.
And now only the new is accurate.

*

Why not go to the source? thinks Willkie, and he is not thinking very deeply, either. In reverie, he begins to hear again some
of his campaign shouting.

Why not go and find out? Go to England and see?

He picks up the phone. He dials and he dials. The circle
whirls. With a burring spins back to rest.

Long Distance? he says. A person-to-person call. To Washington.

*

❨ "What reason did you give for wanting to make the trip?"
"Just that I wanted to go."
"Whom do you expect to see in England?"
"I'll see everybody that will see me."

*

The plane circles over the Capitol. The pilot can tell the time:
the shadow of the Washington Monument falls just right for
noon. The wind will not let him land at the airport.

Let's try the new one, says the pilot, and goes into the landing
pattern for Gravelly Point.

Willkie looks down at the city. At the White House, sliding behind the new-laid airstrip and the trees. Excitement tightens his stomach. Partly because his voyage has already started; but that is not it. It is because they will meet now, face to face.

He goes down the steps, and is driving into the city.

All through the avenues, the sound of hammering. Sometimes it sounds from the next corner, then it will be blocks away, a legend of nails and boards. All through the city. Horizon of children's music, at one moment angry, and now with lightness. A wait of silence. Again, rapidly, the sound of hammers.

The Carlton lobby is jammed as he goes in, a big conspicuous man past the girls in their fresh colors. Girls painted in a scene, incised on the air with their smiles. Everyone is talking, and everyone smiles at him. The young men in their dark suits, and a few uniforms with well-cut shoulders, the young necks held straight. All these heads sharp in detail, all swung around as they recognize him.

Oh, Mr. Willkie—May I have your autograph?

A sound of hammering outside, muted through the thicknesses of the hotel. As if many houses were being built. And digging now, the dragging and striking the ground. Sounds of scraping and nailing. As if a stairway were climbing past the circles, past the intersects, upward through the town

The doors of the elevator slide shut.

*

Emerging two hours later, with him, Yes, says Hull, the President asked me to do this: to make available to you, Mr. Willkie, the information and full assistance of the Department of State.

*

❲ *From the* Chicago Tribune: *Millions of Republicans now see that they were duped. The party will take leave of its late stand-*

ard bearer with the hope that it will never again see him or
he it.

*

The crowd fills the lobby, and as Willkie comes down, they
cheer him. That cheer, for a moment, drowns out the hammering.

Hull and Willkie ride the few blocks. They pass many men,
overalled, carrying hammers. At the corner a work crew on their
way home. The black car turns into the driveway and past the
front gates, past the set brilliant eyes of the Secret Service and
to the portico. Eyes of the last guard. They are calipers trying to
change form, shiny and full of effort. Eyes of an animal pretending to be a machine. Secret Service opens the door of the
car, and they go through the door, and along, past the reporters
and Simmons, taking their hats and coats; past Pa Watson.

Willkie walks into the Oval Room. He stops at the entrance.
Beyond the litter of trophies on the desk, Roosevelt is writing.
In the amazing welter of donkeys, birds made of nuts, dogs, gift-
shop deer, the donkey with clothes on, the harpooner book ends,
the black elephants, the donkey lettered Democrat 1932, the cloth
elephant, the gold screw-and-ball, the carved turtle—past all that
joyful shambles, the sheet of white paper, like a water-candle in
a briar patch, glows. On it the words: If the nation does not recall what its place in history is, it will risk the real peril of . . .
(the President is writing as Willkie comes in) inaction. He
writes the word, looking up.

With their look at each other. Not the quick political smile,
but a slow look of rearrangement.

A new level, a new year; and the cluster of hostility changes.
The same factors in only slightly different constellation.

Willkie's obsessive grip on the man drops away, dissolving its
hold on himself. He looks at this face, as if for the first time.
Here is the face of Roosevelt, changed even since the meetings

of the power fight. Fuller, stronger than on the screen. The hammering rings very loud outside, and is at last related to the papers on the immense desk: they are the sheets of the Inaugural, the workmen have been hammering on the bleachers along the route to the Presidency.

The old dead hatred in Willkie falls away.

I won't be long, he says in a fresh voice, on a curious note of youth. With happiness, he sees the real man sitting in sunlight on his gray velvet chair, the developed head and the chin of his emphasis tilted up, looking straight in his eyes. They are looking at each other like horsemen, legendary riders into the dark forest. In the strong light they look at each other, before the next signs of enjoyment come into Roosevelt's face. He scents this game with intense relish; his nostrils open slightly, for a second.

For Willkie, there is a flash of Indiana. Without a bridge, some gap is jumped and he is hanging in the night, painting something green with a wide fascinated stroke.

I know what it is, he says grinning, to be interrupted while laboring on a speech.

Roosevelt throws back his head and laughs. A strong current runs through this room. Both of them look down at the papers on the wood-red polished desk. I wish, says Roosevelt, you were going to be put on the cold stand tomorrow, taking the oath instead of me.

When I get to London, you'll wish once more to change places with me. And be where the excitement is.

Later, the President takes out a sheet of notepaper. Over the pages before him, quickly, his pen makes the sharp verticals: three sentences and four lines of verse. He hands the envelope to Willkie. For Churchill, he says. This is the actual passport.

And look up Harriman, Roosevelt adds. He's a man of excellent judgment. He put $5,000 in my campaign. He smiles and glitters.

He *is* smart, says Willkie. He put five thousand in mine, too.

Before he goes, he is invited by the President to the Inauguration.

He can't come, he says, refusing solemnly: I have to have my typhoid shot. Appointment, in New York. And a reservation on the early morning train.

*

❲ *Willkie, speaking at the Astor Hotel: Know what they said about Stephen Douglas when he ran for President? "Well, if Steve Douglas wants to run—but I don't for the life of me know why he wants to be President and have to be good for the rest of his life."*

The American people relieved me of the necessity of being good for the balance of my life.

*

❲ FDR GIVES WILLKIE NOTE TO CHURCHILL

ROOSEVELT GIVES HIS BLESSING TO WILLKIE WAR TRIP

Former Nominee Called Agent for Morgan—Chicago Tribune.
. . . *The Presidential blessing was pronounced on Willkie as it was reported in Washington that he is undertaking the inspection tour of England on a confidential assignment from J. P. Morgan, the international banker, who managed Britain's American finances in the last world war.*

At the same time, according to reports, he will seek to sound Britain's future trends for Morgan . . .

Willkie will see just what British officials want him to see. . . .

*

❲ *I am going to England entirely on my own responsibility and am paying my own expenses.*

*

〖 PEOPLE THWART NEW ATTEMPT TO BURN LONDON
∗

I hear the voice invited into every room, the voice declaring
Above the sounds of your houses, the sound of your streets, the
      sound of your cities,
I speak your conflict, now I will speak your hope.

"To us there has come a time," I hear, and the voice arrives clearly, although now and then confusion in the air and the voices in the next room blur single words. He is speaking from the wooden stand. He is braced up and speaking: ". . . A time in the swift happenings, to pause and recall our place, to rediscover what we are and may be. If we do not, we risk the peril: isolation."

I hear the words as I move about the room.

"The lives of nations may be counted, too: by the lifetime of the human spirit.

"The life of a people is the fullness of its will to live.

"Some doubt. Some now believe freedom is an ebbing tide. But we Americans know this is not true. . . .

"These later years have been fruitful. They have brought a greater security in our understanding that life can be measured in other than material things.

"Democracy cannot die," I hear him say. "It is built on the full force of man's enlightened will. Cannot die *when* it is," he says.

"Democracy is the structure of the limitless civilization; its capacity is infinite process toward a developing fullness—the fullness of human life.

"A people, like one person, has a body. To be fed, clothed, and housed. Strengthened by vigor and rest according to our best skills.

"A people, like one person, has a mind. It must be kept informed, inquiring and alert. It must go on knowing itself, understanding the hopes and needs of its neighbors. The neighbors of the mind are all those that live and have lived in the world.

"And the people, like one person, is something deeper, something more permanent, something larger than the sum of all its parts.

"This is it, calling to the future, requiring us to guard the present. This is sacred, and its parts are sacred.

"What is our name for it? We do not give it a name. The spirit, the faith of centuries, born of the multitudes from many lands, mostly plain people, seeking here early and late to find freedom more fully.

"The democratic wish is not a recent phase of history. It *is* human history. Deep in the ancient life it blazed up; then written; and, in the Americas, irresistible.

"This is the New World. In all tongues, to all peoples, not for discovery, but because all those who came here believed they could create a new life—a life always new in freedom.

"We still have far to go. Security . . . chance . . . wisdom," he is saying. "We cannot tolerate distorting poverty or wealth, the slave to itself.

"We will gather all our faith and spirit, justified by the resources and the capacity of the land. But it is never enough to achieve these purposes: clothing and feeding the body, instructing, informing the mind.

"For there is also the spirit. Of which all the rest are parts moving in relation, according to their nature.

"The spirit speaks to us daily, in simple apparent ways—through our processes, the unnoticed days of our counties, our rivers, our cities, our many-ranging land. And in the voices from past the borders and voices across the seas. Voices enslaved, as well as the free. And in the past . . .

"In the face of peril, our purpose to protect, and still create, the structure an integrity of the democratic spirit.

"We do not retreat. We will not stand still."

*

Leaving New York, I looked back fourteen times:
Once when the bridge was cloven, and the driver
Chose smoothly. I saw the city emerge; but you
Sleep somewhere, who in my waking never sleep.

The highway leaps. I look back many times.
Now again, I know the splitting everywhere:
Clouds, roads, words given me from you, this river
Dividing us, locking you back to the dreams of islands,
Locking me now to voyage and to air.

*

You know the green glass tower. Thinking of invasion, we think this morning: the airport is intact. We rebuild it, waiting for him. A revolving light set low, and runways of radiant concrete, first fading, then brightening at dawn, as these do.

A tissue of rays in early morning, linked centrally. Radio beams and their power of origin. One or two planes inclining, taking their signals. Conversations of skill.

Almost half past eight. Blowing over the marshland, the salt spray bringing in planes, over the city, slanting down on the fish-shaped island. Straight to the eye of the fish.

The plane is ready for him. A prancing sound of engines, revving up, prime of propellers.

The landscape straightens here, everything being linked distally, star-shaped, very strict. If you are thinking of the ground and roads. For the air.

And now the reporters order coffee for each other. "This break is nothing new; it was true before Philadelphia; I'd rather have things out in the open," a knotted thin man says. During the campaign, they sat on it. Everything as neat as checkers. All the fine angry advisers, caught in a field of force. Then they clung to each other by threads; then they were surrounded, it boiled up over them. But before that, side by side, they opposed and repelled each other. Each pole appeared; they were opposites, with squares around them. Everything was clear, all the mixed insights, all the corruption . . . "No, we have time to talk. They always get here 35 seconds before take-off. Another cup? Go ahead."

He is leaving at the moment when he is rid of defeat. Two intermixed armies, each hostile to itself. This is the story of a war in which all the cleavages between the ranks on each side are greater than the frenzy between the sides. If you sort out the meanings as the fields of force strengthen, what do you get? What is he to the others? Do you know the terms of froth? A disperse phase. Have you seen cast metal cooling at the mill? Look into the structure of its changes, flowing fire—

But these are not metal. These are people.

Fire turning into honeycomb.

Now Willkie walks in with his friend the publisher and his friend the banker. He looks tired, like a soldier; he looks miserable and turned inward, with his shots and his preventive fevers. All the papers of passage ready. A word to the press, to his old friends.

Before.

The way to keep out of the war, he says, with his blue look, is by giving aid to Britain. Yes, I said that. (Certainly, the answers come, not loud enough except in dream, the way to keep war out is by giving, by giving.) The others ask their questions. Will you testify? And your wife? Were you ever . . . ?

Of course, I'll testify. I couldn't this week, my inoculations. But if lend-lease isn't passed by the time I get back . . .

Mrs. Willkie has been a good sport about my going.

Now it is time, and he walks along to his Gate, still answering them: "Yes, I was. On a trip, six or seven years ago; and then with the AEF . . ."—looking up at the Yankee Clipper: "On a transport, that was." His voice is very sandy now. "Landed at Glasgow."

Exhausted for a second, he feels the difference of that leave-taking. To Winchester and then to France with the 325th. Stationed at Bordeaux then. Shack Miller and he getting lost in Paris for days, looking for some town next to Bordeaux. Searching for it again in Nice. Lieutenant Shackleford Miller. And quite a different crossing, quite a different mission, yes. His foot now on the engineered ridges of the lowest step, the silver plane above him, in his briefcase the cable from Churchill, and his credentials, in the swift audacious pent-up writing. On the envelope, the formal words: Kindness of W. Willkie.

*

([*From this date on, Willkie's concept of "loyal opposition," according to Rosenman, was to precede the administration in urging measures needed to defeat the Axis.*

*

LAT. 10° NORTH, LONG. 45° WEST

Roundabout hours of air, slanting past Massachusetts above the
         slate of rain,
Plane over the hard ocean, construction of rock whose law
Offers its gray erect.   The strength of this bare floor
Appears as ledges where pale moss lies, and the dry ocher green
Of moss in these crevices seems to move a little; lichen the color
         of unripe apples
Or the shadow of walking figures, ice-color hands shivering
Above rock-blue and rock-green.   Figures of clouds.
But these quartz fragments and plains we know are sea.
However classic the crystal lattices,
Speed makes them; this storm is over the mind and the Atlantic.
Work on the chart; and land where you can land.

*

Ice from the wings, a rattle against metal. All right, come down.
At the Azores, the sea is a flight of stairs,
A flight of leaves as spearsmen over flat courtyards
Whirling, the blown archaic curtains of the world.
Red roads of Horta where nothing has subsided.
Not surf, not history, dissipations of foam,
The whips and winds.
And America asking personal questions.
—All right.   If we're to be held up twenty-four hours.
He will in that case set out to see the island.

*

He would do as he had done in other states:
Interview the natives.
A party of tourists, leaning on the wind.

*

They drove after breakfast to a lookout point, where the spinning and flagellation of a wind that is all head and arms, whirling like a formal design and yelling like an uncle, blows at his skull and flaps the cloth of habit. Does he stand firm, still thinking of legs, of a cold wooden hammered-up platform half-ocean over? He decides to forget, in the face of the wind, so coming to the end of a beginning made back there, face to face at the White House.

He shouts and laughs very hard now, the wide laugh throwing itself away into the storm, like foam in tension scudding this green wet field. And across a road frankly hungry, primitive red. A woman making lace (for export) staring out of a line of blank windows in the whitewashed house. Some long-range flickering appetite in her stare, a fantasy of a man with heavy muscles and large equipment and well-fed indulgent brutal foreign ideas of *riqueza* and women. Flash of such demand past glass; under it the pale curve, early apple-color of bosom.

The colors blow. The wind blows the desires past.

You can feel the wind steering the wheels of this car.

All right, stop the car. This farmer in the crewel field.

The man's clothes retell, in crease and color, the short monot-
onous anecdotes, to a tourist looking for anecdote. His face
with its crackle of gullies tells strain over strain, the weather of
adaptation finally glazing his hard cheek. However, the pigpen
behind him seems a simplicity.

Willkie says to the driver, I'd like to talk to him.

The driver bows, dips his shoulders at the lip of the bow,
politeness pours like oil. *Certamenta,* he says, and they hear
something said to the farmer' of *perguntar* and *o governo* and
o presidente. That was the word of the delegation greeting his
arrival. Willkie turns to his friends, in his first confusion: They
don't! he exclaims, reddening. One of the men nods. He hesi-
tates; on the mainland he would avoid this. But here, in a strange
country, in this wind—Yes, he does say. They think you're the
President.

WILLKIE, to the farmer: What kind of corn is this?

THE FARMER: Eatin corn.

WILLKIE: It's Indian corn. (*Shucking the ear. The ripping sound.
The yellow, regular grain.*) A bit stubby; still, it's corn. But
what I want to see is hogs.

Later, WILLKIE: What kind of hog is this?

THE FARMER: Eatin hog.

WILLKIE: (*getting into the pen*) Looks like a Berkshire.

The drive back to the hotel. A small-scale pomp and fake
authority. The tacked-together attempt, when the delay of
planes goes on. Now another delegation.

WILLKIE: (*praising storms, delays, and low ceilings, the sutures
of darkness over the islands*) . . . And I am delighted to find
here Berkshire hogs, and Indian corn; just like Indiana.

The delegates whisper to each other. No one is able to face
this; it is clear that the delegates have never heard of Indiana,

where Mary Sleeth manages his farmers, and, besides, they disagree about the provenance of their hogs and their corn.

DELEGATE 1, doing his best: Nevertheless. Nice things to have
around.

WILLKIE, interested in the disagreement, snatching at it: You
have the vote here, don't you?

DELEGATE 2: No.

WILLKIE: Well, suppose you don't like something. What do
you do?

DELEGATE 3: Get shut up. (*With a gesture that cuts across lan-
guages, the tints of maps, and naval history.*)

*

⟨ *From Chicago. Since the election, Mr. Willkie has been received at the White House and is Wendell to Mr. Roosevelt.*

*We don't know whether Mr. Ickes has had him to dinner,
but at least he has paid for whatever he might eat.*

*When we last looked around, he was indorsing war bill No.
1776; next thing we knew he was on the wing for England. By
now he is, more truthfully than Harry Hopkins, FDR's alter ego.*

*

The forces and surface of the sea. The solid air, and hard
        ridges of water
Immobile from the scanning plane as a dead forehead.
No. Alive. The gray-blue hard morass
And a flash of cheval glass lengthening into
Uninvented track of the sun, shouting There is a curve of ways.
In their green moment, the shallow fields of the sea
When a plane goes into a glide over Lisbon.

*

⟨ *From Berlin: The visits to England of both Hopkins and
Willkie show that the Americans have not believed British re-*

ports. You know how the Americans are: they want to do what
they call "seeing everything with their own eyes."

Cartoon of Morgan, Set Up Like a Mayan Pyramid on What
May Be a Hand.

Caption: *Willkie's Entirely Private Trip.* Additional remarks
about the "mammoth banker Morgan," reportedly supported by
the strong fist of Mr. Henry Morgenthau.

In short, Berlin is told, it is all just the way they like things
in America: highly confused and dazzlingly illuminated for the
purpose of concealment.

*

⟨ In London, among the rumors of official audiences, the press
prepares itself for the Leader of the Opposition.

Statement: We don't want flattery.

Be as frank as you like with us.

*

In secret, in the dark, Portugal descending leftward down, on
a right-moving wheel. Zigzag up Europe to a ritual landing, due
north of the disguise of courses, at an unnamed field.

Where are your escort planes?: to their Dutch pilot.

Clouds be my escort.

*

Radio silence of aircraft over the dense ocean,
The American silence within our flood of sound.
You know that our speed over the clouds of ocean
Cannot approach the cry of a burning city.

You know that this cry arriving is only our own speed
Screaming its own pleasures and names, in flying.
Among this high air only the rage of speed
Can reach us.   How can one child saying Mother?

How can these bone-cold naked men, standing all day
And then forced to sing and then to dig their graves?
I hear the grating of shovels.   Or is the wind of day?
Or songs from all Europe and Asia in the smoke of Poland?

Here the propeller drifts into a rising high tight
Strong infant's cry in China, under gongs.   Noises of flapping.
And the squeaks and grincing of barbed wire knotted tight.
Slower than steps, the tentative walk on the ghetto pavement.

No bones could go so slow as these slow swollen children.
They cover their eyes. Their mouths. You cannot hear their cries.
This is the missile waste, all agony, famine, a child deciding
That life is like this agony that has surrendered its cries.
Sound carrying through sound.
                    Alive, awake, or with all their veins broken,
Waves of their cry to us : Make, for we may not make.

*

⟨[DIESE STADT IST JUDENFREI!—*Words on a banner across an
avenue; a city of Europe.*

*

The plane is shielded, darkened, as it comes over the Bay, over
Land's End, to the airport. They meet him. They show the
travelers his friends to a hut, where a lance corporal stands guard.
Willkie, to the press: I am not pessimistic.
Willkie, to the press: I am not worried about anything.
He is to fly at once to London.

*

Of course the town has been damaged. But the airport is intact, and Come along to the station! they are saying. They walk
down the platform and indeed the train is there. His hosts look
at their watch faces, those most human designs that express most

human assumptions; and pleasures; and irrigations, all in sync. Soldiers on the train checking their watches, too, putting their heads out and waving. The particular inflections and English melody of voice, taking natural delight in tone, after our narrower range. Laughter of soldiers.

Far back for him is a small boy lying on a branch, waiting for a train to go.

The train pulls out of the station. On time. He watches it in its diminishing magic down the track, the geometry of its snuffing out. Then he sees the brilliance of his host's smile; and his other host smiling like a street light. They are waiting for him to be proud. My God, he thinks, the afternoon train, pulling out without incident. I had no idea, he thinks, and cancels out that thought.

He praises the train, he praises the station. He remembers everything the car toads and cherry pickers of America have never told him about timetables. He explains the wheel arrangement of the Mikado—2–8–2—and of the Berkshire—2–8–4—until, at the crest of his charm, he sees the wall.

The rose-pink bricks are balanced on themselves with a delicate and exhausted recklessness. Old brick whose color we will not see at home except as museum color, as general here as poppies. And conveying the balance of stemmed flowers; the colors of warmth and assurance, lifted up as blossom. Season of mutilation, this used to be a house, people were protected here before they were burning. The broken no-house, this wall, constructed and tenuous; its design of chambers, seeming able to defend, now only like the wing of a dragonfly tortured by a boy who hates his father.

A few laths and shreds of plaster still here. Beyond the earth-red brick he can see those pale interior colors, walls of dead rooms. Ivory, light gray, flat white, one very creamy strawberry, painted to imitate the reflective, gentle light.

It is incredible that the wall should stand, open to the big

winter daylight. You would think daylight and the watching of
three men would have toppled it down.

Past the gap, they have cleared the rubble, says his host. He
sees the startle of sky, blue gratitudes. Something turns in him
of shattered years, some mud of the other war. The other season
of this war, with some relief especial to himself. Something light-
headed and noble, drunk on cognac, some buried drowned joy
of standing on his feet in the roadruts of a foreign country. Balanced like the last wall of a destroyed home-building, standing
in a sky half mist and sleepsoft. Among the perfumes of the
smell of earth, cut and crossed by the wheelcars of compulsion.
Destroyed. Gone to mud. Or powder. Fire and dust, while he
lives.

*

The plane flies him into evening London. Absolute quiet.

Quick habitual motion of people on street corners.

The colored arrows, the closed-down slits of color in the traffic
signs, sharp-focus yellow and red allowed, and green as the car
turns to his hotel. Restlessness as the colors darken and gray out,
as the city feels itself low and open to the sky. The balloons up,
becoming invisible. Beasts of prehistory that, after all the textbooks' promises, did in fact coexist with men. Big silvery.

The colored arrows? They point to shelter.

*

He reaches the Dorchester. The door opens on the lit and
crowded lobby. The backs of heads, the broad backs all in uniform; backs of women, their shoulder blades exquisite through
the stout cloth of the services; the crisp heads, and laughter in
cool tides. Not a head turning.

Not one of them recognizes Willkie.

He is a big man in his blue suit and dark overcoat not cut in
Britain; his soft hat brim snapped down over his eyes.

He does not stop to sign the register.

Half an hour later, when the reporters see him, he is wearing his campaign tie, the blue four-in-hand the color of his eyes, woven so that the white stripes spell his name.

The blackout around them. The spotters busy with sky, and the roof of the city.

Still the all-quiet.

*

([Willkie says to the press, I am very glad to be in England.
*

Dined in his suite at the Dorchester.
*

Whatever roams the air is traveling
Over these griefs, these wars and this good.
Whatever cries and flowers, lives and can farther find
Than the threshold of sense; I know the piercing name;
Among all the silence, in pain, the birth-cry came.
Salt of these tears whitens my eyelashes.

Whatever ploughs the land turns into food:
Before my face, flowers, color which is form.
Bravery ploughs the season, turns to birth
Upon the sex-sown people-flowering earth.
A year turns in its crisis.   In its sleep.
Whatever ploughs our dreams is ours to keep.

Whatever ploughs our dreams is ours to give:
The threshold rises and changes.
I give, I perceive;
Here are the gifts of day risen at last;
Blood of desire, the riding of belief
Beyond our fury and our silences.
*

In the morning charging out of the hotel door, like a swimming dog surfacing he shakes his head. And stops; and looks across at the bobby. Things to do, says the tourist briskly. The Embassy car is waiting at the curb. Willkie goes over and asks the bobby, How are you getting along?

ǫ: How *was* he getting along?

WILLKIE: I don't know. He seemed indulgent; touched the strap of his helmet when he smiled. I thought of Virginia Woolf's bobby who said to her, "And, I can tell you, to direct the traffic orderly, at 'Yde Park Corner, Piccadilly Circus, is a whole-time, white man's job." But, then, she wasn't a foreigner.

ǫ: Too bad. Your first go, too. . . . You could have told him you're a black. Know what the Christians are doing in Denmark, about the armbands the Jews must wear? They too are wearing them.

And then the army private on the pavement. Willkie buttonholes him, standing well away from the left arm in its sling.

WILLKIE: How did you get hurt? How are you feeling? How's everything going?

The soldier gives him a pale smile. Polite; he supposes there must be some arcane reason for this civilian, this large man with a look of profits and a stateside accent, and his questions. "Not so bad, sir," he said. (That's a good grin he has.)

Willkie climbs into the official car and is taken to meet Eden. Then, at the Ministry, he tells the press: Go ahead. Shoot your questions and shoot them fast.

They are making notes. "His face alight." "His smile magnificent."

ǫ: And what do you plan to see here, Mr. Willkie?

WILLKIE: I am going to talk to the man in the street and visit towns and cities which have been particularly strafed in the provinces.

ǫ: What towns do you expect to visit?

WILLKIE: Manchester and the Midland industrial centers. I want to find out all I can about your English methods of production. I've got some questions myself.

ǫ: What are they?

WILLKIE: Questions like these: How far can English methods be co-ordinated with American? Where are your shortages? (*A laugh, from one of the reporters. Quickly over.*)

WILLKIE: Are your methods better than ours? (*Sound of factual writing.*) If so, get them put into operation quickly. If some of our methods are better than yours, then you can improve in that direction.

He is leaving with the officials in the official car.

A feature writer watches them go and lights his cigarette. That's one way to do it, he says very softly. The whirlwind touring the ruins.

Do you know where he is going? Past ruined Guildhall, past St. Paul's, spiked and opened by fire. The city is steered by lightning. No. It is not, he thinks, and this tourist has never stood under an insane sky. He forgets what he has never had in experience. He is loud and glib and imperfect of sight and motive. His consciousness is corrupt, he had been tainted by the superstition of his tribe: a mysticism of the material. Nevertheless, in flashes, Nevertheless, in this moving, deep-throated city under torment. He sees the energy, like a tongue-tied schoolboy who has been through a family breakfast quarrel and cannot say his lines. The energy of response, the most human response, although it was nowhere summoned up in time, now functions here. That is what steers the city; lightning is its name.

Whose eyes look into his today? Men I have never known. I met Tommy Atkins. His arm was in a sling. I talked to a bobby. And to Hopkins.

Always to look up after this, even at intact rooms, as he looks past these walls up through the ceiling as a lamp might shine.

At the equivocal sky. The sky of power, with which may be created the refusal or the limitless creation.

*

At lunch with Churchill. Giving him the note.

*

❨ *TO A CERTAIN NAVAL PERSON*

DEAR CHURCHILL:
Wendell Willkie is taking this to you. He is being a true help in keeping politics out of things.
I think this verse applies to you people as well as to us:

> "*Sail on, O Ship of State!*
> *Sail on, O Union, strong and great!*
> *Humanity with all its fears,*
> *With all its hopes of future years*
> *Is hanging breathless on thy fate!*"
> FRANKLIN D. ROOSEVELT

*

Churchill looks at the schoolbook lines come to serve as a bond—simplified, affirming, the large general rhyme.

Now the link between our countries has been made, says Churchill, in President Roosevelt's way.

And how would you define that way? Willkie asks.

The way of emotional precision.

He glances at his American guest. The soft places in his face are braced now and mature. He is the admiral, he is the symbol of stubborn courage now and the breath of drama. And he smiles.

You came to us with a certain authority.

Willkie says quickly, I have no authority and no position.

But there is great interest here, Churchill slowly answers, since it is the opposition that you represent.

Willkie shaking his head, smiles too, and suddenly finds lightness and pleasure in what he is saying: I am here representing Wendell Willkie.

Churchill laughs now, and the game is opened: That is an authority of its own. It should have its will. Since sight is your will, he says, I can assure you that every arrangement will be made by us, with the assistance of the enemy, to let you see all you desire of London at bay.

And again: You do know Hopkins by now—that frail and glowing man? Burning with passion and comprehension, loving the causes of the weak and poor, he lives at the root of the matter, a true leader of men.

Under our English system, Churchill says over brandy, a defeated candidate for high office persists in his connection with government. You in America follow another custom, and I cannot think where your sense of production can be, in this. You most wastefully, as wastefully as nature, send a candidate for the presidency to other occupations, to private life!

Willkie pushes his hand forward. You know I'll defend our system: "loyal" must outbid "opposition." He finds himself falling into a parody of Churchill's hypnotic period, and checks himself. Perhaps we have the advantage over you. Don't you find yourselves having your political figures always with you, like certain other constants? That can shadow the happiest election, can't it?

You play it like the World Series. But, when the banner—the pennant, that is—when the pennant's won, there is still governing to do.

We consider that we have a convenient method: retire them.

Put out to pasture! I think not, says Churchill, in cigar smoke.

And that makes two of us, he says, with all his benevolence. They look at each other, smiling. But the two men are rather repelled by each other and the smiles are smiles of will. They dislike each other so much they might be in love with the same woman. He's more of a poet * than a close-thinker, Willkie says to himself, gritting his teeth. He feels that he himself is thinking very closely today; but some obscure elusive present in this place reminds him sharply of defeat.

Churchill matches this in himself. But he is in power, and formal, and this is a game at which he is a master. No, he says, answering what has not been spoken, and bringing direction to his words. Let us go on talking. For even production, for even the hierarchies of command, even the issues of tyranny, here are joined. At the summit of life—here, in the crisis of a major war—it is not possible, Mr. Willkie, to divide political ideas from military ideas, nor any idea from action. At this summit, they are one.

These words are what were needed. This belief touches Willkie. Or possibly it is the rhetoric of belief that makes him reverse his feeling and clear the mist. The hereditary grandeur, the conviction of magnificence—to offer these as a leader in wartime is his panache. Only when one sees that this may accompany a view of the continent as so many dukedoms, that the trap may be in a set of fealties that exclude more than they bind, that this people who is enduring vast sufferings fiery beyond showing may still be thought of as the donkey to be drubbed with the stick or wheedled with the carrot—can one stand off and analyze. This man can call up bravery. He can make men and women require more of themselves than they knew they could draw on; that is morale. The energies he summons from them are the deep energies of contact with the land, with each other's belief. In the face of the long destruction of those contacts by the forces he speaks for. Glory, England, and the word, Willkie thinks, leaving Downing Place. The stormy island, crowded with

* A very ambivalent term in the usage of this period.

virtues—or manias, depending on your eyes—dominion, repression, control. Island teeming with poets. He has a boy's wish, at that last, to make a face at himself. Well, he thinks. A word can be used in more than one way.

*

The meeting with Bevin goes well. A grand fellow, Willkie feels at once and, just after, No. No. He's too much like our union leaders. Willkie, going from one to the other man, goes back and forth between emotions. There I go—the quick liking, and then the undertow. I shall make you late for the Cabinet meeting, I'm afraid, he says, and makes Bevin late, talking of what is being done in production, and what will be done. Yes, he says then, Mr. Churchill. A most unusual man; a very gracious man. Yes, a great man.

And goes to dine with Lord Stamp. Then sees the press. Some of the faces of this morning, again against blackout, remorseless white and friendly; the ground-animals of invasion looking through their eyes all starved of sleep at this man who is a tourist, a visitor.

The spotters on the roofs. The fire watchers.

*

❨ During the few hours I have been here, I have found their spirit magnificent. I like their nerve. I have not met anybody so far who is downhearted; but I did not expect anything else.

*

After breakfast, in St. Paul's again, he is climbing the great blocks of masonry spilled to the choir floor. Over the ramp, up the side, there lying like arms, there a knee of stone.

Looking up quickly. All quiet. The high altar there, and up through the wall with its shadows, the sky . . .

*

The long sky, disturbed but scarless all the way to the earth-mound.

There are some people in a tremendous grave. They talk among themselves. There is nobody here who asks for mercy or speaks of mercy. There is a sound of an old woman singing; an old woman with snow-white hair. Shouting now. A man stands over the pit, counting to twenty. The old woman is singing to a child. The child is about a year old, it makes a little tune of delight, over and over, over and over, part of the pure sky, a birdcall of nearness. The engineer in charge stands at the pit. Annette passes him; slim, blackness still gleaming after this long time. Annette points to herself and counts off—Twenty-three.

They are lying wedged together and on top of each other. Their heads can be seen; one's eyes make a jumble of the rest, unless somebody lifts an arm somewhere. But their heads start out, and the blood over their shoulders. Otto turns his head. He shows me he is still alive. He does it out of love.

Now the pit is almost full. Perhaps a thousand. The people go on undressing, they stand around in family groups. They kiss each other. Ernst holds the boy's hand. This is his son, just ten. A lanky, knotty boy, with the same look his younger brother has: Paul, now asleep in America, having bad dreams. The son at the pit fights his tears. Ernst points to the long sky. He strokes the boy's head; he is explaining something.

Now can you see who is doing the shooting? It is a man. He is young, he wears an SS uniform. He sits at the pit end, taking time out and smoking. Half an inch to go.

The people are all naked now. The cigarette has about four puffs left. They clamber over the heads of those who are lying there covering the clay steps. They greet those who are still moving; they caress them and speak to them in gentleness. Others come, speaking for the last time in dignity and human quiet. It is our turn now. We are to clamber over these heads. One puff to go.

*

An old rabbi, buried in earth up to his beard, shouting: Green grass outlives Nebuchadnezzar!

*

The sky at St. Paul's. A thin face stops in front of Willkie. "For you. Bit of incendiary that landed on the dome. Souvenir."

They drive through the streets. Now Willkie sees how carefully his route to the city has been selected. If they are choosing now, they are finally choosing to show him. Under the city-colored sky with its light thrown from all the sea and the clouds of Europe, London eaten away.

The truth, and the official present. Montagu Norman and Cardinal Hinsley; lunch with the Labour leaders, Attlee, Greenwood, the others. David Grenfell, telling of his closeness to the States. He has relatives, he says, several of them, there. Most of them live in—he supposes Willkie will not know this town, it is not a large one—live in a place called Elwood, Indiana.

The long room of the Commons. A visitor in the gallery, looking down at the debate; stress of sea surfaces, the turbulence declaring itself.

These sounds of anger are carried through him. This exchange is his food. Attack and defense within these limits make an image of the parents who fed him.

He sits down, listening. He is leaning forward, on his elbow, his big head based on his big palm.

Was there a cry? The cry. One after another, the short jagged crying starts, the sharp cry taking up the alert. While he listens to the sirens, he hears another driving sound, barking upward: the ground guns.

Other visitors look at him out of the tails of their eyes.

Now the barking of other dogs, yapping and answering. What sounds are those? From where?

Overhead, the hum of enemy planes.

He will not ask. Anyone three days alive in England might be expected to know each sound by heart. Besides, he is listening. And soon absorbed in the talk down there, thinking of that, and of the grim air, with nothing but wonder. Triumph and wonder. What had he expected? Anyway, not this. A man thinking for the thousandth time, It is all stronger than they have ever said, the colors are more, the colors of life are stronger. For the denunciation below him is the attack of the Labour member on the officials for the government's recent suppression of the London *Daily Worker*.

*

❨ *He seems to have taken the view, from the indictment alone, that he was dealing with a dangerous conspiracy akin in its nature to treason.*

The charge shows no perspective, no understanding of the nature of our liberties. The forcible suppression of discontent has a long history among the governing classes. Something, no doubt, is due to the atmosphere in which we have all winter moved. But we need to guard ourselves against bias here. There is in this a history which, to our law, lies so near to the boundaries of criminal conspiracy that one may find oneself interpreting the issues of this case upon assumptions which condemn militant protest, written or spoken—before the the issue is heard. Our thinking has at its foundation what Mr. Justice Holmes has called an "inarticulate major premise."

The law is still an armoury of weapons.

What is called criminal conspiracy is still an offense. And criminal conspiracy may easily be held to include an agreement of two or more people to do anything that the propertied classes, and the judges, may hold to be unlawful; and even to do any quite lawful thing by means, or with intentions, which the judges—not the juries—might hold to be unlawful.

Nothing but a strong party in the House of Commons, specifically charged with the defense of . . .

*

He felt a noise between the neck and the shoulder, like the blow of an ax.

He felt a noise like a wild beast's claw.

He felt split by a stroke, a tree half green, half burning. And leaves and serpents descending: the incendiaries.

Yapping of ack-ack guns, answering.

Everything of this reaches him, visitor no more. There are many kinds of homecoming. This is his: the stability is here, the turbulence, all the stresses communicated and acted out. Now he can hear voices and scars.

He stands outside, under the tower and the white spirals signed by planes. It was magnificent—please change that word—he says to a notebook.

It was the most dramatic example of democracy at work that anyone could wish to see.

Mind you, here Britain is, fighting for her life.

Yet a free House meets, people get up and denounce the Administration; and while they're talking, their country's attacked from the air; and under this threat, invasion.

*

❨ *They have given Wendell Willkie his white steel helmet with M.H.S. (Ministry of Home Security) in red letters.*

*

Tuesday, at Transport Hall, where they're talking manpower, mobilization of. The Trades Union Council and the Employees' Federation.

Hello, he says to the doorman. Bevin takes him in. He speaks.

Unanimity—looking at war—working man everywhere—not an imperialist war.

I begin to hear your jokes. To meet your lions. The clerks of the City. The incredible old women, the fire watchers. Now dark chimneys are precious to me, a pail of sand and a rake.

It is like remembering. These metal signs, or the words in the House. Fire spilled over the windowpanes, fire behind the eyes of your children—sleepless faces. My country knowing sleep.

Let me tell you what my first case was. I was just beginning as a lawyer, and I was proud to stand in defense of the tin-plate workers in Elwood, Indiana. Nothing original there. My father was the lawyer for the local trade union.

The Council gives Willkie this blue-bound book. A big handsome memorial, backed in leather. Leather covers.

*

([*The Book of the Martyrs of Tolpuddle.*

These Six have fought to win the beginnings of freedom. They were not the first, nor the last of those whose heroic stand against oppression made working-class organization possible, but their memory is cherished because they suffered and endured the hardships—the most dreadful torture . . .

*

What torture, asks Willkie?

*

([*Torture and hardships. Seven years in prison. The hulks, and the camps. Riveted in irons. To the knees in water, in the cold weather, at the first dawn of day. In the convict ships to Botany Bay. Van Diemen's Land on the floating hells. The branding iron; the spiked collar; flogging, and then the brine bath. Lash-driven; set on by dogs.*

When you're bound to Botany Bay . . .

*

Shaw's picture, asks Willkie?

*

❨ A Shavian Commentary on Martyrs:

I am afraid I cannot say anything, he reads, in praise of the Dorchester martyrs.

Martyrs are a nuisance in Labour movements.

The business of a Labour man is not to suffer, but to make other people suffer until they make him reasonably comfortable.

A Labour agitator who gets into the hands of the police is inexcusable . . .

*

He goes to lunch with Sir Robert Kindersley, chairman of the National Savings Committee. But before he reaches the Savoy, thirty or forty women with empty food baskets are there, stationed, an embarrassment of posters along the staircase from the lobby to the restaurant (sixty, says the *Times*). Twenty more are sitting at tables in twos and threes, some in fur coats (says the *Times*), and I recognize a feature writer from the *Daily Worker*. She does not wish to give her name to me.

—What do the posters say? In quite large letters:
THE GOVERNMENT SAYS WE MUST EAT LESS
FOOD—BUT THE RICH STILL EAT THEIR FILL
and another in blue:
WOOLTON AND THE FOOD PROFITEERS
MUST GO
—What do several policemen do?
Several policemen look on.
—What does Wendell Willkie see?
Nobody knows if he sees at all.
For they have steered him along the wall
And around a little balcony.
And now he strides through the great lobby.
Through the Savoy does Willkie go.
His face so still, you might never know

Whether he knows or does not know.
—And what does the manager say and do?
The manager stands and quotes the law:
Manager: "The law is that the policemen cannot intervene
unless we ask them for help in ejecting disorderly people.
—We don't want to do that."

—And now what do the women shout?
"Food for the workers" is their cry;
And while the management stands by
The law-abiding police stand by,
Employees put one lady out,
Three workers put the worker out,
And now about twelve ladies are out,
While all the other ladies shout.
—And Wendell Willkie?
He goes along the corridor to another entrance of
        the restaurant.
The ladies parade through the restaurant,
Shout one more shout
And then go out.

Times man: Any comment, Mr. Willkie?
Willkie: (tactfully) No comment.

                        *

([Then Willkie goes to see
*Sir Andrew Duncan, Minister of Supply, and Professor Harold
    Laski,*
Count Edward Raczyuski, the Polish Ambassador,
*General Wladyslaw Sikorski, Polish Commander-in-Chief and
    Prime Minister of the Polish Government in Exile,*
Quo Tai-Chi, the Chinese Ambassador,
and later at the Home Office,
Herbert Morrison, Home Secretary, and Ellen Wilkinson.
                        *

In the evening, he went with Ellen Wilkinson to the shelters. Did he look like a young air-raid warden, energetic, full of sleep? Perhaps.

The first shelter was under a market, in the East End. It was early; only the children and their shadows were asleep. Yes, they cheered for America. He comes down wearing a breeze of health; something about the raid, the demonstration, the Tolpuddle Martyrs, even this version of his first case. They cheer, and a woman pulls at the skirt of his coat. "Send us all you can." Tea in a tin cup. Voices arched over with stone.

The second shelter: a tunnel on the Surrey side. Here's an old man who's lived in here for five months. Since that other life when the sunlight lay stretched over the West; when the train raced alongside; who wouldn't want to be what?

Droning of planes. Not a single stick of bombs. Letting him have his little excursion.

Ellen Wilkinson says, "Now this is a more middle-class one—suburban."

"Yes," he says, grinning. Just then the old cabby came up. "I've been in the States," he says to Willkie.

"And what do you think, then—think the Germans will get over?"

"Don't think so, govner; or if they do, they'll all be dead before they take this island."

And one in the center of London:

"Give him a cup of coffee, now. They like it."

"Very good coffee it is," says Willkie. Drinks his cup, thanks them again. "See you again. If I get a chance," he says, and Ellen Wilkinson stares at him, "I'll spend a night in the shelter."

A high voice crackles from among the sleeping: "On a bunk or on the floor?" The shaft opens as he hears this, he has swung all day to and from this clear life, over this shaft; everything he said on the train ignored this life. The holding on of siege, humor of islands; rage, endless stone stairs of rage, and still the

184 · A dance of strings

strings and mazes of official habit were making agreements like
string calendars, a dance of strings to small and courtly music.
To visit their life. To be handed from one to another—their
kindness, the deep colors of bravery in their look. The skill at
judging: production according to potential, help according to
one's own effort. Under the storm of fire their own weather.
Over his shaft.

He is in his room, talking across the ocean to his wife in the
threatless city:

And a little baby, tiny—must have been two or three days old.

We'd never have realized how a thing like this gets you
moved. Congestion. A spirit of endurance. Well yes, I thought
of myself that way: a pretty hard-boiled guy. But sometimes I
turned my head away. Yes.

Next morning, at early morning tea.

Willkie, to the chambermaid: How's the war going?

Chambermaid: Of course we're going to win; but I think we'd
like a little more help from America.

*

《 The National Republican Builders Inc. are sending out re-
leases. They charge Willkie with one thing and another. By
shifting his position on American foreign policy, he has played
"a shabby and tragic hoax" upon the American people.

*

He leans toward Viscount Simon at lunch, asking about the
courts. Still open and free, he is told; still operating under the
old established rules.

But are they at all modified?

Only by war regulations.

A glass of brandy from The Inner Temple.

The Admiralty. Lord Alexander.
Dinner with Duff Cooper.

*

《 *From Berlin: Willkie has not been invited, but the Reich has nothing against such a visit; and, if he should come, he would not be obliged to run for an air-raid shelter while in Berlin.*

*

THE JETTY. DOVER.

Whipping the face.   Europe, with all her winds.
Shore-wind of despair and beginnings.   The big guns.
Whose word is the shape of storm.   Who offer choice
Only of death or growth.

Either a man is a visitor in hell
Or his shoulders become a coast of images:
Fireflood twisting the girders and nave of things
To leave the scars and the spire.
Receding, sees the traveler and the hill
Facing each other in a world of meaning.
Everything else carried its own destruction,
And now again is beginning to be born.

The docks and the steel towns and the shadow plants
Reflect our forms of hope; a man's a visitor
Between the whistling crests of storm.
Storm breaks,
And he in conflict remembers Eden, not dream,
Not womb, not garden, but city of God
City being the form of our wishes for each other,
That burn in cities throughout the human night
Tonight, only a few miles apart.
The chain of lifetimes burning locks his life

To the arm of the jetty stretched into the sea.
To the credence of definite objects, doorsills, nails driven in,
The zone of silence, meaning explosion,
Or Liverpool and Auntie Lizzie McHeice,
A bottle of beer and a notable buttonhole.

The bricks and the spillways of fire,
The pilgrim of surfaces knows these appetites
Deep in the split race of his roots of dream.
He lies down here to bury his old self.
It will restore his earth as fire never can,
Nor blood.   There is no other sacrifice
Beyond commitment, where the terms are born,
Where giving is taking, where all feeds on all
In the human process.   When he wakes
He will venture out into the same besieged
City but smell a difference in the singe
And the air's change.   He will be horrified
To hear himself use the phrases of the other country.
He will look for the fine relations even in his own words.
He will recall, even in death, even in dream, even in his sharpest-
      focused joy
The full birth in its wild simplicities.
He was standing on the jetty at Hell's Corner,
Rings of desire for Europe, no, America, no, the limitless spirit
      of the born and unborn
Fall over his head.
And at his back there is nothing but the future.

*

❲ At the home of the Earl of Derby, Lord Lieutenant of Lanca-
shire. Lord Derby: The worst thing that happened to England
was the invention of the combustion engine.

*

Well, they did cheer him. They did fire the coast guns for his benefit. He loved it all. The American Eagle Club, Claridge's, Lambeth, the ride down to Chequers. To Coventry Sunday morning, seven weeks after the raid, seeing the builders working, Sunday or not.

Willkie: No man could fail to be moved.

Many who saw him are glad the lull of the blitz broke while he was in England. The American reporters found themselves wishing a really thick night for him, and word of it going to the Senate building. Willkie's Benefit, they call these nights, the small bright stars burst upwards from the guns. The deep, rich disruption, when the house shakes and any standing thing rattles and goes. Bury they do, and others come to dig. Dig here for children. Fire engine, fire engine, van, van.

"Was that thunder?"

"Don't you know that noise?"

"Oh, all right. Good. I was afraid it was going to rain."

*

((*A composition of geese, barbed wire, grounded half-blown balloon seen between formal barbed hourglasses.*

Herbert Read says of this war as seen in art: ". . . It may be that the general effect will strike the American visitor as tame or subdued, as too quiet and harmonious for the adequate represen-tation of war. . . ."

Glass splintered and ringing. Laughter of plants proliferating. A bedspring in conversation. The ceiling slowly and gracefully coming downstairs.

Now a great many people grin and brace themselves.

*

HE WANTED TO SEE DAMAGE AND PRODUCTION

   Willkie: Freedom will survive only if production survives.

   Did you know that you can get treasury funds to run an industry in the shadow of the great exciting ones? He says the
typical businessman now thinks, If I can beat the government's
plant enough, I can take it over after the war. There won't be
any nonsense about private enterprise surviving.

Q: What is your opinion, Mr. Willkie—will British industry
   come out of the war socialized?

WILLKIE: Certainly not. And do you know that was one of my
   first interests in coming here?

   From Manchester in a chartered plane to Ireland.

   The boats with their red sails on the stone-green sea.

   In Dublin, three hours with de Valera.

Q: What did you do after that, Mr. Willkie? A few facts for the
   late editions.

WILLKIE: I flew back for tea with the King and Queen.

Q: What was it like? What did you drink?

WILLKIE: Scotch and soda. He poured.

Q: Will you give us your impressions?

WILLKIE: You can have facts. You can have impressions. I'd
   rather talk. Just keep this out of the stories. Duty sticks out
   all over the King. That's all as it should be. The Queen now—
   you know how pretty she's cracked up to be? Partly your doing, but tell the women at home, with that Look they've
   imagined into themselves, all legs and nerve. . . . Perhaps a
   little on the dumpy side. But all in keeping; it all adds up to
   the right symbolism.

Q: Here's the front page from the Continent tonight:
   From Stuttgart: American Observer Demonstrates That
   There Is Severe Damage.

WILLKIE: There is damage. Has somebody not heard?

Q: The Spanish press says you and Churchill had a "stormish
   quarrel."
WILLKIE: A great man. I knew it before. I know it now even
   more.
Q: And as a leader?
WILLKIE: He'd be a rotten leader at some times. The perfect
   cheerleader right now.
Q: And the cabinet?
WILLKIE: A cohesive cabinet. Great Labour leadership.
Q: And Bevin?
WILLKIE: I was disappointed.
Q: Two other stories. After you stayed, say the Germans, against
   Churchill's wishes, adds Spain, you saw damage that "was to
   have been concealed from you."

*

Willkie stretches. He wants to go to a pub.

*

A GAME OF DARTS AT THE CHESTERFIELD ARMS

But they are accurate.   That is a target.
He throws the first.   It looks erect
Far from the eye, over the whitebreast girl
Past thirty years of tulip trees.

The second makes a ray
Across stupidity.   Across his own;
Into the edict.   Life goes here and there
Into the land within the land, the deeper secret.

The throwing of secrets, edged and weighted bright.
Directness to the mind; the woman stumbling home

Where there is no home will fall again.   However.
The idiot running under Orion.   However.

The flight of birds escapes from your planting.
Sharp arrows overtake you and go through you
And surpass you and race with your name into daybreak,
And all this is your riddle and your game.

*

As he stood near the plane, they heard him say:
"I am of purely German descent."
The morning blew his words away.
"My grandparents left Germany in protest."
Prepotent grandfather, your seaports and your sea
"And I, too, claim that right."
I now newborn. Protest prepareth me.
"Tell the German people . . .
"I speak for my countrymen of German ancestry.
"They, too, believe in human rights and Freedom."

*

Where will you be tonight? Past Lisbon, flying.
And your message, tonight? Scattered on Germany.

PART SEVEN

A Proving Flight

⟨ FROM *Berlin: His words disclosed Willkie's opportunism.*

*

⟨ From *Chicago:*

A BAREFOOT BOY GETS TO BUCKINGHAM PALACE

We'll have to take what they dish out.—Quisling

. . . The Republican party, coming out of this trance in which it hears voices, now wonders.

We have heard about the Tibetan powder used in the notorious Russian state trials to make a victim betray himself.

There must have been a heavy run on that powder in Philadelphia in June. It all looks very crazy now.

. . . How did he go about this master deception abroad? He took off his shoes, he went barefoot, taking along only a cane fishing pole and a can of worms.

191

*What did he use his pole for? When he saw a Republican
head he hit it.*

*

On the Dixie Clipper's first regular flight to the U.S. by way of
Africa and the South Atlantic.

A day at Bolama, below Dakar. This island holds the airfield
and good hunting. Leopards, gazelles, and lions. Five years ago
the Bijagos—about 1,600—tried to drive out 400 Portuguese.
Now they go on raising peanuts and rice; they bring hides in to
market.

*

《 *All the hunters saw were a few gazelles and ducks. Willkie
bagged a few ducks. Governor of Portuguese Guinea gave him
a sword. The native chief showed him his twenty-six wives. In
New York, Mrs. Willkie was on the air—WABC's "Calling All
Citizens."*

*

Aboard, Juan Trippe, other Pan-American officials. Willkie
and his friends.

1 A.M. in the navigating room. Captain La Porte is showing
them the charts. The needle of the altimeter swings. Flicker of
needles, crystals that vibrate over the instrument panels. These
are to be experiments to find out how "thick" the trade winds
are. The friend of mariners, the westward-faring wind. Streaming
over the ocean currents, where the discoverers' road was, to split
upon Brazil. Blowing that track always, carried them out, reduc-
ing them westward until they disappeared.

Fallen over the world's precipice, the cliff of expiation. Or
drawn against the magnetic mountain, riveted for all time. Or
eaten by the chimeras.

Or returned to the Prince Navigant with their gifts: ideas of earth.

Earth as a plant floating upwards through all that ocean, floating the continents to the surface, the mountain chains miles farther. Earth as a tree rooted deep; as the garden of four rivers; earth the tetrahedron; earth, heart-shaped.

This wind-rose opening over them, flowering and reaching westward. The roots of wind insisting on the west, as if it were the sun, on which the wind-plant was feeding.

This plane, trying the altitudes, feels out strange east winds on her tail. But between 4,000 and 5,000 feet there is virtually no tail-wind.

Of all the basic air movements, says the captain, this is the most reliable on the planet.

*

The running of the light. Flicker of needles, sure and quite calm because they indicate, but flickering on the panels. Outside it is still dark. We are over the route of the discoverer, as if their lives were one course and we were sailing them. As if their ships were suspended in the sea where they had gone below us, or were all there in a waiting stream, full blown by the wind.

Wind that we do not feel, which hardly exists at the highest altitude. The plane makes its best time at 4,000 to 5,000 feet.

The past gives us our fixed points. Judean astronomers and the nodes of the moon; star-maps from Toledo; the Arabic charts and the shadow-cone of earth.

The wanderers, the planets now that fade, and the Regiment of the North Star, according to the position of the guardians.

Use the clock star.

Use Jacob's staff.

Guess the wind now; check the seven vectors disappearing, the one wind left blowing that track the ocean over to another coast of the world. Check the drift angle.

Behind at a moving of the night. Light that is lifting now, splitting away from the past, tomorrow the sun behind us, making day flower, and the water sun below us on the fact of ocean.

And with the lifting of light, he sees clearly the fires he saw: a tearing of cities like membranes, now the glinting broken cheval glass, light on all splinters. Many lights, but most of all those faces and those lives, a reliable tearing of lives. Of all those threatened, who understand islands. Who see that one way to meet threat is with defense. One way to meet threat is with a leap of growth. To become oneself at the next level, and declare.

The light declares the ocean.

Juan Trippe the president, Willkie the passenger, Captain La Porte.

Below, the glinting variable, daylit ocean. Not rocks and ledges now, for all the power and lift of the air, holding the plane as all things give each other motion. But the sea as lives of the living, faces seen along a flash of rails on endless hours in America, or sleepless and enduring in fire and England. Bodies tattooed with waves, living below; tattooed with glitter of morning in this sky. Honoring blue, a breathing of the sea.

He sees the pattern of waves.

The horizon opens its limit; and the curve of water bends before him like an eye, observant, withholding judgment.

These shy animals put great paws toward him. Actual sea-surfaces, in burning filaments, and fish scales changing their nature; turning into kindling wood, twigs on fire, running smoke and the variable profiles.

Stresses pass over the wave fronts. But, looking down, through motion and less motion, to darkness of glass where we assume no motion.

Fire burning through a house in London. Darkness behind. The tenants in darkness.

Spotters and fire watchers, on roofs, in planes.

But all this is partly predictable. All this deals with an unknown. Unknown to the discoverers, a constant that must be dealt with, requiring skill and belief and trust in human possibility.

*

Wind arrow, wind rose, the wind currents in air,
A spiral staircase down the height of sky.
Chart of the urgencies of sail.
Shrouds tight, salted and glittering,
And the glittering lips of fifty-six sailors
All asleep four hundred years of water
Among the cycles of drift.   Forgetfulness.

*

He is reminded of the living. Now the eyes of a glimpse, a crowd too concentrated to see him, one child hurrying. Craters of memory, opened by siege and return. The moment between loss and blessing that rocks and glitters about the directness of change and the plane.

A flight of this nature is given its own name.

"This," says the Captain, "is called a proving flight."

*

⟨ *The next stop is Trinidad, where the party inspects the United States base.*

*

Later in the day, in the landing pattern over Puerto Rico, he sees the furry green of jungles he used to know, and the ax strokes of mountain rock. Working at Fajardo, he had felt the walls of the fort, the harbor cannon, the legends of Iglesias turning ferocious poverty into the torches and knives of belief.

Plane in its glide restrains, spills motive from its wings. Touches land; rolls past the turn; halts.

A cable for Willkie. MOST URGENT YOU APPEAR HEARING FOR-
EIGN RELATIONS DAY AFTER TOMORROW. SENATOR GEORGE.

*

To follow the hard sunlight on the northern harbor
Into the glint, choppy waves off the breakwater
Where a wife and son and a few frozen newsmen
Wait after headwinds.

Between the little flags, the son of the public man
Runs to the float, while in the middle distance
The wife of the public man and the photographers
Wait at the windows.

Others wait.   Words wait.   The memory in craters
Among the unanswered fires, fire's ancestor,
Power without dominion, to which I testify
In word waking and dreaming.

Power flaking in light down avalanches
Of all their words and faces, days after sleeplessness
Where one man, fed on sleep and food, loved by women
May voyage and wait far past defeat.

*

《 Genoa is now under fire of the British fleet.

The race across the battles to Western Libya.

In Breslau, Hess: Here pauses ready the German war machine,
before decisive battle.

*

《 Now they ask him: Questions, Mr. Willkie. What about Lord
Derby and his curse on machines?

Willkie: There are ways of walking through history and not
   noticing it.
Q: What do you want to say about England's chances?
Willkie: A squeak, I'd say, but still a ball game. Particularly if
   they get that help.

*

⟨ Lindbergh, saying, This war is lost. It is not within our power
today to win the war for England, even though we throw our
entire resources into the conflict.

   Besides, he indeed was saying, you know who wants the war.
Only the British, the Jews, and the Roosevelt administration.

*

⟨ Willkie, remembering and forgetting: I didn't believe any nation could possibly be so united.

*

Say it depends on the interpretation.
Want the romantic?   Talk to the passenger.
The classic, profit-taking logic?   The President is with us.
However, if you demand another arrangement
Responsible, uncorrupt—really?   The truth?
Here is the clean-eyed pilot.

   The pilot, speaking: It was a marvelous flight. *Fantastic!* Not
a single coincidence!

PART EIGHT Open System

(A VOICE, *from London:*
"*. . . all its fears . . . hopes of future years . . . breathless on thy fate!*
"*We shall not fail or falter. We shall not weaken. . . .*
Give us the tools and we will finish the job."

*

They are filling the marble room as if it were a refugee boat. Crowded and low on the water, waiting to sail. Early, at four in the morning, the spectators started coming in the dark. Now twelve hundred people are jammed into the room, pushed against the committee table.

Slight motion when the guards pull another senator, or a witness, through.

Forty feet up, the three photographers on a ledge, collecting faces, the shoulders and hats of the visitors. They collect the boredom of senators; the particular interest of the Vice-President's wife.

The breathing works in the depleted box of air. The flashbulbs say their bitter words in the used-up light. Slick of marble and crystal.

At 2:27 Tuesday afternoon, four cops work the big man through to the little well for witnesses, in the middle of the caucus room. Round of applause. Nickering laughter from three women behind the table.

"Who are they?"

"Well, that's Mrs. Longworth."

"And that one?"

"Mrs. Bennett Champ Clark. I don't know—oh, yes, the third one's Mrs. Taft, of course."

Alsop, making notes: Vivandières of isolationism.

The man from Minnesota, seeing the photographers on the ledge: "My God, they're coming out of the woodwork!"

*

❨ *The Administration will ignore him, and so will the Republicans in Congress.*—New Republic

The aim of the Roosevelt-Willkie-Bullitt combination is for a joint British-American war against the Soviet Union.—Daily Worker

We leave the barefoot boy of Elwood . . . as a barefaced fraud.—Chicago Tribune

*

A visitor from Kansas, who had waited since daybreak, keeps turning to the man beside him, saying, Very fine turnout, isn't it? The pale, intent eyes look at the crowd and back to the man beside him. This neighbor has a city pallor; he sits very still in his dark business clothes, watching the photographers, and turning as they do to the door. Bigger than I thought he'd be, the visitor remarks.

The crowded, used-up air. The man at the center table. His face has changed. His mask of openness is not there, he has thrown it away. What can possibly be under a mask of openness? This time, openness.

What did he say? asks the visitor.

Asked Senator George if he could smoke, his neighbor says. Woman, my other side, says his speech is still being copied.

Grace Grahn, at the Carlton, finishes the job. Copies ride into the huge room, and the reporters get the inked sheets.

Willkie looks at the room, gets his glasses out, and pulls his shoulders close, bending to the papers. In a calm voice, he states his most personal choice, broadened until he finds the range of his full audience, for the first time.

He declares and relates. In the press seats, a concentrated few men begin to grasp what is happening; they see his look, with certain pretensions stripped away, and the words arrive. The room, waiting, had been large and without space, ornate and mottled with a stupidity of marble facing. Columns that raise nothing, a shell of pillar painted around the room. Capitoline nudge; a distant hankering after Rome. Boredom of built-in Senators and Big Stick architecture.

Which the words supersede.

He speaks of the great alternatives before us.

The people can withdraw; build up defenses; become so vast a power no aggressor would dare to strike.

The trouble with the idea that we can withdraw into ourselves is this: it is too simple. There is no regard here for the way the world is actually built. We are this structure together; no map is a true picture, they have set colors and boundaries, a fixed notion of distance before us, and tried to teach us with that; no machine is a true picture, however geared. Nothing is true for us any more that allows mechanical or inhuman withdrawal to be shown us.

Great nations cannot isolate themselves. They are woven into the rest of the world.

The other choice is this: to recognize the interdependence, not only of men, but of ideas and principles.

To see the world alive, to know that an attack against liberty anywhere is a threat against liberty in another part. We have named beliefs loosely; when I say liberty, I mean that principle of which as a people we are made, I mean our commitment.

You have asked me to testify concerning this bill, he is saying —a bill further to promote the defense of the United States, and for other purposes.

Our strength is to make with others fighting for it an area of freedom.

We need to think of the immediate future, at work not for Britain, but *with* Britain in defense of an area of freedom. That is the only defense which declares us. The old empty fantasies of defense are only answers to threat. That kind of answering steps back and forgets, until you feel behind you for the last stage-set wall, with threat behind it and looking you in the face.

He follows this with proposals made in shocking clarity. This room is used to clouds of compromise. He lists weapons and availabilities. Now he is asking; the voice is justified, full of the last weeks' knowledge and faces. He looks at the faces of senators cramped with loathing. He sees a face open like a wall; the dense blue wash of sky, some hours away; their faces. It is about war, an interior voice makes satire, sliding on two sounds. I witness, he answers himself.

To be a united people.

The many work with the minority.

To iron out dispute.

To remove the fears of those alarmed in truth over the matter of power.

The Senators challenged.

No questions. No questions.

One voice in hatred, ringing the mikes like banjos:

THE SENATOR: You had already taken your position before you went abroad, had you not?

WILLKIE: I had made up my mind. I picked up the phone and called Hull. When I got through to him, I said I would like to go to England. I did not fly half way the world, roundabout, to advise this or any other committee.

SENATOR NYE: You said in September that the battle of America is a battle for liberty. You said it belonged at home. Do you still feel the same way?

WILLKIE: What are we doing today? Determining whether we will preserve ourselves.

SENATOR NYE: Was that what you meant at the time?

WILLKIE: What I have meant is an effective America.

SENATOR NYE: About the same time you did remark: "I believe we should keep out of war."

WILLKIE: Yes.

SENATOR NYE: These were your words: "We are being edged toward war by an administration careless in speech and in action. You may expect war by April, if Roosevelt is elected."

WILLKIE: You ask me whether or not I said that?

SENATOR NYE: Do you still agree that that might be the case?

WILLKIE: It might be. It was a bit of campaign oratory.

(*Laughter of visitors, relief of laughter.*)

I am very glad you read my speeches; the President said he did not.

(*Laughter.*)

SENATOR NYE: That is all.

A SENATOR: Mr. Willkie, a while ago you expressed your belief that with the United States England would prevail.

WILLKIE: Just a judgment.

THE SENATOR: Mean to say Germany can be conquered from the air?

*

❴ Speaking of *Willkie's treachery, Bertie McCormick is writing, he's Roosevelt's Charlie McCarthy. "I'm very willing to let Britain have whatever she needs, and I think she doesn't need anything."*

*

❴ From Oregon, the *Nachrichten:*
The man *Willkie reveals himself in an ever more disagreeable way . . . not only a rather shabby character but also a kind of fool.*
We German-Americans are ashamed of him.
WRITE TO YOUR CONGRESSMAN:
AMERICA'S FIRST LINE OF DEFENSE IS GERMANY

*

A SENATOR, to Willkie, among all the stir: Mr. President—
WILLKIE: Senator—you merely speak of what should have been. But in the push and murmur, out of clapping, the men for withdrawal scream at him: Didn't you attack Roosevelt? Don't you remember? Will you play into his hands? Don't you see what it is? Three months ago, God . . . Didn't you . . .
WILLKIE: Sure; sure I did; those are the words. Look. He was elected President. He is my president now. I expect to disagree with him whenever I please.

*

❴ *. . . to be one of the most undefeated Presidential losers*—
Christian Science Monitor

*

When he began to witness, it was not to a journey,
Nor the questions, nor the answers, nor fiery London.   Whole
For the first time in imagination, man in conflict
May tell, as he enters, that there is an entrance.
Fire never yet felled this man's pillar;
His bed is at home, where he knows it is.
Love weaves him in, love guards the locks, and love
Sends his eyes a bravery of language.
But the eyes of the man are the eyes of witness
He will never acknowledge the old polarities.
Question and answer carry the oppositions,
And success.   And defeat.
                              Now no one can declare
With any finality, The Day After The War.
He suddenly says, the open ways are sure,
The certain relationships are Offer and Give.
Even to see that fire
Allows me to witness.   Now I begin to name
The name of beginning and making, the first word.

*

WILLKIE goes on: I have made a lot of mistakes. All I try to do is,
  when I make a mistake, as soon as I discover it, to correct it.
Q. And what do you expect our way of life to be, after the present ordeal overseas?
WILLKIE: I cannot say surely that a way will survive. I will not
  speak of oceans. They are moments, whatever I used to insist.
  Democracy cannot live behind walls of oceans or weapons or
  wealth, or any withdrawal; it cannot live if it contracts and
  becomes negative. Here is our crisis, and I will not turn into a
  politician. People the world over are sick of politicians; every
  hut at every empty crossroads knows barter. We must leave
  our downfall trading; the barter of beliefs can bring us doom.

*

That night, the White House car left him in shadows like fur. Over his head of fur and tiredness, the double doors gleamed as he went in.

Three photographers rushing forward. Collectors of facts, his tired face, Pa Watson's uniform. Full dress for the reception.

The President and Mrs. Roosevelt, to the Army and Navy.

A civilian wheeled past. To the Oval Room.

He is the most civilian. The suit waiting until the uniforms. The outdated blue tie still saying WILLKIE.

When he comes out of the White House, fifteen reporters meet him, between the policeman and the laundry-sorting. What did you talk about? Is there to be a place for you in the administration? Did you make a complete report, I mean complete? He said he hoped you'd stay over—will you stay over?

WILLKIE: It was a very lively discussion. Don't talk about a job for me, boys. That's all. I'm going to the hotel now. New York tonight, I hope The Lincoln Day dinner tomorrow.

Then Rush County. What I want to do is get out and tramp around. Besides, there's something fairly shady going on—12 hogs stolen last week.

A statement? Yes, sure.

*

⟨ *A one-man circus.—Senator Hiram Johnson*
Opportunity is his.—Knickerbocker News
Self-sacrifice, courage.—N. Y. Sun
. . . of the first importance—Alsop and Kintner
*

The eyes of a child also making his statement; he comes to his own moments, wanting his warmth. He comes in without knocking, as he did before. We are this structure together. Down we are. We have to go up again. Who are you now?

Rang and rang, rang in a small boy's head.
Going through the same course: the meanings and knowings.
                    *

A child riding the stormy mane of noon
Sang to me past the cloud of the world:
Are you born?   Are you born?
The form of this hope is the law of all things,
Our foaming sun is the toy of that force.
Touch us alive, developing light!   Today,
Revealed over the mountains, every living eyes.

Child of the possible, who rides the hour
Of dream and process, lit by every fire.
Glittering blood of song, a man who changed
And hardly changed, only flickered, letting pass
A glint of time, showers of human meanings
Flashing upon us all : his story and his song.
The song of a child; the song of the cloud of the world,
Born, born, born.   Cloud became real,
                              and change,
The starry form of love.
                    *

ANOTHER DAY IN A FIELD OF PEACE
THE CHILD, PLAYING. THE CHILD
PREPARING FOR DAYTIME SLEEP

PAUL: Miss Lorence, until I get to be somebody else—big me—
    I'm Timmy Torin.
    My horse at home is not really a real horse.
    I told you that a time ago.   It is not true.
    I love to tell you things.   Some are real,
    Some are not, just fooling.

You don't mind?   I wouldn't, except that I'm older than you
and bigger than you and I can do it.   Big people do.
You know, I certainly do like Ropsie in that little, little skirt
with her fat legs out.
I'll take care of you, Miss Lorence.
Just tell you things sometimes,
Fooling.

*

The child wakes in the morning to enter a country
Where the rivers are striped with fire and the tigers
Say their word before they eat you, and the leaves cry out
And the stars are the parts of song.   They are music
And they stand clear in the blue and risen sky.
The tigers eat them and the child eats them.
Do birds eat stars?
They do.   And morning.   And all doorkeepers.

*

ANOTHER DAY. A GAME OF TOYS.
PAUL, TELLING THE GAME:

One Shall Be the Mother and One Shall Be the Father

The father shall shine. The father shall stand at home. Now
he shall go to work. Now war. Now the father has to wait.
Now the horse shall give him a ride. A hahaaaa.

One Shall Be Mad

Now let one be mad.   Which one shall be mad, the father
or the mother, the mother or the father?
No, the father.
What does he do when he is mad?   What shall he do?
The father is mad and what shall he do?

The father has to hit the mommy.
Then what does the mommy do?
The mommy pushes him off the table.
They have to go up again. Both of them.
Down they are. They have to walk.
They have to get up again.
Make believe.

One Shall Be the Baby

The baby is in the mountains, in the tall mountains.
You know the mountains? I went into my book.
You know my book of mountains. Ice, snow, far to fall.
I was the person who knows the way.
You must not stay in the mountains all night long.
There is a rope, and a man behind.
The mountains are bad.
They can make you dead in lots of ways.
They are prettier than a little hill, though,
Or a rose.
Very big, very pretty, and you can't understand them.
But the man and I went on and he fell.
He fell and fell because he was tired.
He fell in the holes in the snow, and he fell on the rocks, and
    he would be dead all ways but I held him on the rope and
    pulled him back. Safe.
I will tell you more, later on.

One Shall Be Paul and One Shall Be Hitler

In the closet is a man, a bad man.
Hitler shoots. He shoots me if I go there.
Would I shoot? I don't know how to shoot.
He shoots the whole house down.
Paul comes out now into the flat world.

It rains. It rains.
Hitler never lies down.   He shoots.
But Paul lies down.   And now Paul is asleep.
What is he dreaming?
He's dreaming that now Hitler isn't Hitler.   No more.
Hitler pushes up his feet like this.
He is the father.   Is he?
He pushes up his feet like the father.

What Shall All Four of Them Be?

Yes, now they are going to sleep.
It's night.   It's night.

A Dream of Night

He's dreaming.   He's dreaming about the day his father says,
   It's morning
And he has a little baby when he woke up.

Here the Game Ends

*

ANOTHER DAY. THE CHILDREN ARE ALL EATING

—This dinner is too rich for you, Paul.
—Do not say that is so. Anything like that. We are good and
rich.
—Baloney.
—Baloney is not a word, it is a thing. It is a meat.
Words still do tell about things.
The word says what is the thing.
It must be, or how would you know?
Baloney *is* a word, Tom.

—What?
—Oh! . . . You are too little for me.

When I drink milk I put my nose in it, way, and blow, foo, and it makes sprickles, fat.

*

—Oh, he *is* sweet. I do love him sometimes.
. . . Why must one love one's children?
Why does one love one's children?
Out of a sense of guilt at having given birth to them, I suppose.
We used to say constantly—all my friends in England and I—
Oh, how I hate my children.
Here you people never allow yourselves to say that.
Is it so bad to say? I do not see how people can help hating their children sometimes. It is natural.

(She has such a quaint European way of putting things at times, doesn't she? That remark about hating your children! Of course she's had a hard time but it's too bad she's so bitter.)

*

PAUL: The father dreams that he was hid in a tree
And she dreams she is washing the dishes.
She *is* washing the dishes
And she dreams that she's playing.   See?
A dream of houses.
MISS LORENCE: What was the dream that time?
PAUL: I don't know.
MISS LORENCE: About the little baby?
PAUL: That's a long dream.

*

How can you explain to children? It's not so hard to explain to them that there is a war, but how can you tell them that their father is in prison?

*

Now he plays with the other children.
The words recede.   He works through bitter things.
But the war did not stop when bitterness stopped.
His father came not.   And the guns went on.

*

Do you know what I play to be, in bed at night?
I play to be a little baby.   Do you know why?
People take care of little babies.
Of course they don't have as much fun as grownup people cause
  they are so little and can't walk or have knives or eat cake
  or anything, but they do get taken care of.
I used to want to grow up to be big.
That's what I used to play at night in bed.
But I'm going to grow up anyway.
So I don't think about that any more if it's going to be anyway.
I think about if I was a little baby.
I wouldn't have to do things I don't like to do,
Shot by a gun I would be dead
But I wouldn't know why about it,
Because babies are so little little that they don't *know* about
  things.
They are just small and eat and sleep and never have to worry.
So I play I am a baby and do not have to do things for myself
  or worry.

*

⟨ *Youth shapes its own destiny.*—Motto of the Hitler Youth.

*

Among our new-found powers.

*

ANOTHER DAY.
PAUL IN THE MOUNTAINS OF FANTASY.
PAUL TELLS HIS ADVENTURE:

I pulled him back.
Do you know, Miss Lorence, why we were there, in those cold
    dark mountains?   We were running away from a man, from
    Hitler.
He was going to hurt me and to hurt the man worse.
Hitler is a bad thing.   He is the worst thing in the world.
. . . I helped the man.   I did not let him fall.
I helped him with the rope.
Do you know who I was helping?
I was helping Fritzel, my father, to get away from that bad land
    to come here where Mommy and Ropsie and I are, where it
    is safe.
It is safe for a while.
It is more safe than it is in that bad land.
If you say anything or do anything that those people do not like
    they may kill you or hunt you and you do not even know why.
They kill you too if you are a Jew, even if you do not do *any*thing.
That is why I was taking my father away from that land.

. . . This is not true, Miss Lorence.
I just pretend.
I would like to do that.
But I was not really in the tall mountains,
I did not really bring my father here.
When I get bigger I must do this.
But I am too little now.
I used to think I could do anything, like this,

Anything I wanted to, but now I am older
And I know:
I am not old enough to do anything.
Children must wait to grow up.
But I wish that I could help my Fritzel
And there are other people who need to be helped.
It takes so long to grow.

*

—My toes feel like nothing they are so cold. Little sticks of
wood. They'll break off if I knock. What does a stick of wood
feel like, Miss Lorence?
    —Well, a live stick, pretty good I guess. Happy. Full of sap.
    —What is sap?
    —Sap in a tree is like blood in you.
    —You know a thing? About the blood in me . . .
Inside me it is all wet and blood and moving,
But outside so dry and careful.
All the time people are asleep or awake
Their inside is there doing things. Did you know that?
Your insides never stops.
The blood is always there and all inside it is moving
And it is blood and it is never stopping.
So funny, all wet inside and all dry outside.
Everybody like that. I am.
Why, Miss Lorence, you are.
I wonder what you look like inside. Did you ever think about it?
    —People look pretty much alike inside. I could show you a
picture, a drawing . . .
    —A picture that would be for you would be for me too?
    —Yes.
    —Then we are alike, you and me are alike?
    —Yes, but so are most people alike.
    —But their outsides is different. You and me don't *look* alike.

—No, but inside of you is like inside of me, only you are a little smaller.

—But I am a boy and you are a girl.

—Yes, some things are different in boys and girls, but lots of things are just alike.

—*Well*. But why don't people look alike outside?

—Some people look like their mothers, Paul. I do. Or a mother and father mixed, nose like one, eyes like the other. Or a father.

—It is very hard for me to think that you have a father and a mother. Where are they? Are they around here?

—No, they both are dead.

—Oh, in the war?

—No, they just died.

—Well, you don't need any now. You're all big enough to take care of yourself. I'll take care of you, Miss Lorence.—But don't you think it's funny about people's blood being inside their skin? And your insides.

—Yes.

—Are you sure your mother and father were not in the war?

—No, they really weren't.

—Did no blood come out?

—No. They just died quietly.

—In the war there is a lot lot of blood, and people hurt and hurt and die . . . It is too bad that there are children dead who can never never get old.

—It would be too bad not to grow up.

—Yes, lots of fun being grownup. You have to do some things you don't like, though, and nobody takes care of you.

—Would you like somebody to take care of you?

—I can do it pretty well. You come live with me. You can sleep in my bed. My mommy will take care of you. Or maybe I could come live with you . . .

But it doesn't matter where you live or what you do, you still have your insides.

*

He turned cruel. Absorbed in his own cruelty, he drove the children, drove them by will, goading their wills, manipulating everything they began to do. He turned into a dark leader, small and ferocious.

And they were fascinated. They followed. He drove them as if with whips into a dance; and they ran, dancing and hypnotized.

He was full of hatred. He was in torment, hating and defying his grownups, goading his generation to frenzy.

For a while, for a short while, it was full cruelty. Assailed he was, with danger over his life-space. Fretful he was, restless and stern, the artificial boasting king. Loud and unreal to himself, with all his conflict packed for him to carry, and the admiring, the pity of the adults, out of reach.

But at the moment at which the grownups would have stopped it, at the moment when the five-year-olds would have turned on Paul, it was as if he remembered. He was on his journey, he was moving toward his world. The long exchange with Miss Lorence —her cheek bent over him as he lay himself down, her short soft questions, the open feeling of her answers, came back to him like Eden. It had always been there. And his own people, the five-year-olds! He remembered the other life: communication.

He turned back to his own group with his whole life in his act of choice.

✻

ANOTHER DAY
FOR A MOMENT SLIPPING BACK,
AGAIN THE UNREAL KING

Let's throw it. Let's throw ice at her face . . .
You should throw back!
You should *hurt* me, Miss Lorence, not just stand there and laugh.

Why do you let me hurt you?
You hurt *too.*

                                    She throws the snowball.
He howls, the howling biting, the biting sobbing, the sobbing thrown down in a snowdrift.

MISS LORENCE: Shall I go?

PAUL: I hate you. I hate you.
  No, no, you mustn't go.
  I need you. Stay here. Why did you hurt me?

MISS LORENCE: But I didn't really. . . . You know . . . And
  besides . . . why did you cry?

PAUL: You wanted to hurt me. You threw snow at me.
  You were not my friend.

MISS LORENCE: But you asked me to throw snow. You cried when
  I didn't.

PAUL: I didn't really want you to.

MISS LORENCE: Then why did you ask me to?

PAUL: I wanted to hurt you
  So you should hurt me;
  But I didn't really want you to.

MISS LORENCE: I'm sorry I hurt you. I didn't want to.
  I was just playing your game with you.

PAUL: It was not a game.

MISS LORENCE: You really wanted to hurt me?

PAUL: Yes. But not really.
  Often I hate you, but I love you too.
  I want to hurt you, but I don't want you to be hurt.
  (He takes her hand and clings, for the first time in weeks.
  Sighs and gets up.)

PAUL: Well, I guess I could go upstairs now.

  He was soft and quiet all that day. School went on. He painted his pictures and modeled in clay. He was very still, but not dependent.

                       *

The sky is a tree.   It spreads . . .
I fly on the shiny hills to a bear's house . . .
My clock is magic.
I dreamed about the zero
And about Elizabeth
And about Miss Davison.
I dreamed about the mat . . . the doorbell, the whole, whole,
     whole, whole, whole, Miss Lorence . . . the world, the
     world.

*

ANOTHER DAY

Day lilies, yellow daisies, Queen Anne's lace. A barrel, a box of
sand, a bucket of water. There is a child. He looks up into the
young woman's eyes, and away down the path.

Toward him is walking a broad tall man, broader than the
bear, smiling and blue-eyed. Willkie is walking between two girls
in their clear summer colors, on his way up the college hill. He
sees the little knotted boy, and the young woman, dark, in her
dress of the most deep rose, color of inner petals.

He smiles at the girl and the child. They look up at him, their
faces lit from everywhere.

The child goes on playing in the sandbox.

The man stops. Did you want to speak to me? he says,
abruptly.

Yes, says the girl. Did you believe what you said in your
speech?

That's right, he says.

Maybe there should be other words for these things, says the
girl, half smiling.

The students watch his face. I'll tell you, he says heavily, I
never have held with those who blame our troubles on words.

But you used to say things that were—slightly different. Didn't you?

I guess I am—slightly different, by now, he says. But I still like people to disagree with me.

What a pity, she answers, and her smile opens to him. This time, I've been agreeing.

I'd like to talk to you more about this, he says. Later?

Perhaps later.

Fine boy, says Willkie. Although, for him, the child is too thin and pointed, his haircut outlandish, his look not really direct. Your brother?

He's my friend Paul, says the girl, touching the child's arm. A gleam passes over the shallow-featured face.

Where do you come from? the child asks Willkie. He speaks very quickly, with a curious, aggressive charm, like a trace of accent.

Indiana. And just now England.

Indiana? What country is that?

America. The U.S.A. Right in the middle of it. He recognizes suddenly: the child's a refugee, of course. But all my people came from Germany.

Mine too; yes, Miss Lorence? says the child. And through England, too. Yours . . . why did they come here? he asks the man.

Partly to come away from there; mostly to live here.

Oh, says the boy. He is finished talking. He looks down at the sand, and picks up the bucket of water. In a curve of motion, he pours out the water, brilliant under sunlight, upon the yellow sand. Willkie looks down. The water is traveling over; the sight hits him with a shock like pain; as if his heart were turning against him and attacking.

The sand, with the streams running through it, is striking his sight with the shape of a tree of rivers. Gullies, branches, the widened valleys down. Glinting on water. The shadows beside the grains, in his clear sudden sight. Ground coming up, and his sight, swinging through the precise air, until he looks down again at the sand. He sees it as a field under his fall when he fell with a parachute, a long time ago; he sees it as a bowl of food, a small boy staring down at the creases of a landscape, hills, juices, and islands where a small strange child is playing. Waiting before him, strong and running bright. As a bowl of food; as the earth seen far-off; as sand in a box; brown branches traced wet in a strong symbol, where a child plays, pouring out his summer.

*

STATEMENT BY WILLKIE
AFTER RETURNING FROM ENGLAND

It is not only the present that is at stake.
Somewhere in this confusing world we must find—we must build
    —a future for ourselves.
We must now have courage, bravely to do the things that we
    know ought to be done.
And we must lay the foundations for the world of the children.
That world cannot be a closed system.
It must be an open system.
It must be a world in which we share the responsibilities. They
    are many, but they lead to the great prospect—of peace.

PART NINE Leaf

(LINCOLN *was a boy like yours. . . . You never know. . . .*
Have his photograph taken now for as little as $1. (Advt.)
*

(*Your home may be a diamond mine! Are you sure you don't*
have any outmoded jewelry around? Look again! (Advt.)
                                                    Feb. 12, 1941
            *

Among the ways of reaching power: in storm, in whirlwind,
in the cross-rule of state; or the song of unspoken journeying, a
girl lying in the grass of a park. Or cities burning like ships in the
linking night of waves and fire.
            *

(*Even the Toronto press approved of the Willkies. He took*
Canada by storm. He called England our motherland, and

221

smoothed over everything. *He is Roosevelt's official left-hand man.*

*

He has gone into private practice; the law firm is Willkie, Owen, Otis, and Bailey. He picked an outfit that wanted him before he was a candidate, that will give him independence of action on his own terms. Nothing stuffy here, he says, smiling. He is no longer an executive, sweetening loans; he is a lawyer, retained to defend the motion picture industry, accused of producing "war propaganda."

*

During the journey there come moments of waking
When you will find, growing among your dream,
A sense of light.   The setting constellation
Has gone far under while you fade in, fade out,
On the threshold of the recognizable.

Again, far off your road!   But showers of fire
Burst in your body; now you can remember as
If for the first time the other waking that
Spoke one word to you.   Daybreak.   The
Actual day.

*

Century of absence. It could be a time when the soul leaps from its priests: spring, when the old freshness is at last available to all children, and God in the morning is on the lips of love. Not out of the dried blood raining from planes, death given away and very expensive, the spikes or revenge on the cross, on the star, broken crescent and spiral-blown mandala. The solitude of Spain, the solitude or Stalingrad, and now your solitude, America, singing in Indiana through the golden-rain tree, through the iris, through the sycamore, white on the banks of these running streams.

*

A LUNCH AT THE WHITE HOUSE

Willkie and Roosevelt had lunch together in July. After their hour of talk, Roosevelt told Willkie that he had been advised to call in the most skilled psychiatrists in the country, to work with him on influencing public opinion.

Willkie grinned. "Have you heard, Mr. President, about the first meeting of your fifth cousin—Teddy Roosevelt—and Albert Lasker, the advertising man?"

Roosevelt had not.

"Lasker waited in the study at Oyster Bay. Suddenly T.R. burst in: 'Mr. Lasker,' he said, 'I've been told that you have the master advertising mind in the country.' Lasker answered, 'It would be presumptuous for anyone to claim that in your presence.'

"So, Mr. President—I think it would be presumptuous for any psychiatrist to tell you how to influence public opinion."

*

A dark regard is floating down the rivers, along the shores, watching the dreams of the little children turned loose on this countryside. Long plains and seasons away, in China, a mother goes crying, "Where are you playing? Come back home," holding up her dead child's clothes. Little square blue clothes. Wide-swept, the countryside is tortured. Enemy engineers arrive with a new machine that can rip up railroad track. The dark regard moves down the river Dnieper, to the pride of wall, the Dnieper Dam.

These grasslands, this black earth, crystalline rocks of the land-shield. At the river border, yellow of day lily and the reedgrass; farther, the yellow steppes. Larch, elm, birches, in the clear, warm weather. Fall, the time of forest fires, under a bluish lower horizon.

*

Child of the root, among your apples and forests,
I see a bird whose gaze and claws are fire
Fasten upon you. In your shape of becoming,
You and your bird change to a stream of water
Through whom light pours, to the present breaking its banks.
A pride of making, that can destroy its objects.
Looking ahead, to a distant point,
Creation unbegun.

*

¶ *This is the great sin, the refusal to create.*

*

Now these people come to their power. They will stop the outer enemy, they will arrive at the inner enemy: in a summoning up of all their agonies and joy, they blow up their dam.

Torn, twisted, the floods roar down. River, river. Seventy feet of water lowers upon this war. Old rapids in the Dnieper reappear. The tears and torments; a child hurrying through a wild field of this world, lost in his own strength that is about to be born.

Roaring too loud for the skin of man.

Roaring ouroboros, heard in the cells of bone, the chambers of imagery; raging down on the course of the river, noises driven by storm deep in the body of man. Blindness and lifting of blindness in the smoke. Command of thunder. The lightning of human power, linked, striking in chain lightning across the

river. Inexorable light, law looking from the eye of light into
our faces.

Not leaves, not lightning, not that greatness of rivers.
The hand and spirit volunteer.
We think to build again, finer nor before.

The water-spiral turns the fire
Broken upon the miles of air,
Leaps through our furnaces of change
To make and make.

The great sun pours his power down.

*

⟪ *Water power is really a form of sun power.*

*

⟪ *The Hays Office was in favor of playing down the notion that
any motion picture had ever contained any idea at all; it urged
the industry to lie low and wait for the storm to blow over.
Willkie sat up night after night with Hollywood tycoons before
they were to testify, building up their morale, urging them to
stand up and simply tell the story of their lives.*

*

⟪ *It is the Jews who have been trying to make America punch
drunk . . . I myself am not anti-Semitic.*

*

When Clark suggested the remedy—require the companies to
present both sides—Willkie said, This, I presume, means that
since Chaplin made a laughable caricature of Hitler, the industry should be forced to employ Charles Laughton to do the same
on Winston Churchill.

*

A sound of screaming for thirteen centuries.
Look at the clock.   It has never moved.
A sound of weeping for the generations.
Open your eyes.   Monday morning.
In all the cities they are telling fortunes
According to patterns flown by the bombing planes,
And the shape of the Leader's genitals.

Bird-voice in darkness.   Tremor of day moving.
The rocks accept brightness, now we imagine trees,
Across the crystals of time forming, suddenly
Feel the flaw of cold breeze following bird-voices.
The river remade, the invitation of water
Flowing down toward the heart of my beloved.

A small man walks, thin cane, clown's feet of grace,
Imagining in cold air down Charlie Street.

*

([*Willkie: Now I am sick of fenagling.*

Oct. 3, 1941

*

His red face changing color, the Senator from Kansas bleated
from the House floor: "Could a few handshakes with dukes and
earls change the ideas of Willkie? He has asked for the repeal
of neutrality, and the Republicans have split. He has talked over
and above the politicians."

NOT FOR ATTRIBUTION

MC NARY: Shit. That's not going to change a damn vote in
   Congress.
DANAHER: It wasn't a coincidence that Willkie visited the White

House, then went to London with three photographers and a press agent. Figure it out.

Taft objects to his dragging the Party in. But he and Brewster both believe it would be a good thing for the U.S. to go in there and clean up Japan right now. It wouldn't take too long or too much.

BREWSTER: We ought to settle them right away. We know we may have to fight Hitler ultimately, and that if we do, the Japanese will be right on us at the same time.

GALE: Yes; I support that view as a cheap investment for the U.S.—a war to crush Japan at once.

GALE AND BREWSTER: It ought to be a surprise attack—we ought to give the Japs a dose of Hitler's medicine.

RAYBURN: God damn it, let a Republican put the Republicans on the spot.

*

⟨[*Willkie Offered Administration Post; Refuses.*

*

⟨[*Indiana Republicans Bolt Willkie.*

*

⟨[*Michigan Republicans hope Willkie gets hit by something no smaller than a streetcar.*

*

Dewey Short: He is a bellicose, belligerent, bombastic blow-hard.

Joe Martin (off the record): There are times when I wish I was a dictator!

*

Saturday morning in New York. Willkie's desk, and on the side, the tower of papers he has been wanting to read all week.

Frost in the salty harbor air. Flakes of paper, with the shouts of
Betrayal on them. If anyone betrays them, it is not I, he thinks;
and it is almost time for the rain of fire. If I betray anyone, he
thinks in illumination, it is myself, forgetting, fading in and
fading out on my real. Was there a cry? He is remembering.
Recalling London in the giant cry, the raid sirens and the hum
of planes, while in the House of Commons where he sits, he
hears the Member attack the government for suppressing the
Communist newspaper.

He holds this brief in his hand, and the letter from Carol
King, that driven woman, stormy-haired, acute, compassionate,
like his mother a lawyer and driven. Yes, he thinks, I will defend
this man in the Supreme Court: Schneiderman, the Communist whose citizenship they have been trying to take away.

I will speak; there is something I must speak for. There are
things I must speak to: myself and the unknown world.

No fee.

*

(Willkie, whose friends advise him not to take this case, writes
to Bart Crum: I am sure I am right in representing Schneiderman; of all the times when civil liberties should be defended, it
is now.

Dec. 3, 1941

*

Sunday, just after lunch, in Washington. Roosevelt at his
desk, wearing his son's old sweater, about to do stamps. He is
talking to Harry Hopkins. The phone rings. The operator apolo-
gizes, but it is Secretary of the Navy Knox, insisting on being put
through. Roosevelt says, "Put him on. Hello, Frank."

KNOX: Mr. President, it looks as if the Japanese have attacked
Pearl Harbor.

ROOSEVELT: No!
For eighteen minutes, he is silent.

*

⟨ At 2:05, Roosevelt calls Hull. The war is on.

*

Churchill, on the phone from Chequers. Winant and Harriman are with him; they have been listening to the radio.
CHURCHILL: Mr. President, what's this about Japan?
ROOSEVELT: It's quite true. They have attacked us at Pearl Harbor. We are all in the same boat now.
My American friends wasted no words in sorrow, Churchill
said afterward. In fact, one might almost have thought they had
been delivered from a long pain.

*

The argument one hears is: does the end justify the means?
There is no end. There are only means.

*

Roosevelt, writing: "Yesterday, December 7, 1941—a date
which will live in world history. . . ." He crosses out "world
history" and writes "infamy."
Roosevelt, writing: "Long will we remember . . ." crosses
out, and writes, "Always will we remember."
Roosevelt, writing: "I speak the will of the Congress and of
the people. . . ." He crosses out "I speak" and writes, "I believe
I interpret the will of the Congress and of the people. . . ."

*

Willkie, on the phone: I hope for a flying trip to Singapore,
Chungking, possibly Manila. Or Africa, say. What for? Well,
more or less in the spirit of adventure. I'd give anything to go.

*

He is closer to power now, closer to speech, and again he becomes unreal to himself. In his own system, he can speak for
the anonymous. Without status he has the status of those who
do speak, directly, to many lives. The anonymous farmer, the
organizer of responses, the actor in the myth, the woman speaking to one life at a time. But he becomes unreal to himself in
the grip of the appetite for power.

Fading out.

From the fight ring, he broadcasts during the Joe Louis–
Buddy Baer match. I know what it's like to be up against a
champion, he says, and the crowd roars. But then he says *Looey*
by mistake and *Max* by mistake for Baer; speaking without
notes, without mind, his driven will takes over, and he speaks
out of will and ignorance. And then he says we are fighting to
"see American democracy ruling the world after the war."

*

([*He wound up with a statement which may disrupt the allies.*

*

([*It was an evening of fox passes.*

*

A DAY IN WASHINGTON

In the winter weeks, sailing zigzag across the Atlantic, cursing the blueness of the sky and all fair weather in wartime,
Churchill made his secret voyage on the *Duke of York*. All that
month, news of sinkings. After Florida and sun, to snowy Washington he came.

Just as Willkie was about to drive over to the White House
from his hotel, Frances Perkins called with word of the President's plan. Roosevelt would talk to him about it in a few

minutes, she said. Willkie was also hoping to have his speech cleared well ahead of the Mayors' Conference that evening.

But Roosevelt spoke only of the farm problem, playing Willkie along, as he did; and of rising costs. What do you expect, said Willkie, if you let the national economy be operated like a grab bag?

It was time to see Churchill. In a secretive way—or am I making this up? thought Willkie—they went down the hall. As they turned in to Churchill's room (the little room he had taken to be on the same floor), Roosevelt said, Oh, by the way, I am putting your name on a labor panel with Charles Evans Hughes. . . . Hello, Winston.

Willkie stood there: he felt his tongue was hanging out. He was burned up; and he didn't want to speak before Churchill. What was Roosevelt saying? That they'd been going over the farm problem.

I wouldn't have anything to do with such things, old man, said Churchill. I let Attlee worry about things like that. You'll kill yourself yet, worrying about such things.

Roosevelt turned and pushed his wheelchair down the hall, leaving the two alone.

The Far East is as good as gone, said Churchill. Britain expects, he said, to lose Malaya down to Singapore. The rest are all dead bunnies—all but Australia, and it would be a good idea if you'd go there. Accept that invitation you have.

The only mistake Japan has made, said Churchill, is Pearl Harbor. As for Hitler, he underestimated Russian opposition— it isn't that he hasn't the *strength* to beat Russia. But of course the cold, that ultimate general.

And my speech to the Mayors' Conference tonight? said Willkie. It's my duty, as I see it, to point out weaknesses.

I think I understand your duty, said Churchill. But where are we going to get sixty thousand pilots?

It was to Pa Watson, at the White House door, that Willkie

blew up. I'm forty-nine years old, he said, and I'm still active!
I don't want to spend all my time sitting around listening to a
bunch of old men disputing; give me something tougher to do if
I am to do something.

Certainly, certainly, said Pa Watson, singing his little tune.
And then waving to the columns: there are reporters waiting.
In the snow.

On the way back to the hotel, he saw the headlines. His
speech to the Mayors was all a call against the lack of a chief
for American production. The evening papers carried the news:
Nelson had been appointed, to precisely that post. And at the
hotel, as he began to rewrite his speech, which now was cleared,
the phone rang. It was Steve Early, telling why the papers
carried word of Willkie's appointment to that panel. I'm sorry,
he said, but I gave the story out while you were with Churchill.
I had no idea you would mind.

*

The water-hammer, the history of ice,
The rising water and the entrapped air.
Drift-pinned, drift-bolted, the rage beats at the gates,
The crest gates and the wheeled gates' seals give way.
When the forces pass the limits of the dam,
There is pure overturning.   In height, in fetch,
The waves increase, the floors of galleries
Give way.   The roots of the forest trees open a path,
Open, in bedrock, seams.   Scarring and scouring, now
Flood-flow and future floods begin to shine.

*

A SPEECH TO THE MAYORS

Now he begins to speak, real to himself again. After long rage,
fade in.

All of you, I believe, have been elected to public office. I cannot say the same, although I assure you it was not for the lack of trying . . .

This war, he says, goes to the very roots of human relations.

We cannot, he says, seal ourselves against the world.

We are fighting not only armies but ideas.

Fascism, he says, is the duty of the people to do as they are told. It has appealing features: especially, to our people, the efficiency with which it seems to operate.

To free minds, there are things more important in civilized life than efficiency.

But, under threat, we must make ourselves function efficiently. We cannot be saved by the armies of Russia.

The future demands of us . . .

*

In a story, in a song, a stroke of bright green color, the smile of a young girl, heat is brought to our history. The sound of a father's slap, fierce on the face. She is running down the street; she runs into the park of forgetting; she falls down, and there she will be found.

Bells of the threshold; the trumpets of return.
Rang and rang, rang in a young girl's head.
Going through our own course : the meanings and knowings.

*

THE FUTURE DEMANDS OF US . . .

There is a girl in America reaching her powers. This is the threshold that is not celebrated; but she celebrates. One tribe will separate the girl for a while, and then introduce her all over again to the whole tribe that is, to the world of her puberty. We have this notion officially only in our official ideas of death and rebirth. But this threshold has to do with death only as the seed dies and is reborn. It is a passage in the journey, a doorway that often is hardly mentioned.

When Venus is enormous, the morning star; when the mothers fade and reappear; there is a song sung which the boys pretend not to understand. But everyone understands. Everyone knows it all. They have only to notice that they do.

The little bird is singing. Deep in the forest, we all can hear the singing of the bird.

She left home that morning without eating her breakfast. She hated the sounds of their quarreling, and she walked out. They thought she was going straight to school.

They found her in Central Park, eleven miles from home. She was lying face down beside the road, and her shoes were completely worn out. The police were notified that Jennie was found; they came, and took her to the hospital. She was unable to answer the questions as she entered; unable even to answer the first question: Name?

Now, for four days, they take her to another hospital. The building is new, the procedures specialized. A man and woman are brought into the room where she is sitting. They look at her with brown beseeching eyes. She is told that they are her parents. "Yes, I accept them as my parents," she said. "You say they are, so it seems the proper thing to do."

Physical Status. Tests and Results.
Electrocardiogram: normal rhythm rate (80 per minute)
Wassermann: negative
Basal metabolism: within normal limits
Urinalysis: negative
Chest X-Ray: chest normal
Blood: chemistry, normal; count, normal
Electroencephalogram: immature?

Skull X-Ray: skull normal
Well nourished. White. Fifteen years old
No evidence of any pathology

Mental Status. Tests and Results.
Attitude, general behavior: Excellent
Stream of mental activity: normal
Relation of events prior to illness: none, unable
Relation of recent events: clear, concise
Emotional reaction, affect, mood: normal
Sensorium: good
Mental trend: normal
General knowledge: fair
School knowledge: fair
Intelligence: average for her age, lowered by amnesia
Blame of present condition: patient blames her conflict over her
      parents' super-severity
Judgment: good
Insight: good

On the sixteenth day, sodium amytal. After less than 1 grain, administered intravenously, she threw herself on the floor; she cried. She expressed her feelings toward her parents for the first time. I don't want to go home, she said in her crying. Why should I go home? I was never allowed to do anything that I wanted to when I was there.

—Jennie, you must be careful. Don't let boys come too near you.

—Jennie, be ladylike.

—Sit on the children's side when you go to a movie. The matron will tell me if you're not there.

—Be home by eight-thirty, Jennie.

Perhaps if we hypnotize her? But she says, How can you hypnotize me when I'm seething inside?

Do you want to go home for the weekend, Jennie?

—No. Not really.

After seven weeks: But I do love my father.

Before the drawing board. She picks up the black chalk, and the paper spurts, a rain of black; a terra-cotta ground, with curving black over it. *The name of this picture is VILE.*

. . . I went home a couple of weeks ago. Saturday night, I came home from a party with a boy friend of mine, he's from the hospital and it was three in the morning.

My father was standing in the street. Waiting for me.

He slapped me in the face.

First, I was upset, embarrassed before my friend. I sent him away and I went in that house.

Then when we got inside, I saw the room again. I screamed and screamed; the neighbors heard.

Now I want the black crayon again.

Now the orange, that orange-red.

I'm happy with my mother when she is not with my father, and yet I hate my father and love my mother. Or is it the other way around? . . .

Very slowly, the forms emerge. When her friend puts his arm around her, she feels like screaming, she loses her interest in jazz. But, a month later, she comes into the room where the chalks are: I'm feeling wonderful, she says, and draws the picture of it, the rainbow and the seasons, the many lights blossoming on the star-tree, the snow-tree, the flowery, the green, the dark. Her image, now arrived, the world flowering and identified.

*

⟨ *All is leaf. This simplicity makes possible the greatest diversity.*

*

Time, moving the man along. The journey where he moves. Now a movie company. Is he chairman of the board? A political

PART TEN Journey

It is a perfectly simple thing, this going around the world.

We live in an advanced civilization.

Each of us knows someone who has done it.

Here he is, taking off. But the journey is already begun.

On the nose of the *Gulliver*, a huge four-engine transport, they have painted the name in English and Russian, and—since nobody can imagine the Chinese for it—the characters meaning High Level Man.

He crossed to the steps, turned and waved once more. The *Gulliver* takes off from Mitchell Field.

After the plane had disappeared, the reporters begin to fill in. Two "salesmen" of democracy have been sent out, they said, Nelson Rockefeller to South America, and Willkie on the longer, tougher route. Roosevelt has coached them, outlining their work, and his farewell to Willkie was:

(| Cairo may have fallen by the time you get there.

*

This is the end of August, hot, dusty, defeated. In Africa, Rommel is close and advancing full speed on Alexandria. The Russian soldiers are holding Stalingrad, always over their shoulders the image of a falling wall. America is the arsenal; however, not one plane has yet come out of Willow Run. To soldiers, time is an enemy.

Fliers' time is no friend. At the Cairo airport the officials are waiting. The plane is two days late, and an hour after that. Two hours. Quickly the *Gulliver* flies its pattern in, and the big man himself steps out. There is a strong sense of relief in seeing him, the familiar trademark of his rumpled business suit, looking transplanted in the ferocious sunlight. Light gives the blue cloth deep black creases, like creased metal; light punches the sunken rivet-heads of the door, and his sun-helmet. On the Americans, he has the quick curious effect he has always at his best. He fixes something; the jagged long wait, and the crucial unrest of the city dissolve.

At Shepheard's, he heard the rumors. By the next afternoon he wants to talk. He is armed; what he gives them was what he likes to give: production figures, exactly how many planes, and how many tanks a month. He is fresh and combed and pressed now, and he is wearing his colors. He smiles for the cameras and everyone, and his blue eyes, his blue socks, blue of his tie. There he stands, jabbing at Nahas Pasha and talking in ten thousands, jabbing the silk of the Prime Minister's morning coat to drive his point home as they laugh together.

Everyone stands around, the jeeps sinking into the dry sand. Who's with him? Gardner Cowles, Joseph Barnes—ask them about the letters Roosevelt has given Willkie. Are they introductions, or power to act? Ask Captain Pihl, his brother-in-law, or Major Mason, or Kight. No. no one will talk, the censors are not letting go, all anybody knows is the index finger jabbing and jabbing, making the production curves follow it up. Today, the Middle West.

*

⟨ *Willkie in the desert, saying: I've come to the Middle East for a definite purpose. As a member of the Opposition Party, I wanted to show by my presence and by what I say that there is no division in America on the question of winning the war and establishing a just peace. On this question the United States is completely united.*

*

In khaki shirt and slacks, he goes to Montgomery, feeling soft and out of training beside that keen fanatical general. Montgomery has word for him of El Alamein, where Rommel has repeated his method and been stopped at last. Willkie goes out to the plateau, and in the sand, among the swarms of flies, touches the burned-out tanks of that battle. Under the German bombers he sees the front for the first time since London.

A plane spirals downward in flames. The parachute opens, and the pilot floats over him, carried by south winds past the edge of the tanks: All with their tails up, Willkie says, and louder, I just want to say I'm damned glad to see you. God bless you and give 'em hell.

Among the flies and sand he thinks of the mud of France, in the other war. When Montgomery speaks of the Americans, he says, "I liked them for saying they wanted to get home. If they had said anything else, they'd have been liars."

And before he leaves, Willkie tells Farouk what the front signifies. As far as the Nazis go, the glory days are ending. Their high tide is reached—he says, feeling a little embarrassed by his warlike rhetoric—and shortly it will recede.

There is a magazine editor in Cairo who has seen Willkie all through the campaign. After a week, in a different plane—a big, drab, special B24—the editor, watching from the field, exclaimed: Not a single rear-platform speech!

*

Deep in the century of opposites,
The myth of mission is the tourist's dream.
He will fly over the zebra-colored cliffs,
Carrying letters, he lands within a war.

He is the big enigma and mask of power.
The fluid desert war and the sea—hieroglyphs
Holding him while he swims with General Fever
Are the response and law of Africa.

This is the threshold : Spain and Carthage lie
Over the ocean, but he goes otherwhere.
In meteor noon, each flaming with its star
The shifting and the warring pyramids.

Egypt is saved, the general said again.
He cannot dream the double fantasy
All that the battle has sent us from its fire:
The film whose heroes are war and the enemy
The poem in the soldier's Highland tongue:
Worse than all Rommel's guns, that my young darling should
     prove false and a liar.

*

He left in a B24. In Palestine he transferred to a Douglas DC3 with Pan-American Airways lettered carefully on so that the neutrality of the Turks would not be compromised.

Now in the dazzle of the airdrome, he shakes hands with the honor guard, and asks where they come from. Ohio, says one, New Jersey, California, Virginia, Oklahoma, Texas, Alabama, New York.

No one from Indiana? he asks. Brereton says, Sorry, Mr. Willkie. All the Indiana boys are in the guardhouse.

Ankara has an ancient city, and a new. There are the wild smells of old streets, and the glass, shine and mat concrete surfaces of buildings going up. The reporters, whose cynicism cannot be outdone, even by the diplomats of a neutral country, even by American politicians in election year, bet on what powers Willkie has. He is trying to sell the United Nations, they feel, and the people here are trying to sell themselves to him.

In the plane, he has been cramming, reading material that his office in New York has prepared for him about each country he will see. Books are stacked against the wall of the plane: Gunther, Michie. He played rummy as far as Cairo, but once he has tasted the red dust here and smelled the fever smell of the margin of war, he has gone back to the notes and the books.

At the press conference he talks about victory. At the party for him the first night in Ankara, he meets the diplomat with the three platinum ribs. Reporters and officials both flatter him, but even behind his back, they say he is unified. Listen to him now, they are saying. No recriminations.

Beside him at dinner sits a dark, confident woman, with a control of manner which is subtle when it is most direct. She is one of Turkey's most active lawyers. He feels the quickness and excitement of a woman in the first years of chance in her own country. There were moments when his mother felt that in Elwood, that sense of striking out without a word to draw on from any woman, since no woman had ever gone this way before her, in her scene; she knows the exultation that is followed in a minute by a reminder, full of pliancy, that this conquest is in character, that the cutting edge of pride and excitement is part of the life of a woman. These women are always about newness, pride, and the value of the arrangement. This fine skillful woman knows that her value may be in the arrangement itself, the way she finds her solution. That may indeed be the solution.

Driving in the country the next day, it is through her eyes he sees the children learning their antique dances, and the machines just brought in from abroad. Wheat, they say to each other, peacemaking, this knot of diplomats; and he turns to her: Look at it all with me. Over the ocean I read my sheets of basic material and my textbooks. But the first sight of the yellow angles of these cities; the glimpses of burned-out tanks like milestones masked, the crowding of the world with everything distant to me. . . . What he is saying is broken.

You are strange to everyone here, she says. We see the freaks of compromise every day, men and spies who will do anything for advantage. And how are they to know what their advantage is? You look to us. . . . No, I cannot, she says.

Yes, this is the necessary thing. I need to hear what you are going to say, he tells her.

You look, then, to us, she goes on, like the success of the West. The large, effective man, with powers no one may guess, flown around the world in the most wealthy style.

He smiles and looks out of the war window at the young trees. That is the businessman's look: everywhere in the world, shall I be the man who made millions for a power company (no matter what happened to the C. & S. stockholders), the leader of the opposition (no matter that I am not anywhere in the government)? But part of that look was not to declare oneself, at any frontier.

Then I find it is better than that, she is saying. You are no more than at the beginning of your miles. You will see the places. And if you are undermined now, in any way—although I assure you nobody you do not tell can suspect—perhaps we all stand a chance. Whatever powers you have! And perhaps you stand a chance, too.

What chance would that be? he asks.

But that I do not know. It is so seldom that the Americans

see, I think. Whatever they are like in their own country, I think they—you—can be very curious when your feet are moving. Or even when your plane is moving.

I don't know that I'm curious, he said, smiling at her. I look like anyone else. In Indiana, that is.

It is not only that the street-people open up before you, saying "Big," she tells him. It is this American thing that I think will be so hard for you to do and so murderous unless you do it. Because you feel suddenly to us like not a new country at all, like something, in your phrase, about the dead hand of power. And, one by one, your countrymen and your women are going to have to communicate somehow with all the rest of us through that. And it has not started.

Part of that I go along with. But I am on this trip mostly to see.

Ah, the eye, she says.

The eye. That's exactly it. I know what I can say to your people about production, and about victory. But under that, as you say—

All the assumptions are there.

And my assumptions are something else, is that it? All right. And what can the eye do here? What can the eye do?

One of your writers made a proverb, she says to him—about the bells, which call the congregation to pray, but cannot themselves go in. That is very beautiful, at first glance; and I am sure it reminds everyone of some grace he cannot reach. But, if you look at it, you see the nonsense: what a silliness, to think of the bells as separate. They do not exist by themselves. What nonsense, to think of the eye as separate. It is your self who is doing the seeing. You, riding in this car through Turkey! She looked at him, the keen look softened, and laughed again. And my guess is that you will write a book.

There will be a book, he answers.

All right. If your name is on anything, it will be what you

believe. We will welcome it. I will welcome it, she says, and she looks away again, at the Anatolian plain.

*

⟨ In answer to a puzzled editor's question about U.S. policy toward Vichy, Willkie says: I don't want to discuss that. My views about our policy don't correspond with those of the Administration.

*

Three days later, looking at his audience of dark Lebanese and Moslems in red tarbushes, Yes, he thinks, she was right. I have been thinking in my own terms. Completely. These men: self-government is what they want. Also, the price of bread has gone up sixteen times since the war.

Those who give the most get the most, he says to them. But immediately after, he hears himself saying: "If you want to see the United Nations win, don't just sit in the bleachers and throw pop bottles." They all stare at him in complete blankness.

I'm a fool, he thinks. He ends the brief demonstration in an attempt to speak of a sport of theirs.

"Bet on the winning horse," he says rather desperately, and he sees Barnes smile and Cowles nod his head—"which is the United Nations."

What do I know of this? he admits, the chasm opening in the hot blue day, as he is driven to De Gaulle's residence. Too late, he says to himself. The face of the woman in Turkey is very clear; she said to him, Nobody here believes that your political life is over. But what can I go on now? he thinks, and his eyes fill with darkness.

Staring at De Gaulle, his eyes still hold that darkness. In the cream-colored, tree-shaded mansion, among the salutes and the bugles, he enters the immense room. Distances and perspectives align themselves, among pillars and curtains, and De Gaulle takes his place among them, like a tall lay figure in an architectural drawing. How many times, thinks Willkie, have I said— and aimed the remark at Roosevelt—"always distrust a man who keeps a bust of Napoleon in his office"? Here is De Gaulle in his white uniform, with two portraits of Napoleon looking into the distance over the General's polished hair, and at the General's left hand, on a pedestal, a bust of Napoleon.

Perhaps I am making the mistake of cultures, as I did in talking baseball this morning. Perhaps, to the leader of the Resistance French, Napoleon is a hero of law and freedom. No, he answers himself, and runs his hand through his hair; he and De Gaulle are talking now about compromise. But, De Gaulle is saying, on matters of moral principle, I, like Jeanne d'Arc, can make no compromise.

Next morning, from the clinical aluminum seat of the DC3, he sees the hills of Lebanon; the big sea; and Galilee; the Jordan; the Mount; the Garden. The old birthplace; birth of the rages; birth of clues past the wars we have made to life. Birth of the truth of contradictions, in which parable is the method and can contain both poles. Must contain both poles. He looks down at the old silver places, dusty, heartbreaking to any human being of any belief. Suppose there were a way to use our contradictions, he thinks. Suppose the energy with which we feed the conflict were used? And if a flash fell across our own wildness, and we saw.

They take him on a quick tour of Jerusalem, with a quick look at the Church of the Holy Sepulchre. They were making it possible for him to do what he wanted. And what would you like to do, Mr. Willkie? I would like to confirm my hunch that two Semitic peoples could live together. If undisturbed, that is. And at the Wailing Wall he sees the prayers of tears.

The Consul General arranges his interviews. He has arrived on the eve of two sacred festivals: both Ramadan and Rosh Hashanah start tomorrow. But all day long, through a house which allows enemy visitors to miss each other by ten seconds, simply because one is ushered out one door of a room at the moment before the second enters by the other door—all day long the interviews with the Jewish and the Arab leaders parade past.

Yes, says Shertok, I'd say two million more Jews would make the foundation of a real nation. Ruhi Bey Abdul Hadi tells Willkie that this is Arab country, but the Arabs like British rule. Dr. Aeieh Altman wants a fully-developed land of ten million Jews. Awni Bey Abdul Hadi, who comes in the door as Dr. Altman disappears, swears that the Arabs will defend the country "to the end."

Well then, thinks Willkie, it's Jewish immigration that is the crux of the whole thing.

Late that day, with sun on the windows of afternoon, he looks at the flowers in a bowl. The worn, perceptive face watching him has earned its look over eighty years. This is Henrietta Szold, and the great discrimination in her look has gathered there in countless choices: all the choices ruled by that generosity of meaning: to work, to teach, to pour out years, since it does not seem likely that persecution has come to an end. As she talks, he too feels the pouring of ease. This has nothing to do with victims only: this is the instinctive power of trust; he knows its strength at once in himself. And, talking to her, he knows that the qualities he has judged by—his yardsticks—ever since law school, are not enough. Sincerity, he has always said, as people do in America, and high ideals (still with hardly a feature defined against our time), these will do it. Now, he goes on, if these qualities are matched with perception and with what this white-haired woman says, the truth that there need not be antagonism between "the hopes of the Jews and the rights of the Arabs"—then a political work based in reality might be begun.

Based in reality, the words echo. Something he had said about population. Henrietta Szold is talking in terms of people. When the old words are used, they remind us of land. Country. Nation. When you use the ancient term, people, the future is included, and the past, and a relationship to the land. In the map the mind makes he sees the great tree of control of the Tennessee and its rivers.

And if it is never a question of the "natives not being ready," of the "natives not wanting anything better"? If there is a process here in which the giving has to do with a human right, in which the giver, the gift, and the receiver are all set free, as we say—turned loose on the road to human power? If there is a process in which the act of giving is creation, and multiplies? I should have come to this some time ago, he thinks, and then at once—No, I could not.

In the speed of this voyage, it is morning again; he sees stream under his plane all of tilted Jerusalem and, a little apart, Bethlehem. Cutting over the river and the salt sea, the plane enters the cloud. Emerging to the sparse and blistering brown country, land raided long ago by generations after Genghis Khan; and at noon, the palms and sand of Baghdad.

The streets of Baghdad have been sprinkled for Willkie. No parking is allowed, and no torn awnings, or even dirty awnings, are to be put up. Ramadan has begun, and nobody eats during the day. In this two-day visit, Willkie reviews the Guard and lays a wreath on Feisal's tomb, and talks to the coppersmiths in the bazaar about his own coppersmith ancestors in Germany. He lunches with the British ambassador, has cocktails at the American Legation, and there is a State dinner reception then.

At Teheran, he lands for the official greeting with the Russians in the red sand. He talks to a group of tank repairmen; they find him as "popular as a movie star."

Now he is reading again on the plane, and making notes.

The Shah goes up for forty minutes and returns, delighted, from his first flight.

Taking off again, the big *Gulliver* heads north. A glimpse of the high snow mountains, the long line of the Caspian surf. The red delta and later the limitless flat fields along the Volga. He is close to the German front now, and not aware of it.

A cold wind is blowing in Kuibyshev, where late September lets him shiver after the dizzied light and heat of Teheran. He says, "No statement," shivering, with his trousers flapping and the flags flapping over him. But when he begins to see the city, he tells himself that if he had not known he was in Russia, he would have thought that this was Detroit or Hartford. And if a man's life were to be told in terms of landscapes: here are the farms, the size of any one of his five farms in Rushville, but worked by women and children in the war; here are the cattle of a new breed, and the Duroc Jersey pigs, and the prize watermelon; and here, on the Volga Bend, the place where a dam is planned to produce twice the power of TVA, Bonneville, and Grand Coulee combined. All right, Willkie thinks, if they decide to build a big dam, what do they do? they go ahead and build it. And he asks one of the engineers, What would you say the main idea here is? The young man smiles at his delicious chance, and answers, Like American industry, wouldn't you say? To do the job as fast as it can be done.

Willkie admires. God, he thinks, looking at the enormous, muscular river currents, I'm not dealing in morals, it's just their way of doing a job.

These were the weeks when the north wind brought the smell of torture. Many were locked in the barns, and the barns were burned. Many thousands were walled into their cities. Over the cornfields, color of joy, the shadow of a plane racing; you might look up too late, these planes are fast. Some of these long low countrysides under cumulus stretching up forever have been burned over, explode. It is the purple bruise-color lava land now. A young soldier lies in a ditch in Stalingrad. Suddenly he feels water flowing over his body and face. Not water, not water, not water. He knows what it is: the mice, hundreds of thousands of them, leaving the city. His pockets are full of them; he shivers and shivers, as they pass softly over him. This goes on for a long time; it is hard to say how long.

They say some fields are bare. Then there are the pines, and snapdragons, clover, buttercups, flowers we know.

They have heard the lost children and their cries.

I'll show you my drawings!

Take my poems!

Find my father!

Help me find my father!

Adopt me.

Here's my diary, take it.

Willkie is asked daily about a second front. The term is in constant use, and during this period it means the Allied invasion of the continent. No military man likes to have this term mentioned, at least not in the United States, and Churchill is saying that he believes the notion is a Communist harassment. Willkie says to the reporters: The Second Front has become almost a symbol for the Russian people of the kind of aid they feel tney are entitled to receive from Great Britain and America.

This is the man who has always refused to believe in tne power of symbols.

At the Bolshoi Theatre, they are dancing *Swan Lake*, Tchaikovsky's ballet. Tikhomirnova is to dance the full four-act performance.

That's an amazing thing, to dance both princesses, says one of Willkie's hosts to him in the box. Willkie murmurs. This is strange to him (what is he talking about? a voice in himself is asking), against the deep humming sound of an audience speaking an unknown language, after a day of assault and tension. One of the facts that he will bring home is the likelihood of Russia's forming a separate peace. There are powerful groups in the United States (at the ballet, of all places! another voice in himself remarks), who have wondered all along whether Russia could put up a good fight against Germany—for one reason or another. (One ballet that lasts all evening, how is that possible?) A long, unconscious, haunting note in music. Now a phrase of five, the colors of haunting.

Just at this moment, the curtain goes up. On the lawn before the castle stands the prince, and the music begins. Singing doom, doom, echo of all wild legends of division. Now it is clear that the prince must choose a bride; and his guests dance their stately, courtly requirings of him. Overhead, with a floating note and a liquid release in mystery, with an involving sorcerer motion, the flight of wild swans. The vow of the prince and his nobles to go hunting tonight. To hunt the magic down.

This is all very well: Willkie is uncomfortable. Theater weather has set in; and to be among these hundreds of people, all taking great pleasure in this very formal and very boring . . . Part of a trip around the world, he supposes; but a most unlikely part. Passepartout had no such . . . the theme has begun again; it floats over all of these people, and now recurrent, enters them in a strong echo of magic, enters even those refusing music. The brilliant autumn, today's weather, dominated the castle in the first scene, when the courtiers were golden and apricot and bronze and green. Now the satins of the men, the clear lilac and blue and sugar pink of women, have all given way before secrecy and moss, ruin and the threat of pain. For here before us, on the lake, ride swans; and of these swans, the first is crowned. There are soft caverns, where swans disappear. Hunters come now, all going through the forest. The prince is alone. In this country of fireflies and warm leaves, when he looks up he must see the Swan Queen. She is fantasy-white, and a woman, she is here, it is deliverance she needs. For, from crowned midnight to crowned dawn, this is her form. Under enchantment, she is a swan all day. Surely his love will give her deliverance.

Willkie's head has rocked a little forward. If a reporter asked him now about *Swan Lake*, he would say it is meaningless.

In love, in ecstasy, the prince dances with the swan-woman, and the music lights the air like snow. But they cannot embrace. The Owl Magician, the White Owl, flies up from the ruined chapel: he cannot be defied. With a huge white gesture, he opens his wings. In the dim night, the wings brace open straight across the water—a white dam forbidding music.

Willkie sits bolt upright now. The hunters and the swan maidens are here again. Willkie looks around the theater from his gold box. Clearly a famous passage: storms of clapping coming in quick bursts. They are applauding some technical achievement: the girl dancers, he thinks, and very nice they are. As though his fortune were being told and he believed it, he is impatient: the next word to him comes from the Swan Queen and the Prince. He has sworn to marry her and break the spell. She is to come to the bridal ball at the castle. But it is dawn! The flow and beat of the swan-music rides the lake with the swans and one gliding, crowned, and shackled swan.

Intermission, with its talk. Some strong part of his life, of himself, is fixed now and apart, waiting for this to go on speaking to him.

The castle is lit; in all its lights suspended, itself a cluster of light. In doom and splendor, the ballroom waits; the possible brides are here, the huntsmen of the tapestry, the Prince in state with his mother. Now the dances of the brides' countries are opened before us: the "Half the Night" of Spain, in black, pink, and gold; the Hungarian "Fire I Carry; Do Not See It; Who May See It, May Not Say It"; the "Paper Children" of Poland, and a tarantelle of Naples. All of Europe. Nevertheless, a black stranger stalks into the castle. It is the Owl, masked now as the Knight of the Black River; and with him into the spinning castle he brings his daughter the Demon Swan, who by sorcery wears the face and body of the Swan Queen. The Prince is down from his throne: It is the Queen! And he chooses her, and dances with her in their dance. All joy, all frightfulness, burst into their whipping, blazing turns. The Prince takes the hand of the false Swan. Now at the towering window, the great true Swan, beating with her wings. The sorcerers vanish. The Prince breaks away from the constraint of magic and from the castle; he must find the Swan.

Running, running, the Prince at the lake edge, beside wavering water. He tells the spell; and the Swan does forgive him.

But now the ordeal comes.

Now the lake water rises, flooding and storming, flooding the forest. All the threats have arrived. And at this moment, the Swan Queen, saved by love, spreads her strong soft wings and is, herself, in love, the great bird of deliverance. She bears the Prince to a cliff above the flood. There all the twinning and the enchantments come to an end. They have saved each other in a double act of faith; now she may take her own, her human shape.

As Willkie sits there, curiously opened, illuminated; something further happens. A deep-colored bouquet of autumn flowers is handed to him from the back of the box; and, on one turning motion, everyone in the theater is staring at him. Without a thought, he clears the rail and is at the stage, filling Tikhomirnova's arms with flowers. She stares at him for a second in amazement and what looks like horror; five days later he understands that she thinks he is going to make a speech. But he does nothing of the sort. He takes her in his arms and kisses her; and from then on, says Joseph Barnes, he can have Russia. All that Tikhomirnova says is, smiling, *Dadon sumpathichny Amerikanets.*

The correspondents wait at the Moscow airport in the driving rain, Sunday afternoon. A little after two the *Gulliver* (called a Flying Fortress by the Americans and a Monster by the Russians) comes through the overcast and lands on the wet field.

Willkie is cold and has put on a tan sweater with green stripes over his powder-blue suit; but he takes off his hat for a picture.

Well, hello, Eddie, God bless you, he calls to Eddie Gilmore, who notices first the strong light in the blue eyes, and then the deep pouches on Willkie's cheeks. They stop to talk for a minute. The Second Front is all that anyone wants to hear; and as soon as the correspondents understand that, Willkie is telling about the Americans who believe that Russia cannot fight, and will make a separate peace, and probably should be set at the throat of Germany, anyway. Ah, well, says one of the men. That may explain why the Anglo-American strategy hasn't been better co-ordinated with Russia. It's been a real strategical blunder. The force here is a decisive one—given a Second Front.

WILLKIE: The front in Stalingrad is as much American and British as it is Russian. The war is global.

CORRESPONDENT: Has this been your position, Mr. Willkie?

(*Laughter*)

WILLKIE: (*Laughing too*) I used to be skeptical, you know that, boys. Then I had one look at the Middle East. There, as you know, the trick's been turned. I'm glad today that I carry in my pocket a letter to Stalin from Roosevelt.

Now the black Packard carries him away. In Moscow he is staying at the Foreign Office Guest House, where dinner begins with caviar and smoked salmon, cheese, tomatoes, and calves' brains; and then goes on to beef, chicken, ham, and sausage, with grapes and apples, and of course vodka; not to forget the choice white wines, and the brandy and coffee.

The press hasn't deluged him, says a reporter. Bet it's not like London last January—fashionable hotel, lots of feature stories. . . . Here the leaves are falling, thick and gold; but the people are cold gray metal. He'll see.

The first morning, he gets up early, eager to go out. Out the front door he walks, with his official bodyguard. There are some stares, but not for him. He has had only a paragraph or so in the papers. The stares are for his clothes or for his bodyguard.

Willkie walks at once to Lenin's tomb. It is closed for the day. He walks past the Kremlin.

His invitations have reached the correspondents: two or three of them have been invited to every meal, beginning with eight-o'clock breakfast. The American cigarettes have not all gone; besides, he says, he wants some good bull sessions.

At the Lenin Library that first morning, he is surprised to find out about the exchange set up between Moscow and the Congressional Library. Everyone has told him that he will be stopped continually; rather looking for interference, he goes to the card catalogue. Ah, that's fine, he tells the librarian, that's fine that people can choose books for themselves.

At the Red Army Museum, he looks at captured German exhibits. But in a case he sees something that moves him: the photograph of a young and good-looking soldier. There is a shadow along his cheek. He looks more closely. It is a scar, and this is one of a set of pictures showing work done on facial wounds.

He wants to talk to clergymen, he says, and that afternoon he sees Father Brown. Later, there is a jazz concert. His first day has left him with the feeling that the people were wrong who insisted that he would not be able to learn anything. It is talking to random people, like that Siberian girl who used to be a Moslem. She was with one of the newsboys, and when Willkie asked her whether she thought Russia was a free country, she said, Of course; the Soviets have done away with the veil. That is a part answer, but it is hers.

His second day is cold and crisp. His walk through the sunny morning city is toward the subway, but he passes near the unfinished Palace of the Soviets, the prize building. He likes the subway ride and is impatient to talk to the workers in their black clothes, and the early shoppers, and the Red Army girls. But he is still surrounded by official appointments: Sir Clark Kerr, and, after lunch, his meeting with Molotov.

Later, at the Moscow Conservatory, he hears Shostakovich's Seventh Symphony, the work that has come to stand for the siege of Leningrad and has its own stories, ranging from the soldiers who stand to hear it on the hot sands of Camp Young to the records that are bootlegged in the East, to get past the union ban on recordings which Petrillo is enforcing.

Life takes his picture during intermission, with his arms around the shoulders of American and Russian officers. When he is asked about his first days, all he says is that he is asking blunt questions and hoping for blunt, frank answers. He hasn't made his mind up about the difference between state capitalization of farms in Russia and at home. The contrasts, though, he finds staggering.

The next morning he visits the defenses of Moscow and eats with the soldiers in a dugout. He praises the rich vegetable soup and says that this black bread is Russia's Yorkshire pudding. There is a reception at Admiral Standley's in the afternoon, with a Walter Pidgeon movie, *6000 Enemies*. "Starved for our own movies!" says a reporter. "Imagine clapping like that!"

In the cool evening, Willkie drives up to the Kremlin. Stalin and Molotov are waiting for him in the office, and when Stalin rises behind the long birch table, Willkie is surprised at his shortness and at the strong colors of his dress: pink whipcord trousers, black boots, gray blouse.

Stalingrad is the center of their talk—the battle that seems to be drawing to its climax. Stalin speaks, with the admiration that moves Willkie, of American industry, of industrial methods, of the belt. Sorting his words out carefully, he speaks of the need of products from these great workshops. We will be most grateful, says Stalin. But I suggest you understate the case rather than give anyone the impression that we are to be patronized.

As Willkie goes, after introducing Barnes and Cowles, Stalin invites him to dinner on Saturday, when he returns from the front, and says, in parting, the words which convey more truth

than any other recommendation. He says to Willkie, Tell America all that you've seen here.

Willkie and his party start for the front at midnight. In the
jeeps they changed to, they jolted through a wet dawn over the
ruined country.

The sound of guns all day.

The exhausted prisoners.

The dugout and the naked bulb.

A body decomposing. Another. Many.

The shivering of the Nazis.

A muddy hill.

Shell bursting. Shell bursting.

Question: What about a Second Front?

And if there are no military answers?

Returned to Moscow, he goes to see *Onegin*; and, after the
theater, he has at last the talk he has wanted. Thinking of
Gunther, thinking of the people at Irita Van Doren's, at Dorothy Thompson's. But this talk at night includes Simonov, Ilya
Ehrenburg, Voitekhov, and Valentina Genne. Willkie proposes
not only that Shostakovich be sent to America to help in building understanding between the peoples of the two countries, but
that writers be sent on exchange trips. Simonov's response, that
both Russia and the United States hang in the balance tonight
with Stalingrad, and that it is foolish to send a musician who is
also involved in the war to show Americans what has already
been made clear to everybody, leads Willkie to discuss production.

We have the planes, and tanks, and arms; where shall they go?
That depends, he says, to an extent you cannot imagine on
American public opinion.

We have elections of one kind or another every year. The
Administration is extremely susceptible to public opinion. England knows that, and has sent writers and cultural leaders.

The Americans have learned, he goes on. Pearl Harbor . . .

soldier look after him and say, He's just like Stalin. *Willkie made
himself felt here, not through a publicity machine, but because
he admires in America qualities which the Russians also admire:
optimism, technical advance, health—and he admires the efficiency here, what Stalin calls "style in work."*

*Willkie pointed out the areas of closeness between the two
people. And it cannot be said too often that we are close in these
two places of our past: both the U.S.S.R. and the U.S. entered
the war after it began, and we both worked for peace as long as
our ideas of national honor allowed.*

*

What do you know of America? I asked a little Russian school-
      girl.
—Money, fat men, skyscrapers, lots of ships and airplanes.
And what do you think of America? I asked her father.
He thought a little, then said, A land where democracy
Will at last break down injustice, where many shrewd eyes
Look steadily and with hope into the future;
A land of brilliant techniques and plenty,
And of people who, like us,
Strive to a distant point.

*

A man in a plane looks at the surface of land.
Down, he stares down; he sees the narrow papers,
His information on China and the book about China;
He sees his legs and his feet; he sees his hands; they are still.
Far down air crumpled, old ranges, the green of the silk route.
You cannot know, you cannot share, this land, the papers say
      to him
Or the last country or the ones before.   And do you know your
      land?

You on your ignorant journey.   He sees : It is my journey.
He sees that he does not know.   But the voices blow through
      him.
He sees that he has not spoken.   But the voices are here.
The world not beneath him, however sheer he flies.   The world
Around him and through him always.   O to be home, now.
He stretches, a big man in a plane.   Home, he thinks.   I am
      not great enough.
I wish I were home.   Before the voices speak,
Any of the voices, he knows.   He surely knows:
The journey is my home.

*

When the *Gulliver* spilled power out of its wings, heading
down into the green field of Tashkent; when the *Gulliver* glinted
silver over the silver Altais, the boy in his furs looked up from
the hillside. Huge flew the plane, the first American.

Tashkent, he goes, high to Urumchi, then on to Lanchow.
Ranges of surface, the crossing over.

Willkie plays cards, reads Gunther, reads the pages prepared
by his office for him. To play, to cram himself with the weathers,
the lands below: earth tattooed with signals, smoke, seadogs
among fog, fogflowers, beards of dawn. Surf of all Asian hours
white on that country. India, ranges past that narrow rounded
wing.

*

Into the air far.   Into the opposites.
Driving through sky into the otherworld,
In a real plane with four real whirls before him
Carrying him into his fantasy.
Now the dance of split and deliverance

Opens in swans before the wings.
Flowers, clouds, a game of paper kings.
And will you kill my dark lord down
Who stares the fiery lady?   Luck
Is not the mirroring, is not the word,
Not the skillful red and black.
The enemy, the enemy.
How fare the wings around the wind,
Spun blade and angle of attack?
How take the ancient mountains of the soul,
And play, the flight forward being flight back?
My drink is airy gold.   The cards I held
Are the same cards my card-hand hold,
While minutes, great miles of Asia, pass.
This jack, this red jack, this statistical crowd,
Two-colored, while we're flying to the world.
Around the world, we say.   I might have known
There's no way round my life or round the world.
There is only through.

Where all his meanings lead:
Into the fantasy of the opposite.

*

The city is cut out of the rock, in the place where four rivers
meet. Rock living as pillars has been blasted, floated away; the
rock being opened by twilight-colored hands. The city is deep in
the peaks and cliffs. Here the dogs bark, a dawn of astonished
barking, if the strange sun ever clears the eastern peaks.

A boy turns his back on the new runway. It is ready. It is
thirty-two hundred feet long, carved from the solid rock of the
Chungking Mountains to accommodate this plane.

*

Over the route opened by Marco Polo, in the *Gulliver* with its Chinese name, meaning High Level Man; over the Tien Shan range, the deep lands of dream. A cart piled immensely high with white bales, out of all proportion high with the bales of wool, bales of salt, bales of tea. The shafts leaning down, for mules or coolies; a few men waiting, they have been waiting, they will wait. Two mules stand, their forelegs spread, as the plane goes over, braced against the sounds of dream.

Coming to Lanchow's tiled roofs, a look of corduroy, of a hat shading a shadowy face. The walled gardens, the many-celled gardens, cells made by tile-topped walls. They land. The little children smile, their legs curved down in apricot-color faces; they smile.

Paper flags, banners, a parade for Willkie. They have been cleaning Lanchow for two weeks for this moment.

They are brought to the central street, and here are flags in their hands, and rows of flags. What can this be for? they say to each other. Nobody tells.

To Chengtu, where the colleges are refugees. Where the scholars of China and the students, cherished, until very recently not allowed to take part in the war, are waiting to hear him. Four thousand of them. And six thousand more have walked in over the hills. They stand on the slope to hear him. He stands at a small column, with a microphone and a flag. He sees them and does not see them. They look at him; they are in their "great fearlessness," as Sun Yat-Sen told them. He hears out of his Indiana youth the scraping sounds of deference as he once called for the making of the road to come.

But all of it rises in his mind, released by opposites, the long disgrace of the mind, buried deep in his life; in our lives. He spreads his legs, big legs in crumpled pants.

*

⟨ *Willkie: I have had many experiences in my life, but this is the first time I have had a college president to translate for me. I rather enjoy this experience because, since I left college twenty-six years ago, I have wanted to make one of those fellows work for me. As a matter of fact, my six years in the university were not devoted so much to the acquisition of facts, but rather to the outwitting of the faculty and the increasing of their discomfiture. I can't tell you how much I am enjoying the passing of this on to you through a college president as my Charlie McCarthy!*

*

For the flight to Chungking, the *Gulliver* is too big. They move to the transport *Heavenly Mountain*. The last leg of the flight takes them into the battles; there has been nothing for four thousand miles but an enemy scout plane. Moon Chen, their pilot from Kuibyshev, takes them in.

*

It is the sixth year of the war in China.
The children of the first winter help with the babies.
Not even a clash in the north for some time now.
The Long March is legend; Taerchwang's a song;
Splinters of autumn drift over this year.
How can strangers be told?   A soldier stands still,
He wavers on his feet; the army has stood for three years,
Lacking the strength to advance.
The boys who went away to war five years ago
Wrote a letter or two, then died; anyway did not write.
The soldiers waver, are thin in their torn clothes.
But they hold.   The cliff-city holds.
Not the blazing, not the wild turning, not the lonely stand.
There was a silence then; but now the fire has fallen
On the exotic silent cities, in a storm on London.

Not alone, not unknown here, faces endowed with stillness.
"The general's white hair, and the soldier's tears."

*

Over Chungking, Willkie put away his papers, and the book
Inside Asia. Here it is: the place of four rivers. The beginning
of a world. The plane comes down.

He walks down the steps, bigger than any of them. The Mayor
is here with a delegation, all neat, compact. The Mayor hands
Willkie the hottest steam towel he has ever felt. He turns to
Joseph Barnes: What the hell do I do with it? The Mayor smiles,
bows again, clasping his own hands in greeting: We think you
will find it most refreshing.

There is nothing in the books nor the sheets from the office to
tell him that travelers reaching cities in China are given hot
towels to do their hands and faces. That they long for this com-
fort as others long for a drink; a deep bath; a cup of tea.

The road to the city, with all the paper flags: red, white, and
blue swarming and blurring. Glimpses of the misted, walled city,
swept clean for Willkie. An order has gone out: all rickshaws
and load-carrying coolies are to be off the roads he takes for six
hours around the time he is expected, so that his sensibilities
may not be offended. Banners stretch over all the streets he visits.
The police, on motorcycles, rush before him, flags on the handle-
bars. In the dim alleys, the little quilted children are playing;
they have American flags.

He goes to the garden house across the river from the American Embassy. This is the guest bungalow of the Chinese Government. Out the windows, past all the rhododendrons, he can
see the great ridges and the colorless shacks fading at evening
into mountains. These cuts in the rock are the deep cave entrances: thin poles in front of them fly the laundry. Now people
come out into the broken sunlight, carrying their loads. The
young ones are fighting the river, crossing from eight gates. From

one landward gate, they go out to the roads: Chengtu, Sian, Peiping. Bright-green and deep-blue rice fields.

A long man is walking a bridge in a profile of mist.

❊

❲ *The Missimo has seen to it that the garden house (which is famous for its radio, its cook, its soft toilet paper) has new silk draperies and American daisies; ancient paintings; priceless porcelain ware.*

❊

Whom does Willkie represent?

Is Mr. Roosevelt irritated at Willkie's call for a second front?

Is the American point of view being improperly put before the Chinese people?

How can American Army procedure be adapted to thought in China?

Can Willkie understand General Stilwell's tasks and interpret them to America?

Can any more be asked of the Chinese war effort?

What truth is there in the stories that the civil war in China is on ice until the war with Japan is over?

How closely does the Chinese economic structure concern America?

❊

❲ *Willkie is doing a timely service to the United Nations against heavy odds. Time is better treated as an enemy than as an ally.*

❊

The Generalissimo gives a banquet on Willkie's first evening in Chungking. Three tables form a U. Western foods are served: cream of tomato soup, steak, besides almond soup, fish, and Yunnan ham. Willkie sees Madame Chiang as very beautiful; she wears a sheer black dress with a little white flower design.

Willkie talks with the Gissimo. Everyone can see that the Chinese are enjoying Willkie. He could do a lot, they say to each other at the banquet, particularly if he has brought assurances of military help.

He is trying to eat with chopsticks, but after a while he goes back to his fork. He is talking, through the Missimo: I have learned, he is saying, that the ordinary citizen loves liberty and wants action now. He is ahead of his leaders. It annoys him to see that much of the might of the United Nations stands idle, waiting.

The Ministry of Thunder begins; the Moon of the Hungry Ghosts is just over. Day before yesterday, the two weeks ended with a feast of ghosts. All Souls, when food is prepared for the ghosts with no descendants, the hungry ghosts.

Now the noises and lamps of the great city, filled with the life that has poured in to resist incredibly, and to live on another level.

*

Sounds of night in the country of the opposites.
Music for the first time, on incredible instruments:
The rapids of a river, a woman's kitchen stove,
A village crossroads with its forgotten language;
Clank and chuckle of gambling; one line of a song;
The strings of lost limitless time.   Music.
Voice of a cat you knew before you learned to speak.
Voices of waterfalls, steel whirls, many small flowers,
Voices of a dream of the animals of heaven
  Raised through the hungering
Of some one thin wavering unransomed boy
  In starved and golden air.
A sheer black music, rare-lit joining of waters.
Night-sound in the country of the opposites.

*

The next morning, Willkie goes to visit the cotton factory on the Chialing River.

He is shown the cotton mills, legs of metal overhead, thread coming down in diagrams. In the caves, they are printing, among the wires, and the sheets of rock above them are flecked like pages of unlearned language. The mottled, journey-written *Gulliver*. Stains of growth; the field spotted over, lichen with pictures, reaching out dark as moss in agate, accretion of the classic urinal wall, limited in all meanings except the meanings of form —or the characters of the unlearned life. Morning in the country of the opposites. Smiles, the life of the sex.

He has met the smiles of the manager and the factory officials. Then he stops. He looks around for a moment. This is one of thousands of inspections; there is nothing to make it distinct.

What I learn, what I make of anything depends on me, he thinks. When it is related. In flesh. Among the opposites.

There is a clerk in the corner, almost invisible. Obliterate in any culture. But now the gleam in his face; unique. Willkie crosses to him, and bows a little. And gets that fellow, the interpreter, to sing his translated questions about pay, games, what he does for fun, for doctoring, and his house, and where he went to school, and what the training is of a statistical clerk in a cave in China.

Down the line of spindles, with the thread glinting and pouring in. He asks a girl how she lives. Is she married? Yes, says the girl, looking back at him with a dense soft black look. A dream of sound in the night. And your husband? asks Willkie. He's at the front, says the girl. All right, says Willkie, taking breath, and his heart rings. And peace? Would you want China to make peace with Japan? Your husband could—he raises his big head— then he could come back to you.

The girl says something rapidly. A pulse flickers on her throat. The interpreter makes a long answer out of it. No peace until— he begins—we will ask for no peace until America—Britain—all the united peoples with China—achieve together a final victory.

He is raised among the opposites. Something has healed back in his boyhood, brought up in a double tradition; from faraway, a breath from the chieftain stalks and a gaunt man among purple flowers reaches him in this cave. Something is made whole for a moment, and he thinks, Final. Final. This moment is final; nothing but a moment is; and from all this hard delicate bravery turns to the commonplace.

In another plant, saying: I'm not really impressed by a place this spick-and-span. I notice that when I inspect my own plants, the next paint bills are always higher than usual.

At the power plant, the American engineer smiles at him and speaks in a flat familiar cadence. Indiana? Willkie asks, and finds here a contemporary from Purdue. Remember the time we beat you out of the football pennant?

Down the polished steps to the river, Willkie running: 373 steps to the shining water. And across, he takes them two at a time to the top, waving at the sedan chair waiting to carry him up.

Willkie: I am not that old.

*

There is a monkey, the story goes, who fights his enemies this way: hard-pressed, he will pull ten thousand hairs from his body, fling them to the ground. Now they leap up, turned into monkeys, each hair fighting as strong as he does. When one of these monkeys is cut down, it falls, you see it fall in the dust and change: monkey-hair again. They are doing monkey-hair fighting, these years in China.

*

The officials think Willkie is napping after his long morning. But he has asked that another visitor be invited to the garden house, rather quietly, things being as they are. This visitor is

Chou En Lai, called The Teeter-Totter by some. The delicate boy who sets himself disciplines. The man who fell in love in jail, and knows the coal mines of Europe. Served with Chiang Kai-Shek, escaped from Chiang Kai-Shek. Emerges in brightness here, for an hour of good talk.

Later in the day, at a China Relief tea party with the Missimo, Willkie hears a chorus of little girls. They sing their song, "Work, Work, Work." They are all ten years old, scrubbed for the party, and proud of the clean dresses and the cake he has given them. It is a big cake. These are the war orphans. There is a child who had run back from hiding during an air raid, to find a pit where a house and a family of ten people had lived together half an hour ago. But the child is not now here; is not now sane. These little girls smile. With the scarf over her head and the butterfly on her dress, this little girl offers Willkie a slice of cake. She smiles delicately; she is charming.

And the Missimo smiles, in the bright day. They are beginning to talk of Willkie weather, these photographers, pleased with their clean lights and shadows. The Missimo says, delicately, Wherever you go, the sun shines.

The photographers and the newspapermen come forward for his speech. Something is forming for him, out of his own lost childhood, doubled then and split, with both his parents there. He stands up, grown broader and taller than anyone here, and says, There is this question which we have to answer: Are we fighting this war to re-establish a world under which these children lost their parents—or are we fighting to eliminate imperialistic spheres of influence, mandates and the like, which only sow the seeds of future wars?

Madame Chiang and I are going to howl and howl—the *Times* man looks up, startled—for the right kind of world when this war is over, so that all nations can be free, and seek their own just aspirations.

The reporters come crowding up to him.

What about the second front, Mr. Willkie?

No more second front talk.

And, in answer to the surprise of a Chinese correspondent: I've always had the bad habit of saying what I think.

And when the *Life* man asks him what he thought he'd answer the Missimo about the sunshine, he smiles and shakes his head, and she sees his blue look. In 1940, he says sideways to the *Life* man, I attempted to answer the master charmer of the day. That was easy. This is tough.

The evening is reserved for Chiang. Tomorrow: Chiang, Stilwell, Chennault.

*

([Confucius and his disciples walk down the yellow road. They meet a woman, who tells them her story: her father died in the sudden floods, her husband fell before the tiger; the big snake came for her brother, the icy fever for one of her sons.

Confucius: And you remain in this country?

Woman: The government's not as bad as it might be!

*

([The Chinese, you know, invented everything, even the Europeans.

*

([The news agencies say that Willkie's formal clothes have been sent in a special plane. Willkie has no formal clothes. He is wearing the same slate-blue business suit to all functions and on all visits.

*

THE ANVIL. THE PINCERS

Two concepts of the war: one is that China is a great anvil against which America can hammer the Japanese until they are

smashed. China is required only to stand firm. The other had
China as one arm of a pair of pincers. America is the other arm.
As soon as the arms begin to function together, give Japan one
year.

The Chinese, says one of the best reporters, like the concept
of the pincers.

But where are they to get that strength?

But where, that skill?

*

Tumble of boards in the house, and a broken basket, a tall-
backed chair down. It might be the flood country of Alabama.
The golden baby, smooth, her mother holding her up.

The child with his ink-brush. His concentrated face.

Two men walking a water-wheel, leaning on the stream-worn
timber; rods of their collarbones, rods of their ribs, their smooth
absent faces filled with a wish like homesickness.

In the rush of heat striking Chungking, Willkie works naked
at his desk. And then the Americans come, the Army people,
asking:

Q: Are woman's auxiliaries really going to be sent out?

WILLKIE: I thought you boys came over to fight.

Q: Are you speaking for Roosevelt these days, Mr. Willkie? Do
you know he said your Moscow statement was not worth
reading?

WILLKIE: I've been commissioned by the President to do certain
things. But when I speak for myself, I'm Wendell Willkie,
and I say what I damn please.

*

The Chinese now give him his Chinese name: three words
saying Powerful, You, Foundation—which mean in English,
strengthen your inner self.

*

❴ *Mr. Marco Polo Willkie has already caused more embarrassment to the Allies than any man abroad.—Rankin, in Washington; hoping the people of the Orient do not take what Willkie says too seriously.*

*

In his talks with Chiang Kai-Shek and Madame Chiang he can see clues to next steps. Come back to America with me, he invites her; they will be moved, will be swayed by you; come back on the plane. On the next plane, they think.

The Gissimo has just returned from his talks with Nehru, and has caught that flashing of all of Asia. It flashes newly for him, and fades. Willkie knows that forgetting, but he is there on the edge of a real voice. He has been to see Asia, curiously, through the ovations to himself. He sees what they want him to be.

He has caught, from a way of standing, from the music of balance, from the enduring tension that carries its own rest, a word that speaks to him. In the public confusion of this journey, and in the flashing inward times of light and attraction, he has reached for the second time his own voice.

Not elected; never elected; he has never had anything like the power he imagined. With no status except the status given by a moment before a microphone to which he brings his lifetime. No weight, like the moment in love when the body lets go of substance. A gathering of splendors like memory. He looks at the instrument, complex black and silver giving him possibility, his voice. He speaks to whoever will listen to him—a world of listening, as if he were speaking to one woman who gave him words. Or one man, a life to a life.

Toward world unity, he says, and begins to talk of four things he has in common with all the ordinary people with whom he has talked:

Deep in war, they want the UN to win and to take the offensive.

All want the end of the war and the chance to live in liberty.

All doubt, in their variousness, the readiness of the leading democracies of the world to stand up and be counted upon for the freedom of others after the war is over.

Doubt kills the quick whole act, he knows, the "great fearlessness" in which the Chinese trust.

Now he says: the winning of the peace.

Without the real support of the common people, he says, the winning of this war will be enormously difficult.

This war is not simply a technical problem for task forces.

The winning of the peace will be nearly impossible.

It is also a war for men's minds.

We need more than arms.

We need a passion for the future.

This war must mean, he says.

We believe this war must mean an end to the empire of nations over other nations.

No foot of Chinese soil, for example, should or can be ruled from now on, except by the people who live on it.

The world's job is to find a system for helping colonial peoples who join the UN cause to become free and independent nations.

We must set up firm timetables.

We must establish ironclad guarantees that they shall not slip back.

Some say these subjects should be hushed until victory.

Exactly the reverse is true.

Sincere efforts to find progressive solutions will bring strength to our cause.

Remember: the opponents of social change always urge delay. There is always a present crisis.

After the war, changes may be too little and too late.

*

TO CHINA. A BROADCAST

. . . Mankind is on the march. . . .
The old colonial days are past. . . .
To you people, who have fought for five devastating years
We owe a duty to assure;
China will be completely free.

*

⟪ *His is a curious position. History may call him the first UN statesman; a man without power in any country, who has suddenly developed enormous power in all free countries.*

Somewhere on the road, he has met the democratic upsurge, and he has recognized it. You cannot invent this stuff. You have to feel it.

Willkie has merely read the faces.

He has become suddenly powerful, not because he is a charming man, but because he has read it straight, and said it straight.

*

⟪ *The American Embassy at Chungking was as disturbed by his recommendations for China as had been the Embassy at Kuibyshev by his demand for a second front.*

*

He talks to Chennault, the seamed and stormy face.

He goes now to the front at Sian. Now he will come to the four hundred million.

Willkie weather, say the correspondents, driving to the airport past bamboo and red maple, in the sun of autumn. Bright October, scarlet among the mountains, the meng leaves falling, the heads of chrysanthemum. There is a party and a brass band, out on the edge; an American thinks of the Washington swells who set out to look at Bull Run. "De luxe struggle and strife," says the old-timer.

At half past four Moon Chen takes the plane under the low ceiling at Sian, running in toward the dripping buildings.

Banquet and lanterns. They go to their sleeping car. All night the guards pace at the railroad siding. Early in the morning, the little company climbs into handcars in the chill; they sit on the benches, wrapped in their brown lap-blankets. Exposed to the wide air and the wide land, they watch the backs of the men pumping the little cars along; and see themselves diminish, the world traveler become a man along a small and endless line. An old-fashioned train moves along a track which takes them narrow and cold to the stale front of war. Now they are moving on a single line, drawn by a child; now the line itself thins out. It is the knife; it is the sword blade along which a man crawls between the attempts of death. There! there! in puffs and spatters of the air, the Japanese gunners, racing in their planes, fire at this track. Many know stinging green of Malaya; and far in the snow, in Norway, a tall blond boy works his shoulders down deeper in his hillside, and word comes, sparse news: Willkie is now in China. A kind of gladness reaches one distant blond anonymous boy.

The hunter plane turns away on a wide curve of space.

The front has been changeless for four and a half years.

Willkie walks the narrow roads of this war, deep-cut through yellow loess. These roads rise up around him, cramping his arms. Grave-cut. Through. Yellow dust of tall paths, lanes for slender men.

Here he is thick and tall, exposed again, and marked; staining the shoulders of his clothes with yellow, rubbing the walls as he walks through.

In a distinct clear glimpse, he sees through his telescope two Japanese artillerymen leaning against the mouth of their emplacement in the sun.

Will you have Chinese troops perform for you? They run through a practice assault, taking—in mock—a steep defile, the overhang green whistling under bangalore explosions. They have defended the mountains of the Great Farewell. The enemy is long past the Peak of Peach Blossoms. The high peak, Rich Damask, died for many times. And the Mouth of the Stone Gate.

The guests go back to their special train. With lunch they drink Graves, Peking beer, and liquor captured from the enemy. The train takes them under the sacred mountain, to flatlands where among winter wheat the reserves form a hollow square. Ten thousand men he sees in the wheatfield, stocky, sturdy he sees them, in perfect health; the exquisite, fit veterans. Under their planted feet, yellow-green blades.

And a flashing of red and yellow, the pennants riding by. Then the guns, then the mountain guns. And the infantry; and tanks— "A hodge-podge handful of antiquated tanks."

On the walls of a town in ruins, at the crumbled bend of the Yellow River, words written in English:

"We want more tanks. Guns. Airplanes."

This river that leaps and overflows—China's Sorrow.

The river given a new course, manmade, four years ago.

The fliers, when they dove to machine-gun the train, killed six men in a coach car.

At Suad station, the band was playing for them, in snatches of strange music blown away. Sian again; five miles of cheering, the band music carried in from the central tower, thin sounds and faraway. The eyes; the eyes.

*

❨ They are emotionally starved; and trying to tell America they like her.

*

A gift of swords, captured from Japanese.

Now the gold-rimmed western mountains.

Now the crows, flocking low, rapid and piercing, low over China to the temple groves.

Two anthems. In the plane. Lifted away.

*

Leaving Chungking, at the airport rest house, Willkie said: One falls so much in love with the Chinese people that it is difficult to form a critical and fact-finding judgment.

Back to Chengtu, for the *Gulliver*, and then northward over Mongolia. He reads Gunther again: "Outer Mongolia is such *terra incognita* that Tibet is Coney Island." This is the last of China, older than rocks. These people almost a fourth part of all of us, with one single written language, and an idea of the truth which can never be proved, but can only be suggested.

Now the joy of the journey is in the air and land and in dream: to be a conscious part of the streaming life that is forever creating, one life in all things.

And now, over fall, the time of forest fires, over beech, birch, day lily and redgrass; the velvet tree, the Asian fir, the climbing grape; rose-color lotus where the streams are warm; Korean pine; more larch, sedges, black birch. Amur linden, peony, the relict plants, and fern under the dense tree-cover. Clearings and burning over. The river valleys where cold air flows down. Living among their smoke, those in Siberia; and secret on the slopes, the grain-manse, the raccoon dog, and the nocturnal hare. Pheasants, and the great lord of the woods.

Chita, and then Yakutsk, the marks on the roads fine drawings from the air. Landing among the firs and the eyes almost shut with laughing. The hunter in the forest of little birches. The dog-sled and reindeer sled before the low hut, with the laughter and all the pipes smoking.

*

Eastward, in laps of flight no American plane had made.

Over the Arctic of Siberia; over the Bering Strait to the glacier's stripes and the great green lake.

*

⟨ *Roosevelt says everything is all right with the Willkie tour, as far as he's concerned.*

*

WILLKIE IN THE GULLIVER

When after the screens of the evening of defeat
You try the remote clean air, withdrawal, think of him.
He was like many of us.   He had lost.
He flew to the many, making a crisis of choice
Lead toward the solving of barriers; learning, flying, crossed
Level after level of process, where we come
To ourselves, to the voiceless many who never in time
Choose against life.   We find the direct voice.

Remembering limits, in the days of death,
All the faring that follows our first sight of the face
Of all things beginning again past deepest defeat.
Think now all of us of our loved and great,
Traveling new to make human the bonds of breath
After defeat; for all men; by God's grace.

*

Down the straits flying, looks at the surfaces.
Down, staring down, he sees the narrow places,
The opposites and the space between opposites.
He sees his legs and his feet; his big hands moving.
A narrow place like the road like the endless channel
Yellowing his shoulders with mortality;

Narrow as the knife of his life and death, a blade of rail along
    which he ran, and they shot at him.
Narrow, a running spark between opposites.

He stretches, a big man in a plane.   He thinks of a woman
Who is a sea of meanings, whose flower of rivers
He knows as a speaking of dreams.   He wants his speaking
Out into darkness like a speaking to one woman.
Forever; whether it be narrow; whether it be his death
—A clenching of the heart, in an instant hidden—
Or whether his life, a spark between opposites.
Striking a firefall in which there flare no fears
Doubled, no poles, for between runs fire.
The journey is his; how can his voice be him?
My voice, my life, he knows; my life, my home.

*

Then down at Fairbanks, to astonish them. Mrs. Willkie, at
Rushville, has been told he is back: she is thrilled, and Phil, on
a ten-day furlough, is waiting at home with her. Whirling October evening at Edmonton.

Next afternoon at Minneapolis, where the signs say LASALLE
BUILDING; COLLISION WORKS, Willkie is telling the newsmen he'll
go to New York tomorrow, then home to Rushville, when he
learns that Roosevelt wants to see him first; tonight or tomorrow.

He rages; clamps down; goes on with his praise of the crew's
performance and the amazing skill of Major Kight.

"Willkie carried good weather in his pocket," says Kight, and
names the *Gulliver's* achievement:

First round-the-world passenger flight via the North Pacific.

First to fly China—Alaska—U.S.

First American plane over the Gobi Desert.

First American plane over the Mongolian Republic.

First American plane through Siberia in wartime.

First American plane to enter China through Russia.

Nobody is going to let him speak, to a woman, or to the American people, no matter how he stretches and rages in his rumpled clothes. Among his savage dreams his broken inheritance. Endure, grandmother of all music.

His sense of the real is with him.

Angry, full-sighted.

Will go to Washington.

*

⟨ *All day Wednesday the skies hung low and dripped. The Potomac River had already overflowed its banks. In the distance, the sodden newsmen and the photographers, the newsreel cameramen heard the drone; past leaden skies nobody saw the plane. Then, minutes later the flying box-car picked a hole in the cloud of fog, expanded gradually into reality. Circled, came slow in, hit asphalt screaming. A shrill of brakes.*

*

From the open door of the *Gulliver*, three soldiers; Willkie, clumsy, steps down to the runway.

Newsreel fixer, yelling: Say something!

Willkie: I'm damn glad to be back!

Newsreel fixer, apologetically: I'm awfully sorry. We didn't pick that up.

Willkie: I'm damn glad to be back!

*

"How do you feel, Mr. Willkie?"

"Never felt better. The trip cost me—the word 'cost' slightly shifting—ten or fifteen pounds. Yes, I ate well. But I lost a lot of sleep."

The telephone rang.

"What did you think of Chiang Kai-Shek?"

"You might not believe it, but Madame Chiang is beautiful beyond belief. She is not only beautifully attired; her conversation is wonderful. She is the most charming woman I ever met."

"What did you think of Uncle Joe?"

"Who?"

"Stalin."

"Oh, great guy. Dresses colorfully, likes a stiff drink, and—"

"You mean pink pants?"

"Yes. Tosses off his vodka without a chaser. Frank. Smokes a pipe. Good sense of humor, seldom shows. Simple. Childlike admiration of American Indians and the assembly line."

"And Russia?"

"With the possible exception of the United States, the Russians are the most effective people in the world. They just decide to do something, to build a big building, and then go out and build it.

"If they decide to build a big dam they go ahead and build it. The idea is always to do the job as fast as it can be done. I am not speaking, of course, about the morals of their system of doing things. I'm just talking now about their way of doing a job."

Somebody else comes in. "What about Stalin?"

"Well, he's very short and he likes his liquor. He has trouble making himself understood, even in his own language. But when he really wants to get something off his chest he doesn't have any trouble at all. You get what he's driving at."

The telephone rang for the eighth time.

Joe Barnes answered it. It was the White House calling.

Into the Presidential audience, in the limousine.

*

Later, in the pall of smoke, he answered questions, sat cross-legged on a round mahogany table.

"Somebody give me a cigarette. . . . One thing the President did tell me was that any report that he had been critical of me is wrong.

"You will recall that I wanted one head of the military—MacArthur. And certain military men said no layman should talk.

"No, I have no special military knowledge. Flatly, no. But a wide experience in evaluating the reports of technical men.

"Win the war? Certainly. But how soon? At what cost? I don't mean cost in dollars and cents but cost in human lives and human values. And what kind of a world are we going to have afterwards? It makes a lot of difference just how we win."

*

Later. A battery of cameras. He looked terrible.
Don't you want to button your coat, Mr. Willkie?
Willkie: No I don't.
Tie askew, belly over belt, bottom button the only one hitched. Hat on uncut, uncombed hair.
Willkie: I don't give a damn how I look; but my wife does.

*

⟨ *He has discovered the East. It was a typically American response to the sights he saw and the views he heard. The New World we are accustomed to locate here is no longer here but there.*

Actually, the airborne traveler's capacity to take in Russia, China, and the Middle East in a single eyeful, especially when the eye is fresh, makes clear that what is taking place in the East is really a "process."

To behold men and women on the march not in one place but everywhere is to recognize a universal.—THE NEW YORK TIMES

*

❲ "The kind of peace that Americans will wait upon will bear a direct relationship to the kind of war they have to fight."
                    —Wendell Willkie, NEW YORK TIMES MAGAZINE
                                        *

❲ The Willkiean blast is not distinctively his. It is simply the discovery of the most important truth in Asia, expressed by Willkie, with a world audience.
                                        *

❲ What that speech did was to give the folks back home the sensation of reality.
                                        *

    Q: Whose reality?
    A: Their own.

PART ELEVEN Dam of Silence

To THE NATION, by radio, Willkie: Our thinking and planning in the future must be global. The two hundred million people of Russia and the four hundred and fifty million people of China— people like you and me—are bewildered and anxious.

They know what they are fighting for.

They are not so sure about us.

Many of them have read the Atlantic Charter.

Rightly or wrongly, they are not satisfied.

They ask: What about a Pacific charter? What about a world charter?

*

❨ At first there was a disposition by many world leaders to say that Mr. Willkie was talking out of turn.

Then the dam of silence broke—and now, the deluge!

*

⟨ Roosevelt, saying: It is perfectly clear that the Atlantic Charter applies to all humanity.

Roosevelt, of himself and Willkie: Not a controversy in a carload.

Patman: Instructive . . . hurtful . . . belittling.

Norris: I don't criticize him. . . . But I think some of the things he said were impractical.

Rankin: He gave encouragement to the revolting elements in India.

Jed Johnson: The American people know what we are fighting for, even though Mr. Willkie may not.

*

⟨ From India: We are the disease; not the doctors. But I have faith in the spirit of man. Moreover, I maintain that if you look deep enough into the heart of your enemy, there you will see your twin brother.

I have faith in the fact that nothing is static. . . .

*

Dreaming we were awake, we heard the rivers
And seeing in sleep through the eye's meteor
A forest of light through which all rivers run
We ran, we ran upon the waves of stairs.
We juggled our entrances, losing our inner time,
And thought of the dead, who have entered the universe,
Running and running to the fading door.
The living will be giving us one song.
Congregation of sperm, in related music.
Sing down the legacy : Dominion solving hope!
O my own heart, forgive me, let me live.

*

Hitler, dreaming he's a Jew, moving his hot head from side to side.

Churchill in the desert striding and crying, Rommel, Rommel, Rommel, Rommel!

Goebbels cursing statistics: They prove and lie. Whoever depends on them is sunk.

Lord Bennett: Willkie proposes to sabotage the British Empire.

*

⟨ *Benefits! said the Kanaka chief. Too many benefits! Before the foreigners came we lived at peace.*

*

⟨ *This United Nations charter has in it an international Bill of Rights and certain economic guarantees of international peace. These must and will be made more specific.*

There must be an International Bank and an International TVA—including, say, an International Dnieprostroi Dam, for that matter—based on projects which are self-liquidating at low rates of interest.

—*Vice-President Henry A. Wallace*

*

Churchill, saying, We mean to hold our own.

Does Willkie attack? He does; remembering Wilson and the faded silver dream of League, he calls for agreement of purposes among the people of the United Nations. There is no conflict among the hopes of peoples.

Now he defends Schneiderman before the marble court. This man, the Secretary of the Communist Party of California, has not read Foster's acceptance speech, and Willkie says: I doubt that any Presidential candidate's acceptance speeches are ever read. He talks of the things said in the heat of elections which might reflect on the rights of the native-born. Or one of the editors of *The New York Times* who advocates revolutionary changes after the war. How lucky Mr. Hazlitt was to be born in this country! He can't be deported because he has some ideas.

He argues that a man's beliefs are not proved by the beliefs of his party. You might as well prove mine by showing Ham Fish's. He reads from Lincoln. He reads from Jefferson. They talk for revolution in certain circumstances. Now Schneiderman is "a man with a strong social urge." As for the theories: "If he can understand them all he's a better man than I am." He wins his case.

And in New York, begins to write, in the mornings at Irita Van Doren's, writing his words: *One World*.

*

❨ America is like a beleaguered city.
  I have been outside those walls.

*

In Africa, Eisenhower makes a military decision. It is for a military purpose, he says, and it includes an arrangement with Jean Darlan, a French admiral who is head of the fascist French government in Africa, who admires fascism. Should De Gaulle be the man? He is not in Africa. This is all a matter of policy, say the foreign correspondents when the outcry starts. All a matter of ideology. Or morality, they are trying to write.

*

❨ *Churchill to Eisenhower: Anything for the battle, but the politics will have to be sorted out later on.*

*

❨ *Former Naval Person to Roosevelt: Nevertheless in view of the dominating importance of speed and of the fact* . . .

*

Stimson phones Willkie, asking him not to attack the Darlan deal. Your speech may cost sixty thousand American lives, he says, and persuades him with these lives.

Then he calls Roosevelt, who quotes him a Balkan proverb: If the devil offers to help you over a bridge, don't go on the other side. It takes Stimson twenty-five days to think of the answer: it is the story of Joshua, taking Jericho with the help of Rahab the harlot. Roosevelt, delighted, roars. In thirteen days more, the admiral is assassinated.

*

He swings through all the states again, attacking the government, demanding we take our lead in the United Nations. All through these months, even with Willkie Chairman of the Committee, the break is coming. He will not move for a third party; and as he finishes his campaign, the primaries begin.

Wisconsin, April 4: Dewey 17, Stassen 4, MacArthur 3, Willkie 0.

He re-reads *The Count of Monte Cristo*.

*

❲ *Madame, I never eat muscatel grapes.*

*

He closes his headquarters in the Grand Central Building.

*

❲ *The sea is the cemetery of the Chateau d'If.*

*

In June, he is not at the convention. Left out of the Party's councils, given no share in shaping the platform, he is not invited to participate in any way. The ticket that Spangler sends him is not even a delegate's admission. With the professionals coming out for Dewey, his supporters are very few and crowded far out. Go to a convention on a visitor's ticket! He stays in New York and sends his telegrams. Fade out.

In July, Judge Rosenman makes the secret appointment at the St. Regis. Do they meet in a hotel suite, with Willkie dodging into the bedroom when the waiter is heard at the door, to keep the whole thing dark? They do. Are the chances opened from another side? They are. Does Roosevelt want him to run for Vice-President on a new slate, breaking across all party barriers? Can there be a combining of liberals, with these antagonists bridging the gap? Across the disappointments? Across the defeats? Now, what will he answer? Tired, he is, in the great stony heat of this New York July. Betrayed, he is. Played out, is he? No, he is saying, to every question. No, I will not. And what does this word mean, No? Fade out.

He refuses them all. He is very silent now. Silent in Maine, in the hot stir of August, the flow of wind at Moosehead in the nights.

Again and again, political suicide. Mist, indecision, and his pure voice gone. Now to move further into purity. He is the voice; he is the enemy; he is the journey; and the waiting powers.

*

Light falling on that filled will drives
The mares of energy, breakneck and black,
Into our days, into our days.
A man's life and the buried life,
Leading and losing.   A leap upon the dark.
They cannot find him now who gave him gifts:
His throat is vulnerable.   His endless body
Now is his strength, it is his penetration:
His appetites, his hope, are his wide images,
They are the world that enters and they are his own self.
Women like images, friends like ideas of man,

Arrive in meanings that are hated and found.
Find him.   He is somehow yourself.   His eyes your eyes.
The myth of your journey, your living traveler,
In the middle of life breathing the sequences
Of revelation; your story and your song.

PART TWELVE

The Double

Death

It WAS IN the train, on the way to Indiana. Taking him by the
heart. Lurching down the narrow corridor, a road deep-cut
through journey. He reaches for the handle of the heavy metal
door of the diner. He feels his shoulder crash against the wall,
a great painful grip about his chest. Missing the handle, he tries
to reach once more. Pain leaps down his arm, its harpoon striking down the veins of his reach; the heavy door stays shut and
heavier; he leans gasping against it. The breath will not come.
For a minute, he is a child far out on a branch over a train, seeing his own rough hair, his crumpled arm through the roof of
the train turned suddenly to air; he hears the rough from that
distance rough sawing of his useless excellent forgetting breath.
Nothing happens. Arms of his wounded days refuse, refuse.
Pain runs through time, past time, and looks at him. Nothing
happens. Again he reaches for the savage door.

*

A parade of images begins to pass, as he put his hand out: faces, thighs, tall glasses, breasts. Of what importance? he has thought, denying. The steel track. The excitements: the certainty of wildness, each breathing a flame of its own. Bells, hammers, bells, lurching within his chest. The secret bells, that never deny never.

*

To keep the weakness secret. To deny it and break through. In the dream of chieftains, the corn distinct again in gold-white tuft-feathers. The roads all paved, stony, savage; the knocking in the chest resumed.

Your father has a passion for freedom
Rang and rang in the small boy's head.
I will go to the doorstep of a woman will keep me secret. He stands, in Rushville, on the threshold of Mary Sleeth's house. I've known her long, he thinks; she speaks out, she'll keep a secret; and stares at her out of his cloud.—Take me in and keep me here.

—What's the matter, Wendell? Come in.
—Thanks. Nothing. At all.
—You look as though you need a doctor, Wendell.
—Swear to me now.

The man sits in the rocking bedroom, claws
Hooked in his heart: anger denying rage,
Pain and refusal of pain, an image of himself.
Chill, and renewed, the animal, predatory,
Grips a stone statue of a stone hero.

—Swear to me you will not call a doctor, Mary.

*

A woman hiding the exposed hidden man, whisper of green in the night, weakness like blood over the green night,

Seed blown by the wind over rock.   Cracks in the rock.
A great flight of clouds.   The cry of meteors falling.
In a rich sunny autumn, this implacable cold.
Mary, Mary, hide me!
Concealing what the man has always concealed
From his own eyes.

Now that the sunburst throws over him its sack of nails,
Torture and a jungle of kings and monkeys,
And pain prepared in darkness so the muscles lock
Flowing away in confusion.   My wounded king,
Father of pain.   He will not think of the man
Finding a newborn son, himself in the pool.
Hide me, he hears his stripped heart wanting said.
Hide me from eyes and voices.

I am the man hidden in incident,
The boy as fluid as the tulip tree,
The angel, his glowing shoulder to the stone,
About to roll away all dead things.
Wounded.   Now hide me, Mary.
I cannot be that man, boy, angel, stone.
There is a hunting animal on my soul.
I refuse the smell of his breath!
You hide me now.   I am not done for yet.

*

She swears. She turns down the bed and draws the blinds.

*

Not given to any great power. Not a party. Not a state. Not
a rule; nor war; nor peace. There must be something besides war
and peace. He hears a shouting of newsboys, Paris rejoicing.
The tank-tread stamped into the avenue under little trees, the
kiss drinking itself in bright wine.

Now do you know what you were searching for? Hurt. This time will you forget? Or move on for once from what you this moment know.

—Let me get the doctor now, Wendell.

—You promised.

He hides the flaw tearing open his chest; his life hides its appetites that saved him many times. When most torn he was.

*

In your time, there have been those who spoke clearly
For the moment of lightning.
Were we all brave, but at different times?
Even raped open and split, even anonymous,
They spoke.   They are not forgotten.
But they are.   In late summer; forgot; caught at cross-purposes,
Interrupted in an hour of purity,
Their lives careening along in the fierce cities,
Through atrocious poverties and magnificence,
The unforgotten, the early gone forgot.

Late daytime, and nothing left to hide but an eye endowed
With the charred, guilty, gouged by war, the raging splendor;
Despised like you, criminal in intent; sunburnt, in love and
        splendid;
This heart, naked and knocking, going in clouds,
Smoke and a cry of light.
In pain, the voice of pain.   The shadow of your cry.
And never forget : you are magnificent beyond all colors.

*

All right, he says at last. I'll see that doctor in Indianapolis. And he goes in, out of the hot, heavy, endless roaring of the cornfields.

*

It's one thing to go back on what you know. To forget, or be defeated, I forget how many times. I spoke up pure, I think of three or four occasions; I'll speak up again, and stay with that music. Betrayed, betrayed. By all the roaring. Outwardly now. Now this; just as I began to know.

*

My best advice to you is, he said, looking straight at his face: go into the hospital.

*

Written off as an old man with a bum heart. No. Moving in pain, like a rejected lover, he climbs on the long train to New York.

Wheels and galleries of the control of tears,
The cries of parting, and the claws of ferocious
Pain with its filth coating the sharpened claw-tips,
Rot of the will in concealment from itself. Distance,
Fear; smell of the city of pain.
His wife.

Billie, he says, finding her look, sad, startled and glassy in the glass vault of the station. Leaning hard as the taxi leaned around the turn, going home: he said, and his look leaned hard —I'm afraid this is something I can't lick.

*

MARY SLEETH

> So going slowly now
> A man from his green,
> In a hid groaning light;
> So ill concealed
> The grinding of his pain

Amazes my square house
With its dark rays.

Lights my days now
With betraying,
A man against himself,
His life broken open,
All his refusals
Reflected back again
On his blue eyes.

He always ready
To break down doors
Stood in my doorway
Begging my hiding—
Nothing will keep him now
From his soul and the world,
Least not his own self,
Its hiding and its cries.

*

In bed at the Lenox Hill. Only when the hospital door opens broad, runs down the hall the whinnying fanatic humor of the old man dying at one end of the floor: Bed*pan*, bed*pan*! Doesn't anybody here speak *French*?

The negotiations are off now, for the Chicago *Daily News*.

He is unfortunately unable to go to California on legal business.

He cannot hurry the editing of his book, *An American Program*.

He cannot decide where his support will go in the coming election.

He will not be able to see Roosevelt now, to talk about going to Europe for the President after the armistice.

He is trying not to smoke.

He sends letters from his hospital bed: Of course, as a Republican Governor, he writes to Saltonstall, you will want to support him formally, but for God's sake don't sacrifice your principles.

Formal support! He is taken by the throat. Among his sedatives, he might be dreaming of his faraway train, when his throat deserted him. The lurching of this train being implacably the lurching of his own. Cut loose from itself. And sex and power gone. Claws hook in his heart. They close again. He knows the legs of a wounded man. He knows the network of belief, Osiris in his veins praising the world away, risen innumerably now, the voices of contradictions made pure for one more time.

The claws hook in his throat. He hears old words loud in his head, something about a grandfather; and the huge man's hands out of his childhood are on him once again, black rags flapping, purple flowers, prairie phlox speaking to him. Bells, bells.

Fourteen heart attacks in the hospital. The news stories say he is run down, he needs a checkup. And rest. On Wednesday, the pain in his throat is named: streptococcus infection. On Thursday, his fever is up. Penicillin will take care of that. Who is with him now? Love; separation.

*

⟨ *Willkie has been seriously ill; but, as this goes to press, he is out of danger.*

*

That was Friday's paper. Saturday night: cardiac condition, acute.

*

When the true things meet us at the place we reach, they are
    all real, all dreams,
Hidden by incident, often, they stand clear, here they are;

The mottled frayed fish in the pool leaps, the magnificence,
Epiphany among the sparks and rags of God.
Before the opening of the world, in our own time,
When the air we feed on gives us magnificence in conflict,
A naked man in this stream may leap, may pour his energy
Into all lives, pouring himself out on the forming light
Where power-crossed creatures soar, trees up and over us,
Our joy, our meaning, our love, even in dream.

> To go   to make   to flow
> To rise   to break   to grow
> To shine and to stand;
> To join and to separate
> To give and to take
> To destroy and to defend
> All beginning in end beginning
> Spirit through world acting
> World without end.

*

The beggar in his cloud and Saint Venus this evening. The growth of this world. Cast thyself into the journey of the world, fear not, the air of this journey is bitter but full of lightness; though words and wounds be bright in suffering, the words are those of the air of lightness too; the journey has been known to thy self, born and unborn moving to wake, always.

*

The man of anatomies, his beard flowing like time, learning the climate of the past from the rates of growth recorded by the rings of trees, according to their thickness that year.

*

The brilliant, the full-bodied, the real of the world in their
    powers,

The faces of these people always with their lights, one face,
      one face.
The process being the hero and the song.   And the light in a
      face.   One darklit voice.
One deaf musician with his two hundred amens, his endless
      climbing of life, saying "peace" to the trumpets.
The singing of all the voices, your chance and your choice,
Making your acts
And your imaginings.
Related to finding, whether or not we are found.

*

((*Died late Saturday night; early Sunday, that is; of a coronary*
thrombosis.

*

. . . The curve of regeneration being the skew curve of
growth . . .

*

. . . Survive, being given, give off; in this process yielding
energy . . .

*

HE HAD A QUALITY OF GROWTH

No one ever walking this our only earth, various, very clouded,
      in our forests, in all the valleys of our early dreams,
No one has ever for long seen any thing in full, not live
As any one river or man has run his changes, child
Of the swarms and sowings.   Death nor the woman, seed
Of the born, all growing, going through the grass.
However deep you have looked into the well of the cradle
Or into any dream or open eyed the grave

While the soul, many-leaved and waiting,
Began to assume another exact flower.
Smoke and smell in the wind, a single life!
However true you tell, you never have told.
And even that is not altogether true. It changes, we say,
    changes, for yes,
Indeed we all know this, any, any of us, there are secrets known
    to all.

Was it indeed shown you in a flash of journey, the flicker along
    change?
In the fine shadow between the curve of lips, shadow of days
    lengthening,
In the flicker of meaning revealed by many windows;
In the form of the eye, the form of words, of the word; mean-
    ing that formed
These marvelous genitals, nameless as God;
Or in the informing light behind his dream, and he was dream-
    ing of you.
Did his own self escape him, now to reach us, reaving the edge
    of cloud?

Has a gift then been given, each other giving our lives?

As air is given to the mouth of all?

                                *

TIME HINDER NOT ME;
HIS ARMS REACH HERE AND THERE

I WILL NOT CARE FOR TIME. FORBIDDING ME

   The Senate, years later, after many deaths, is asked to consider a man appointed for a job without a history.

MR. WHITE: Mr. President, under the heading of the Atomic Energy Commission, the name of David E. Lilienthal.

THE ACTING PRESIDENT: It is so ordered.

MR. HICKENLOOPER: We have no pattern to guide us. We do not know where we are going in the future.

MR. BRIDGES: Now the Senate, instead of debating on the ablest, are on the lower level of trying to determine the worst qualified; whether Mr. Lilienthal is too bad for the job. In my judgment he is.

MR. HICKENLOOPER: I will say that I am not certain in my own mind exactly what kind of a man should be chosen. We have no history of atomic energy.

MR. BRIDGES: Will the Senator yield?

MR. HICKENLOOPER: May I finish? There is a question in my mind: Do we need the best scientist in the world? Do we need the most capable businessman? At the top, we will need administration. All scientists work in laboratories.

MR. BRIDGES: In Mr. Lilienthal we have neither. He is neither a good businessman nor a good scientist.

The record of Lilienthal: Trained as a common-law lawyer (Anglo-American).

*

⟪ Lilienthal: *It is the very basis and the great heritage that we insist on the rules of credibility of witnesses.*

The record of Lilienthal: *Chairman of the TVA: 1941-1946.*

*

⟪ Lilienthal: *I believe men may learn to work in harmony with the forces of nature, neither despoiling what God has given nor helpless to put them to use.*

I believe in the great potentialities for well-being; though they do hold a threat of enslavement and frustration for the human spirit, I believe those dangers can be averted.

I believe that through the practice of democracy science holds out the greatest opportunities in history for the development of the individual, according to his talents, his hopes, his willingness to carry a free man's responsibilities.

We have a choice: to use science for evil or for good.

I believe men can make themselves free.

*

MR. BRIDGES: He probably can spend Government money. The taxpayers' money, faster than almost any other man in the country.

MR. HICKENLOOPER: I do not know. But he is a completely excellent administrator.

MR. BRIDGES: Will the Senator yield?

MR. HICKENLOOPER: Yes.

MR. BRIDGES: The Senator said, as I understood him, that we have no pattern of the past: we are going into an unknown future field. The Senator cannot decide, can he, what type of man he wants?

Does not the distinguished Senator from Iowa think he has a very distinct duty to his country and to the Senate to look into the background of this man, to look for the slightest fault?

MR. HICKENLOOPER: The President appoints. Our job and our obligation was to see whether or not the appointee was able.

That is the limit of our responsibility.

MR. OVERTON: If Mr. Lilienthal is of the very high type,
The very high type the Senator has portrayed,
Does not the Senator think he would,
When he knows,
    as he must know,
The members' objections,
Of his accord withdraw?
Must he not realize that if he is confirmed

He is confirmed under a cloud?

MR. MURRAY: There is a smokescreen here; there are baseless charges; a substitute for proof. Double talk.

MR. HICKENLOOPER: Mr. President, this matter is vital to the American people.

*

⟨ *With the surrender of Japan, and the lack of any clear peace-time method of handling this new force, he said, and with the future mysteries of atomic energy still unsolved, progress abated somewhat.*

No program prepared for the control of the science, he said, and its advancement.

Imagination running riot here.

Doom cried, and the millenium. Doom cries, sweeping the world.

No program for this process: war to peace.

*

Peace the great meaning has not been defined.
When we say peace as a word, war
As a flare of fire leaps across our eyes.
We went to this school. Think war;
Cancel war, we were taught.
What is left is peace.
No, peace is not left, it is no canceling;
The fierce and human peace is our deep power
Born to us of wish and responsibility.

*

⟨ *Because there was no legislative program provided for the immediate transition from war to peace, it was necessary for the military to retain full and complete control, under military terms, of this going plant that had been built.*

*

Until a program of peaceful handling.

Meanwhile, a year of uncertainty.

The drift from the project.

No one could be sure of the final program.

The military could not run peacetime, or program the future from the standpoint of peace.

A Commission has been for 4 months in control.

The world cannot afford further delay, nor we of the world afford to brook further confusion, uncertainty, and inertia.

This work is part of the guaranty of our system. Human freedom, he said here, human hope. No excuse to tomorrow, he said, as if to himself. Confusion, suspicion, fears, delay.

How can we be certain, he said in a full voice, how atomic energy should be handled under a permanent peacetime policy?

*

MR. HICKENLOOPER: The evidence further establishes Mr. Lilienthal as of high intelligence, great administrative ability, and vigorous devotion to his enterprise. I might disagree with him on important political matters; here is one field that must be above pure partisanship.

The Dies committee, after all the suggestions, the penetrating emotional innuendo, the insinuation, held a hearing; seemed satisfied; pursued the results no further.

MR. BRICKER: The Senator from Iowa mentioned a moment ago that Mr. Lilienthal is a man of high or great administrative ability. I should like to have the Senator give to the Senate his definition of great administrative ability.

MR. HICKENLOOPER: I have been in the Tennessee Valley. Not to inspect it; but I have talked with people, people I know well, who have lived in the Valley for a number of years.

I know an engineer; and other people.

They all speak of efficiency. The TVA's.

The examiners do; the auditors do; efficiency, orderliness, progress, size.

I know there are quarrels; but after all, it is run as Congress voted.

MR. BRIDGES: The Senator should examine the records. He would find the resistance to an accounting of money.

MR. HICKENLOOPER: We tried to follow the leads; examined the reports of the audits.

There is not one word against the last 2 or 3 years.

Lilienthal is vigorous; he advances his views: I understand that he fought for his philosophy.

MR. MC MAHON: Congress is responsible to itself and the people to change the organic TVA act, instead of blaming Mr. Lilienthal for, shall we say, advocating that it be kept as it was.

MR. BARKLEY: The Senator from Louisiana suggested a man might withdraw his name, in opposition. Do you recall Brandeis? And Mr. Hughes? If the past or the present requires our withdrawal because there is bitter or intense opposition, the nation will lose by it, the future will lose.

MR. BRIDGES: Justice Brandeis! Justice Hughes! I resent Lilienthal among the great men.

MR. BARKLEY: I do not have the Senator's contempt, but I do entertain, no doubt, the reverence.

MR. BRIDGES: There is no contempt. This is the first time that an attempt has been made to choose a man to head the Atomic Energy Commission—to develop a force which may destroy this country and the world.

MR. HATCH: A while ago Mr. Bridges said we might reject the nomination unless the person was the best qualified person in the United States for the position. I certainly hope that the people of New Hampshire will never adopt that rule when they select their Senators.

MR. BRIDGES: I will take a chance in New Hampshire, just as the

Senator will in his state, and I will be in the Senate as long as he.

MR. HATCH: I was merely trying to be facetious.

MR. BARKLEY: I thought he was trying to pay a compliment.

MR. HATCH: I failed in trying to be funny. The funniest thing in the Senate is the attitude of the Senator from New Hampshire. I well recall he has never been friendly to TVA. I can well understand his opposition to Mr. Lilienthal, who has made such a success of it. I remember his protest, many years ago, against TVA's purchase of a certain jackass. I also recall George Norris, challenging him on his position in favor of private power.

MR. WHERRY: Would the Senator vote to confirm because of Mr. Lilienthal's scientific background?

MR. HICKENLOOPER: Not necessarily.

MR. WHERRY: Because of his business ability?

MR. HICKENLOOPER: First, he's outstanding; second, he's able; third, he's honest.

MR. WHERRY: There are 140,000,000 American people who are honest.

MR. HICKENLOOPER: We are in a pioneering field.

No one knows the future of energy.

We know we can make a bomb.

We have some ideas in biology.

We have no experience with this energy in peacetime.

There is no pattern to go by.

We do not know, over the next 20 years, whether a specialist in atomic energy or a businessman would better serve this energy in the United States.

I do not know; but I believe Lilienthal can do this job. I am for him.

MR. WHERRY: He is not a scientist. He is not a businessman. The record shows only he is an administrator.

MR. MC MAHON: Until this period, TVA was the largest business enterprise this Government ever engaged in. It has been a success. Its success is attested by the people who live with it.

MR. WHERRY: During 5 years, we have given $626,000,000 to TVA. It has paid back only $17,000,000.

MR. MC MAHON: I suppose there are several tests which can be applied. 100,000 planes in 1 year could not have been built and flown abroad without it. The whole character of the Valley has changed for the better. Private enterprise has grown and flourished.

MR. WHERRY: Is that success—spending $626,000,000 and getting back $17,000,000?

MR. MC MAHON: The question is not to be stated in terms of dollars—the investment of dollars and the return of dollars. The Congress which passed the Act never proposed that. Physical assets; human resources; these make one balance sheet.

MR. WHERRY: The measuring stick for financial ability and business ability is dollars and cents.

MR. MC MAHON: That issue should have been met when he held that office.

MR. WHERRY: I think that is very unfair. I have not said anything about this man in the TVA.
I ask the Senator about ability,
about financial ability and success.
What is his measuring stick?
If it is dollars and cents,
we have appropriated $626,000,000
and we have gotten back $17,000,000.

MR. AIKEN: If we have $625,000,000 invested and earning $17,-000,000 a year—

MR. MC KELLAR: Oh, no, Mr. President. It was $17,000,000 all told.

MR. AIKEN: There probably is not a private corporation in this country that has invested $625,000,000 and is amortizing $17,-000,000 a year.

MR. MC KELLAR: And it has not been done here.

MR. AIKEN: That means it would be paid off in 36 years. And $625,000,000 was not spent for power. Some of it went for navigation, some for soil improvement, some of it—Very few persons can equal this record.

MR. BRIDGES: If any amount of that money ever came back, very little of it ever stopped in the Treasury.

MR. AIKEN: It was reappropriated. More capital extension.

MR. BRIDGES: But little of it remained.

MR. AIKEN: It could have stopped, if Congress had stopped it there.

MR. MC KELLAR: Dr. A. E. Morgan built the dams!
Lilienthal did nothing to build the dams!
As soon as Dr. Morgan got through with them,
so that he knew they were going to be built,
Lilienthal came here and honeyfugled
around our good friend, Franklin Roosevelt.
He just sat around and pussyfooted with him,
and teased him, and begged him,
and got him to give him Dr. A. E. Morgan's place.
Dr. A. E. Morgan built the dams.
Lilienthal took all the credit for it.

MR. BRIDGES: I had no objection to him on TVA—but this could destroy this nation. Or the world! Entirely different, far more important issue.

*

(I realize the consequences of that which was done on the desert, at Alamogordo.

*

The work in the loss of mass.
The work in the lifetimes of the fixed stars.
The work in ideas of unstability:

divisible and transmutable as matter,
divisible and transmutable as idea,
The inner passage of lifetimes and of forms.
Relations of stars and of the stages of life.
The half-life of the forms.
The laws of growth and form.

*

(*Arthur Haas speaking, in 1927, in Vienna: If atoms or nuclei colliding with light-quanta were in enormously rapid motion, then the frequency of the light-quanta could be raised. Collisions in speed with these particles might give the light-quantum that needed frequency. It then would be transmuted to hydrogen.*

It may only be necessary for the light-quantum to enter a swarm of corpuscles at the speed of radium disintegrating. If there were time or place in the universe for these velocities, that gas in speed might, perhaps, help allow the transmutation: radiation to matter.

*

I have tried to show the atom as a source
A source of energy.
I have touched on another question:
Might energy become a source of atoms?
If this relationship is real,
The universe passes along a way of cycles.
A process of matter dissolving in the stars,
Turned into radiation, passing through forms
Again to matter; again, perhaps, to birth.

*

MR. MC MAHON: I sometimes think that very unfortunately the implications of what was done, on the desert sands of Alamogordo, in July 1945, are not sufficiently appreciated even yet by the American people.

Because Mr. Lilienthal has made a success of the Tennessee Valley Authority—that is only one reason why I am for him.

MR. MORSE: I think the point needs to be made that of course the primary objective of TVA was not a business objective at all. It was a great social and economic experiment. How are we to measure the value to the nation of the conservation program in Tennessee? Of the increase of standard of living of thousands and thousands of people? How measure the wealth created, in benefits to business in the Valley? Wealth has flowed from the experiment.

Where is there any private enterprise that could possibly have done what Congress decided ought to be done in the Tennessee Valley? Industrialists say they could not carry it out. The utilities of the Pacific Northwest plead today, Go ahead, build the great dams. . . .

MR. WHITE: May I inquire of the Senator from Iowa whether he cares to proceed any longer this evening?

MR. HICKENLOOPER: I will be happy to yield for a motion to recess. . . .

RECESS. THE SENATE.

Nine days later.

MR. MURRAY: Mr. President, the matter before us, on its face, appears to involve the simple question of the confirmation of a Chairman of the Atomic Energy Commission.

The real controversy, however, does not appear on the surface. Viciousness runs underground.

For a month, the press has paraded unjustified and unsubstantiated charges, power lobbying, political doubleness behind the scenes. They undermine the American people in the integrity of their faith.

We must look beyond the smoke.

It seems clear to me from the character of the opposition to Mr. Lilienthal, and the unfounded abuse leveled at him, that he is being opposed because of his splendid administration of TVA in the public interests as against the private power interests. It is recognized that he will guard the public interests in the administration of atomic energy.

Mr. President, I do not question the motives of those opposing Mr. Lilienthal.

I believe they oppose him because they have been led to think that he is a Communist or a Communist sympathizer.

It may be difficult for those who know the record to imagine this. Nevertheless.

No doubt some oppose him because he has been in sympathy with the progressive policies of our late President— particularly the Roosevelt policies which led to TVA.

The propaganda let loose on the country by the power interests and other monopolies hostile to Roosevelt's policies has deceived many.

Psychiatrists claim that we in the great majority are susceptible to the effects of modern propaganda methods.

It was declared that as a result of the confusing, contradictory, and conflicting propaganda, the United States has become one grand "transmogrified" lunatic asylum.

Evidences have been displayed in the Senate many times during this debate.

This fight is not a fight against a man.

It is a fight of private power against power development in the interest of all the people.

It is a ruthless fight of lies and fear against one who regards the development of energy wholly in the public interest. Free from monopoly control, this energy will have a fundamental effect.

*

❨[*The Neanderthal wing of the power industry is fighting hard against Lilienthal, using all weapons available.*

*

MR. MURRAY: The part played in the affairs of Government by the privately owned power companies is well recognized. Here in Washington, one can never tell from day to day what public interest will be scorched next. They reach every town in the land. They express their emotions on a wide variety of matters. Some of these matters seem only remotely connected with the electrical industry. Taxes, housing, trade at home and abroad, floods, insurance, rural electrification, more often than not, whatever the issue, must weather out these attacks. They arrive in the voice of the electrical companies, who speak with a single voice.

The private companies have a public-relations system, working at all our levels; a single-purposed lobby; their tactics have been exposed as vicious and un-American, calculated to bring the democratic processes into disrepute.

They direct government from using the God-given riches of natural waterfall.

They seek to stop the TVA method of unified approach to power, flood, expansion.

They seek to dominate the development of water power, unless they may dictate the terms.

Mr. President, does anyone doubt that they would, if they could, undertake to gain the same character of control over atomic power?

MR. OVERTON: Mr. President, will the Senator yield?

MR. MURRAY: I am limited to 10 minutes and must proceed without yielding.

THE PRESIDING OFFICER: The Senator from Montana declines to yield.

MR. MURRAY: Mr. President, it seems to me that the real reason for desiring the defeat of Mr. Lilienthal lies with the liking of those who do not wish to see atomic energy controlled and directed in the interests of the people.

We have seen the thought and suggestion: our resources— our minerals and forests, all our fuels, are being exhausted, the chances of capital are drying up; there is a need that private industry control this energy.

There is an apparent belief, behind this opposition and the schemes we know of, that there would then be opened up one of the richest fields for private exploitation that American monopolists have ever been offered.

Are they waiting and ready to get aboard, just as the buccaneers used to board the galleons of the Spanish Main?

And this bonanza, mark you, was completely outside the realm of possibility until . . .

*

〔 *The Edison Electric Institute—the propaganda agency of the power monopoly—has distributed an "analysis" of TVA's financial set-up.*

This has charged all TVA activities, all the munitions plants and navigation locks, against power sales.

Thus, New Orleans should pay for the levees of the lower Mississippi!

Thus, the dams of the Ohio should be items on your power bills, you in the area!

Some time ago, our people united, and for good reason.

*

〔 *ALL-OUT UTILITY DRIVE AGAINST U.S. POWER PROGRAM*

1. *Campaigns to emphasize efficiency of private companies— and their taxes.*

2. *Equally strong campaigns to undermine Government pro-grams.*

3. *Power lobby (private) (Washington) to oppose appropriations for public power.*

4. *Support of Federal agencies which do not include power.*

*

MR. MURRAY: In spite of the witch hunters and the Edison Electric Institute combined, TVA stands. Its record stands: a system of greater value, greater service, greater earning capacity, greater potential.

It takes time to catch up on the "big lie," but it will be done.

*

⟨[*In war, they provided power.*
In peace, they offer a key.

*

MR. MURRAY: New energy requires new approaches, to its use and control.

MR. MC KELLAR: Two systems of economic life are in the world: Mr. Lilienthal is the exponent of Government ownership. This is not a question of private utilities or public power; It involves the whole philosophy of our way of life.

For my part, I believe thoroughly in the American system. The Atomic Energy Act creates a power pool to be owned by the Government, but to preserve free competition in private enterprise.

We must insist that the man we appoint believe in the system of competitive private enterprise which is spoken of so aptly in this declaration.

Mr. President, Napoleon once said he could control Paris with a whiff of grapeshot. The man in the United States to whom the atomic bomb is entrusted can control the United States if he wills to do so. David Lilienthal has described himself as a man who believes in a government of men and not of laws.

MR. VANDENBERG: Mr. President, I have been a member of the Senate Atomic Energy Committee which sat as a jury in the Lilienthal case. As a result, I have been driven away from the adverse prejudice with which I started. I have been driven to the belief that logic, equity, fair play, and a just regard to urgent welfare combine to recommend Mr. Lilienthal's confirmation in the light of today's realities.

What are the realities in the instant case? We, the Congress, have declared by law that the control of atomic energy must be the tightest Government monopoly ever set up in the United States—pending the day when the destructive use of atomic energy shall be outlawed for keeps.

You all voted for it. It passed the Senate unanimously.

We solemnly and unavoidably decreed that Government ownership and management is an indispensable public necessity for the sake of national security in respect to the control of atomic energy.

To leave this world-wrenching mystery, involving life and death, in private hands or under private enterprise at the present time would be a shocking outrage upon human values. It would violate every element of public trust. So we, the Congress, declared for a primary Government monopoly.

It seems to be a fact, despite incidental arguments, that TVA is one of the most successful public institutions on earth. It is the nearest thing, if not the only thing, comparable to the far-flung empire of the Manhattan project.

It is not Mr. Lilienthal's chairmanship which makes the

job a public project. We, the Senate, did that unanimously months ago.

Whether we like it or him or TVA, this sequence leads logically to David Lilienthal's door.

MR. TAFT: The distinguished Senator from Michigan has referred to the endorsements received from many scientists. None of those scientists have read the account of Mr. Lilienthal in the TVA. None of those men have anything except a casual social acquaintance with Mr. Lilienthal.

These scientists have not examined his philosophy of government. All they know is that Mr. Lilienthal is an attractive man who has taken very largely the point of view of the scientists.

Unfortunately, the scientists, who have endorsed the Lilienthal-Acheson report, do not realize the dangers of international power, any more than they realize the dangers of an arbitrary Government control of various operations, no more than they realize what we have been up against here for the last 10 years in trying to cut down the tremendous power of the Executive to make regulations to regulate the lives and the very existence of the people of the United States.

*

SENATOR MC KELLAR: You are willing to admit, are you, that this secret, or the first history of it, dated from the time when Alexander the Great had his Macedonian scientists trying to split the atom, and then Lucretius wrote a poem about it, about 2000 years ago?

And everybody has been trying to discover it, or most scientists have been trying to discover it, ever since.

Did it not seem remarkable to you, who have never even been an engineer, who knew nothing in the world about the splitting of the atom or about atomic energy and its discovery, that the President should turn to you, now, one who is not an engineer, knowing nothing in the world about it, and appoint you the head of this Commission? Was that not a little striking to you? It was to me. I will say that.

MR. LILIENTHAL: I did my damnedest to keep out of it, but I failed. I am sorry.

*

A GAME OF MEMORY. OR OF IMAGINATION.
ONE SHALL BE THE QUESTIONER
AND ONE SHALL ANSWER

SENATOR MC KELLAR: Now, is it not a fact that while you sell your fertilizer to these cooperatives you also furnish them free of charge about $2,000,000 worth of fertilizer a year?

MR. LILIENTHAL: I don't remember the figures, Senator, but it is a substantial figure.

SENATOR MC KELLAR: Well, what did you sell your fertilizer for per ton?

MR. LILIENTHAL: That I don't know.

SENATOR MC KELLAR: You do not know?

MR. LILIENTHAL: I don't remember it.

SENATOR MC KELLAR: Yet you are proposing to go, if the Senate confirms you, into the most important business, probably, that the world has ever known; certainly one of the most important discoveries ever made.

MR. LILIENTHAL: I just don't try to carry figures like that in my head.

SENATOR MC KELLAR: You do not carry them in your head. You do not see any use of it. You will not see any use of it when you go into the atomic energy field, will you?

MR. LILIENTHAL: That is what books are for, and assistants.

SENATOR MC KELLAR: That is what books are for and what assistance is for, and you just go according to the books?

MR. LILIENTHAL: Some people keep their heads full of things of that sort; I just don't. But I can get the figures for you.

SENATOR MC KELLAR: Mr. Lilienthal, did you, acting for the TVA, complain of the price of ammonium-nitrate fertilizer?

MR. LILIENTHAL: Senator, I don't remember. I can get the file in, and we can see.

SENATOR MC KELLAR: I think you had better see. You do not carry that in your head, although you were the head of it, and you really were the TVA.

MR. LILIENTHAL: I am sure that the men who did these things were responsible men, and whatever they did I was responsible for.

SENATOR MC KELLAR: You endorse—

MR. LILIENTHAL: I am responsible for them; I do not endorse.

SENATOR MC KELLAR: I want to ask you another question. I believe you admitted the other day that you belonged to and sponsored the Southern Community of—what was the name of that organization that you sponsored with Mr. Pope and Mr. Clapp? The Southern Conference for . . .

SENATOR MC MAHON: Human Welfare?

SENATOR MC KELLAR: Human Welfare. You sponsored that, did you not?

MR. LILIENTHAL: I may have. I don't recall.

SENATOR MC KELLAR: The truth is that your sympathies are very leftist, are they not? What about them?

MR. LILIENTHAL: This I do carry in my head, Senator.

SENATOR MC KELLAR: You do not?

MR. LILIENTHAL: This I do carry in my head. And I will do my best to make it clear.

SENATOR MC KELLAR: Yes, sir?

Lilienthal said : I heard him saying words like these.
Almost like these words:
My convictions are not so much against, as for.

I believe—and I conceive law to rest here, as does religion—
The fundamental truth, the integrity of the individual;
That all we build be designed to promote and protect and
     defend
The integrity and the dignity of the individual.
This the essential meaning of our nation,
As it is essentially the meaning of religion.

Any forms, then, which make men means rather than ends,
Which exalt any institution above the importance of men,
Which rest on an arbitrary power over men,
Are contrary to that conception and my meaning.
That I deeply oppose, and I deeply disbelieve.

Out of this central core of a belief
That all men are the children of God
That their lives come first and are sacred,
A great belief grows in civil liberties,
In their protection; a repugnance to theft
Of these liberties and a human being's good name,
By innuendo or by open lies.
Here is no ethical standard, nor in the state
Which exercises blind powers over the human heart.
Occasionally, all these things are done
In the name of democracy.
They can tear our people apart.

I believe in the capacity of our central belief
To survive its trials, provided only we
Practice, in daily life, daily, our truths.
They are affirmative.   That is their hope in the world.
This I deeply believe.

In Praise of Process

Breaking the nets of the world, in glimpses going
Among the mountains of light and the mountains of darkness.
All of his gateways were the opposites.

If you should mourn him now, you will know whom you mourn.
Whenever you hate him, and he must be hated,
You will know what you hate.   Whatever in him you love
You will see in yourself who are your brother.
All the legends are for him and against him.
When he saw his life false, founded on oppositions,
In the face of love, in the masks of judges;
When he knew he was strong and heard every summoning;
When he fought, when he drank, when he walked into the
        world;
When he forgot the moment of revelation.
His monsters, his valleys, his waves, his rains of paper,
All spoke to him, and all the masks of power.

Wounded he lay.   And for good reason.
His wounds our wounds.   His masks our milestones.
The guardians of recovery be our guardians,
Exultations of towers sting our healing;
—The leap that fulfills him, the laugh and the forgetting,
Are all your dreams, are all your dreams.

The nets of sleep are broken.   The four colors of daybreak
Shine clear where the wish stands, having body and knowing
These rooted forests are familiar country.
The nets of the opposites and the nets of refusal
Swing at the pliant windows of our birth.
Nets of his emerging all can see.

Fire of making streaming over the lives
Of our fathers' youth gave him, gave us our fire.
Stony constraints, the lips of a judge denying
Found weakness everywhere wishing to be Holdfast,
Repeating rejections and a mimic doom.
The rivers of all grace streamed through his years,
Even among the iron islands, chance;
And in the acting-out, the rivers are changing:
They are a net of snare or a living tree.
For in the breaking of things, continual choice
Is the glimpse of birth, given him, given all of us
Who know in ourselves his fullness and refusals.

Now light says Amen to shadows and takes all things
Into another morning where the moment
Offers necessity at last its flower,
Offers the meanings which are the clues of form.
The man who fought off human meanings finds
All avenues full, a procession of images
Confronting him with the chain of his lifetime dreams.
For all things grow, remade as rivers that time
Turns to resolve hostilities of power.

*

He is breaking the nets in his wildness for the real.
Rivers, and wrestlings, the theater of time
Disclose his need to grow, which is the bond of man.
The holy linkings acknowledged and the search
Seen with its meanings, and the love of man
Seen with the meanings of the lives we praise.
Identified with our flesh, the living flower
Of consciousness, the soul which is the form,
Giving the human power.

Most human power of the bonds of man!
All things are taken in the net of meaning,
Assuming form.   The form is the light of day,
The net, the need, changing desire, the morning
Of man in our full value whose name is peace.
Peace is the growing form and the cry of Holy
In the city of the world, in the eyes of children.
The light on the rivers and on the poor is peace,
Light that by being requires, from all who see,
Beauty and change and life.   The life of peace,
Peace the necessity of growth, clue of our ways.

Music of growth, the world's magnificence,
Is born, the break of day, child of the world.
        Now in the net of forces
The stars of these migrations being our days
Do take their changes, another constellation.
Although today their broken-crested light
Shines on our blackened poverty of wars.
There is the seed of the gift diversity
Declaring the pride of man, allowing lightnings kneel
On the horizon of difference, shocking the blaze awake.

The central mysteries and dance of initiation,
The language and links of making, and the process

We bless that discovers self and the self of the world
In one law moving and given : the form of the love of growth.
By that light, by that infinite rich darkness
Many shinings of truth making aware,
A flare against corruption and forgetting,
Declare and create that the human light of meanings
Let us give us ourselves
Linked, given, and in glimpses going.

ABOUT THE AUTHOR

MURIEL RUKEYSER's first published book was a collection of poems, *Theory of Flight*, which came out in 1935 when she was twenty-one years old and recently out of Vassar and Columbia. By her mid-thirties she was the author of six more volumes of poetry (her *Selected Poems* were published in 1950) as well as a book which is now recognized as one of the classics of American scientific biography, *Willard Gibbs*. Her work has appeared extensively in magazines and anthologies.

In addition to her poetry and her work with biographical forms, she has been active in films, television, and the graphic arts, and as a lecturer and teacher. She has been the recipient of a grant of the American Academy of Arts and Letters and a Guggenheim Fellowship. Miss Rukeyser has recently completed a play based on the life of Harry Houdini and is now working on a biography of the great anthropologist, Franz Boas, and a selection of his work.